TRANSCENDING
NEOLIBERALISM

TRANSCENDING NEOLIBERALISM

Community-Based Development in Latin America

Henry Veltmeyer and
Anthony O'Malley, editors

KUMARIAN
PRESS

Transcending Neoliberalism: Community-Based Development in Latin America

Published 2001 in the United States of America by Kumarian Press, Inc.
1294 Blue Hills Avenue, Bloomfield, CT 06002 USA.

Production, design, indexing, and proofreading by ediType,
Yorktown Heights, N.Y., and Charleston, S.C.
The text of this book is set in 10/13 Adobe Sabon.

Printed in Canada on acid-free paper by Transcontinental Printing and Graphics, Inc.
Text printed with vegetable oil–based ink.

∞ The paper used in this publication meets the minimum requirements of the American National Standard for Information Sciences—Permanence of Paper for Printed Library Materials, ANSI Z39.48–1984.

Library of Congress Cataloging-in-Publication Data

Transcending neoliberalism : community-based development in Latin America / Henry Veltmeyer and Anthony O'Malley, editors.
    p. cm.
    Includes bibliographical references (p.) and index.
    ISBN 1-56549-125-4 (cloth ; alk. paper) – ISBN 1-56549-124-6 (pbk. ; alk. paper)
    1. Community development – Latin America. 2. Latin America – Economic conditions – 1982- 3. Decentralization in government – Latin America. I. Veltmeyer, Henry. II. O'Malley, Anthony, 1947-

HN110.5.Z9 C646 2001
307.1′4′098 – dc21

                                                         00-067382

10 09 08 07 06 05 04 03 02 01   10 9 8 7 6 5 4 3 2 1   First Printing 2001

Contents

Tables

Acknowledgments

The authors would like in particular to express their appreciation to Gisèle Morin-Labatut at the International Development Research Centre (IDRC) of Canada. Financial support of a conference and research workshop in which the collaborating authors were able to present their findings and receive critical feedback was an important contribution toward the intellectual project embodied in this volume. In addition, through the good offices of Ms. Morin-Labatut, IDRC contributed directly toward the publication of this volume. This support helped bring the project to completion and is hereby acknowledged with appreciation.

The authors would also like to express their appreciation of the interest in the manuscript and support provided for its publication by Linda Beyus of Kumarian Press. Kumarian Press was by far the publisher of choice for the authors and editors of this manuscript, directed as it is toward the broad and growing international community of development scholars and practitioners.

ONE

The Quest for Another Development

Henry Veltmeyer

The End of an Era?
From Modernism to Postmodernism

We are, it has been said, on the threshold of a new era. This era, it is also said, is characterized by an epoch-defining shift in the dominant forms of social and economic organization, the globalization of associated practices and processes, and new ways of thinking about the world and doing analysis.

In the late 1950s several sociologists (C. W. Mills and Daniel Bell, among others) wrote of the end of the modern era and the coming of another that was postmodern, postindustrial, postcapitalist. The modern era, as they understood and constructed it, was based on and characterized by the quest for enlightenment, scientific analysis of the laws that govern the workings of the economy, and a better if not perfect form of society in which people could realize fully their human potential. Such a development was seen to be the result either of a *process*, and thus subject to forces that can be understood and manipulated but not controlled, or of a *project*, and thus realized by appropriate action on the rationalist principles and universal ideals of freedom, reason, and equality. Modernization, so conceived, has entailed a protracted process or struggle to overcome the obstacles in the way of economic progress, social justice, and democracy, the three critical dimensions of a modern form of society and the emancipatory process involved in bringing it about.

By many accounts this image and notion of a new postmodern,

1

postindustrial, and postcapitalist form of society were somewhat premature, given the unfolding at the time of a far-reaching international process of economic growth, development, and modernization. In hindsight, however, these early voices could be understood as prescient, presaging as they do developments and ways of seeing that emerged or became apparent decades later. In any case, in the 1980s there were many additions to and permutations of this notion of a new postmodern era, leading to a radical rethinking of the process, or project, of economic and social development. Gone was the Enlightenment belief in the idea of progress, the universal principles of alienable human rights, and the ideal of a rational form of society and state in which freedom and justice would reign—a community of free and equal individuals capacitated and empowered to realize their human potential.

To be sure there is no consensus on this point. On the one hand, there are those who remained convinced of both the necessity and the possibility for the radical changes needed to institute the rationalist principles and ideals of freedom, equality, and progress—to complete the modernization project of the eighteenth-century Enlightenment. After all, there was widespread evidence of a growing worldwide development gap and a significant increase in social inequalities, the result of development that was appropriated or enjoyed by a small, privileged minority but that mired large masses of people in poverty and misery, excluded from these islands of prosperity and well-being. On the other hand, there was an equally widespread disenchantment and a growing chorus of voices (and all of the instrumentalities and power of the nation-state) raised in objection and denial, in rejection of both the possibility and the necessity for radical or revolutionary change. Consolidation of and adjustment to the existing system and its globalization and other processes, rather than social revolution, were here projected as the goal of the development process. And between these two points of view, both of which were taken to their extremes, there was a proliferation of voices in the search for another form of development and an alternative way of doing analysis.

At the center of this search was the notion that development was both possible and necessary but that it had to be conceived and put into practice in very different terms. Development, it was argued, should recognize the radical heterogeneity of experience, the existence of multiple paths toward development, the local community as the basis of the process involved, and people themselves as the only effective agency for change.

The Crisis of the Dominant Model

A model is a simplified theoretical representation of reality that makes analysis possible and provides a framework of ideas for the construction of theory. Economists and sociologists have constructed a number of models and theories for the purpose of explaining the salient patterns of international development. These patterns are complex and subject to the most diverse forms of interpretation.

First, it is possible to identify profound changes in economic and social organization associated with, if not caused by, a technological revolution that has transformed available forms of communication, the nature of society, the system of global production, and the possibilities of meeting people's basic needs and realizing the human potential. There is an ongoing debate about the driving forces behind these changes and developments. But there is no question about the centrality and importance of new information and communication technologies and the enabling policy framework of stabilization and structural adjustment measures. Nor is there any question about the need for balanced accounts and fiscal discipline — liberalization (of trade in goods, services, and capital), privatization (of the means of production), deregulation (of economic activity), and downsizing (of the state and capitalist enterprise). These measures constitute the key elements of the neoliberal model (or New Economic Model [NEM]) designed by the economists of the international financial institutions such as the World Bank and today in place throughout the region (Bulmer-Thomas 1996; Green 1995; Veltmeyer and Petras 1997).

There is an obvious downside to this model and its acknowledged achievements. The north-south development gap has grown over the years in spite of impressive rates of economic growth and social development exhibited by a number of countries in East Asia. The social inequalities and inequities of market-led growth have proliferated, and the ecological limits to economic growth and industrialization have been exceeded, leading to a drastic, if not fatal, deterioration of the underlying ecosystem and an unsustainable growth process.

On the one hand, the post–World War II economic order that has generated these negative developments has been renovated with the institution of what in Latin America and elsewhere is labeled the "New Economic Model." On the other hand, there is little or no question of progress as conceived by the proponents of modernization. The progress promised in terms such as justice and equity, growth and development, modernization and advances in human development has not materialized. However, within the framework of the NEM, the lack of such progress is not seen as a failure. It is seen as evidence that the notion of social justice and the associated ideal of a classless society — a community of free and equal and empowered individuals — are an abstraction from reality, a utopian ideal incapable of realization. The NEM, it is thought, creates the best of all possible worlds in which there is not so much (or at all) equity and social justice but individual freedom and an efficient distribution of rewards on the basis of productivity: to each according to their contribution (to production).

In this context the collapse of socialism as actualized in the Soviet Union and elsewhere in the socialist bloc is seen as signifying the triumph of free-market capitalism and with it the idea of individual freedom institutionalized in the trappings of liberal democracy. At the same time, for a number of intellectuals it signifies an end to the belief in the Enlightenment concept of universal progress and the possible state of social justice. In fact, the intellectual certainties and mobilizing beliefs and ideologies connected to the project of emancipation, modernization, and development have been abandoned. As François Lyotard, an exponent of this postmodernist perspective, has put it, what characterizes the emerging intellectual position is "skepticism and distrust of all metanarratives," a distrust of any and all theoretical representation of reality in structuralist form.

Over the course of the last fifty years, the concept of development has been the object of innumerable reflections, studies, reformulations, and criticisms. For some, the concept retains the mark of its origins in the Enlightenment ideals of emancipation and universal progress, its underlying belief in human reason and the capacity of bringing about or instituting changes based on the universal values and ideals of progress, freedom, and social justice. However, for Gustavo Esteva, Madhu Suri Prakash, and other proponents of "grassroots postmodernism" or counterdevelopment, the obvious failure of the development project, despite decades of concerted effort and long-term planning and market-led development, signifies that development is a misbegotten enterprise both in theory and in practice. What is needed, it is argued, is for each people, with reference to their own values and on the basis of autonomous action and grassroots organizations, to craft their own cultural foundation and to construct their own futures from that foundation. This social construction of reality, the conditions of which are subjective and political rather than objective and structural (economic), is not based on abstract universal principles, rationalist discourse, and the grand narratives of modernist thought — the universalism of human rights, the notion of the autonomous individual, the idealism of democracy and liberal (or socialist) internationalism or globalism. The efforts of "people" ("ordinary men and women who autonomously organize themselves to cope with their predicament") in the most diverse specific cultural contexts to come to terms with the conditions that affect and shape their lives escape the "monoculture of modernity" (Esteva and Prakash 1998, 3). This project has a new center of reference: an emergent grassroots epic of localized struggle, the drama of everyday forms of resistance, and "a wide collection of culturally diverse initiatives and struggles of the so-called illiterate and uneducated non-modern 'masses'...pioneering radical post-modern paths out of the morass of modern life" (Esteva and Prakash 1998, 3).

Between these two responses to the crisis of the postwar development project — neoliberalism and grassroots postmodernism or counterdevelopment — there is a broad range of diverse approaches and schools of thought united only by their shared commitment to an alternative form of development. In this commitment there is no unity. What defines the diverse conceptions of alternative development are the recognition and valorization of radical difference: the notion that development in its diverse dimensions is heterogeneous and that it can and should take multiple forms; that people should construct their own development on the basis of autonomous action of community-based local or grassroots organizations;

that development be participatory in form, human in scale, and people-centered.

Despite the respect paid and commitment to the principles of cultural heterogeneity and difference, there are observable patterns in this search for Another Development. It has even been argued that all of the alternative approaches toward Another Development share a worldview, that in effect they constitute a "new paradigm." If this is the case, what are its constituent elements? Are there common definable statements of principle to guide thinking and action? On the basis of these principles, is it possible to formulate or identify one or more theoretical models that can be used to represent reality? What theories, if any, have been constructed on the basis of these principles and within the framework of these models?

Models of Another Development

The search for Another Development has reached the proportions of a major social movement of nongovernmental organizations (NGOs) that can be numbered in the tens of thousands on a global scale. In every region of the world and in many countries today it is possible to identify several nodal points in the search for Another Development in the form of a research group, a program of activities, or a journal that provides an outlet for collaborative research, programmatic statements, and news. An example of such a nodal point is the Instituto Intercultural para la Autogestión y la Acción Cultural and its journal, *Revista Iberoamericana de Autogestión y Acción Comunal* (*RIDAA*), at the Universidad Autónoma de Madrid. Other examples include the Stockholm-based Dag Hammarskjöld Foundation, the Society for Alternative Development, and the journal *Development Dialogue,* all of which can be traced back to 1974, constituting, in effect, a foundation stone and a pillar in the movement to establish an alternative form of development; COLACOT (Confederación Latinamericana de Cooperación y Mutuales de Trabajadores) in Sante Fé de Bogotá, Colombia; Equipo Pueblo in Mexico City; the Alternative Development Network and its journal, *Interculture,* in Montreal; IFDA (International Foundation for Development Alternatives) and its *IFDA Dossier;* and several operational agencies of the United Nations, in particular UNRISD (United Nations Research Institute for Social Development), whose conferences and publications over the years have been instrumental in the propagation of the idea of a community-based, people-led, and people-centered participatory form of development.

Manfred Max-Neef and Human-Scale Development

On the basis of this organization and institutional development there have been a number of attempts to construct a community-based and participatory form of Another Development. One such attempt is associated with the ideas of Manfred Max-Neef, a Chilean economist whose reflections and work on "human-scale development" constitute an important reference point in the search for Another Development (see Max-Neef 1986; the work was first published in English by the Dag Hammarskjöld Foundation in 1982 as *Human-Scale Development*). Max-Neef's reflections were based on his experience as an international consultant with indigenous peasant communities in the highlands and coastal regions of Ecuador and black artisans in a microregion of Brazil.

Max-Neef (1989) distilled several lessons from his reflections on the development process in Ecuador, Brazil, and elsewhere. First, with reference to Ernst Schumacher's perspective on "economics as if people mattered" (small is beautiful), he argues that it is of critical importance for economists to escape or get beyond

1. an obsession with size and a biased preference for the large-scale;

2. an obsession with quantification and measurement, which leads to a failure to appreciate the centrality of and to gauge the critical role of nonstructural, cultural, and intangible moral factors in the development process;

3. a mechanistic and technico-managerial approach to theoretical solutions based on an orientation toward scientific rationality, technological progress, and management;

4. a tendency to oversimplify and objectify the critical conditions of the development process, with an associated lack of understanding of the need for a moral vision, a sense of history, and an appreciation of social complexity;

5. a tendency to bring into analytical focus and theorize essential categories and forms of development (the domestic labor of women, subsistence activities of the poor, etc.), the cultural (and structural) conditions of which are rendered invisible; and

6. a failure to recognize the antagonism and lack of balance that are often found between existing cultural forms of socioeconomic organization and the underlying ecosystem.

In terms of such considerations, Max-Neef (1989) argues for a form of development that is human in scale and based on a balance between and integration of human values and natural limits (integral ecological humanism).

Luis Razeto and the Economy of Solidarity

Luis Razeto, a Chilean economist connected with the International Labour Office's (ILO) Santiago-based Programa Regional del Empleo para América Latina y el Caribe (PREALC), has written a number of book-length studies that constitute critical points of reference in the regional search for Another Development. These studies include *Economía de solidaridad y mercado democrático* (1988); *Crítica de la economía, mercado democrático y crecimiento* (1985); and *De la economía popular a la economía de solidaridad en un proyecto de desarrollo alternativo* (1993).

In these studies Razeto explores a number of variations on the same theme. At issue are various forms of autonomous action and organization formed within civil society, a sphere of social action and organization that can be differentiated from both the state and the market, the two critical institutions in most theoretical models of economic development. As Razeto sees it, the emergence and construction of a vibrant civil society as an independent arena of struggle, action, and organization were responses to regionwide conditions of economic crisis in the early 1980s and the stultifying operations of the state and the market, both of which created forces and conditions beyond the capacity of people to control. The emergence of this civil society is associated with the growth of a popular movement, the formation of grassroots and nongovernmental organizations, and the impulse to democratize existing institutions as well as to expand local spaces for decision-making power on development issues of importance to ordinary people and their communities.

The central issues raised and addressed by Razeto are whether (1) the forms of action and organization pioneered within civil society are able to overcome the conditions of marginality and poverty that gave rise to them; (2) these popular organizations are able to generate the social forces capable of converting them into agencies of collective development; and (3) the economies of solidarity established in the process have achieved sufficient dynamism as to constitute a model of development.

The first point established by Razeto is that the economy of solidarity created by the autonomous action and organization of the urban poor, occupants of a burgeoning "informal sector," is a defensive response to a situation of dire need. The great variety and diversity of such responses, he notes, make it difficult to evaluate and determine the degree of effectiveness of such activities and organizations. In many cases the economic activities or operations of economic exchange are not mediated by money; they are neither commodified nor monetized. Nor are they based entirely, if at all, on rational calculations of self-interest or utility. In many cases, economic activities are dictated by social conditions of solidarity or collective sharing and distribution of scarce resources and are motivated by a sense of community — or solidarity. The object of economic activity is to meet the basic needs of subsistence and to do so on the basis of ties of communal solidarity.

Another problem addressed by Razeto is to see if, or how, an economy of solidarity can be inserted into the broader structures of the market economy and the state as well as the globalization process. The problem, in other words, is to move in theory and in practice from the local to the global. Can an economy of solidarity operate on a larger than local scale? Can it constitute a model of national development? To these questions, however, Razeto has provided no answer.

Jaroslav Vanek and Abraham Guillén:
The Economics of Workers' Self-Management

The economics of workers' participation and self-management is the optimum strategy for developing countries and provides a useful model for the industrialized countries. This is the conclusion drawn by Jaroslav Vanek in a study published in 1974, a year that saw a number of initiatives to which the current worldwide search for Another Development can be traced. The strategy formulated by Vanek on the basis of diverse experiments and government-supported experiences in Yugoslavia and elsewhere has several requirements and conditions:

- internal and external self-determination in the political sphere;

- economic self-determination, implying the self-management of workers within the enterprise and the existence of a market that functions effectively without recourse to compulsion save for exceptional circumstances; and

- surplus generation as well as an equitable distribution of productive resources and the fruits of development among the members of the community.

There have been innumerable studies based on Vanek's proposals, but the experience with social-property enterprises in Chile under the regime of Salvador Allende (1970–73) has been particularly instructive. Studies of this experience, conducted by, among others, Juan Espinosa (a Chilean collaborator of Vanek and Andrew Zimbalist and the author of the classic *Economic Democracy* [1978]), were generally supportive of an argument advanced in numerous studies by Guillén (1988, 1993, etc.), perhaps the major intellectual figure and theorist associated with the Instituto Intercultural para la Autogestión y la Acción Cultural and its journal, *RIDAA*. Guillén's thesis is that workers' self-management is the essential condition of an alternative (that is, socialist) form of development, the best if not the only means of people in the developing countries becoming subjects of their own history.

Without popular participation, Guillén adds, there can be no full or authentic democracy; without collective management by the direct producers or workers, there is no escaping the alienation of labor; without a direct control over the means of administration, the state inevitably places itself above society in the interests of the dominant class or elite. In short, without the participation of workers in the management of production, economic democracy based on social property, and political democracy, the state remains an instrument of class domination and not of collective development by citizens of government and the state (Guillén 1993, 66–67).

Roberto Guimarães: Cooperativism and Equity

A critical departure point for the reflections of Guimarães and others on the Latin American experience with cooperativism is a series of studies and reports commissioned by UNRISD, coordinated by the Colombian theorist of social action Fals Borda and published in 1974. On the basis of extensive field research and case studies, these reports concluded that cooperatives generally were ineffective forms of organization relative to meeting the basic needs of the poor and as an agency for social transformation. At the time it was widely assumed that effective development required and was predicated on radical institutional change or social transformation, an overhaul of the social and political structures of economic production. In this regard, cooperatives were clearly deficient, a conclusion that differs radically from the lessons that others were drawing from experiences as diverse as Mondragón with worker co-ops in the mid-1950s[1] and Antigonish with producer co-ops in Nova Scotia.

The general conclusion reached by the UNRISD team, and largely supported by Guimarães, who now works with ECLAC (the UN's Economic Commission for Latin America) in Santiago de Chile, on the basis of subsequent and extensive experience with the cooperative movement in Latin America, can be summed up in three statements: (1) cooperatives are not agents for change, producing few benefits for the poorest sectors of the population; indeed, the strengthening of cooperatives in most places led to an unexplained increase in income gaps; (2) co-ops tend to reproduce the structure of community relations and conditions rather than transform it; and (3) they tend to reinforce as well as extend and deepen preexisting social inequalities, an inclination that can be traced in part to the tendency for groups and individuals who are accommodated to the power structure to control the key committees and the administration of co-ops; and in the few cases when co-ops actually represented the interests of and were composed of poor peasants they were manifestly incapable of promoting the interests of their members (Guimarães 1989, 285–86).

The one surprising feature in Guimarães's review of cooperatives as a factor of development in Latin America is the obvious presumption in many earlier studies that cooperatives might or should constitute an agent for social change — of what in the contemporary context and discourse is referred to as "social transformation." It is clear enough that like so many NGOs in the 1980s, cooperatives (see the OAS study reviewed by Guimarães 1989, 290, 292, 295–98) were never set up or organized to this purpose. The strategy of development pursued by these cooperatives was generally characterized by respect for the institutionality of the existing and dominant economic system — by the search for development within the interstices of the capitalist mode of production. The same could be said of the wave of NGOs formed in the 1980s under very different conditions of economic crisis and a redemocratization process. A number of essays in this book explore this issue.

At issue in diverse attempts to understand the role of cooperatives in the development process is the structure of their internal organization and political orientation. As indicated, cooperatives generally operate within the institutional framework of the dominant economic system. On this basis the means of collective production are not socialized; nor is the enterprise collectively managed. However, this is not so when cooperatives of workers see and organize themselves, and are instituted in relation to the state, as unions. This applies, for example, to SEWA (Self-Employed Women's Association), a cooperative union of self-employed poor women in Ahmedabad, India, that has been manifestly successful not only in promoting the interests of the poorest of the poor but in promoting effective social change. It also applies to those cooperative unions joined together under the umbrella of COLACOT (Confederación Latinamericana de Cooperativas y Mutuales de Trabajadores) in Sante Fé de Bogotá, Colombia. Like other such organizations, COLACOT operates with a social economy model, an "economy of labor" based on variations of the following four basic principles: (1) the supremacy of labor over capital; (2) social ownership, in one form or another, of the means of production; (3) an association of the direct producers; and (4) collective self-management of the enterprise.

At the level of principle and that of internal organization, the issues are clear enough. The problem is to determine how, and under what conditions, such an organization connects to and operates in terms of the broader economic system and the state. This problem is also addressed by a number of studies in this book in a more contemporary context of conditions found in Latin America today.

UNRISD: Participation as Social Empowerment

"Participation" is a term that first appeared in the development discourse in the late 1950s. Development practitioners began to notice that common people were almost completely excluded from the formulation and implementation of development projects. It was thought that the inclusion of local people would increase efficiency, leading to the improvement of development. This view of participation is now widely accepted by most NGOs, development workers, and even national governments. In fact, these days it is taken as a matter of principle with regard both to the design and execution of development projects as well as to the process as a whole. Thus it is that the concept of participation serves as a primary tool for project evaluation by the World Bank and other donors and aid agencies (Blaikie 1985; Cernea 1987).

There is, however, an alternative conception of participation, treated not as it is by the World Bank — as a means of ensuring greater efficiency and cost effectiveness in project design and implementation — but as an alternative form of development that is both socially empowering (of the people involved) and transformative (of the broader institutional structure of society).

In the first view, the development agenda is predetermined, objectives are defined, and solutions envisaged long before local people have an opportunity to begin participating. In the second view, propagated by scholars such as Anisur Rahman and, in the Latin American context, Fals Borda, among many others, participatory development requires societal transformation and leads to social empowerment. This perspective was widely aired at a number of conferences organized by UNRISD in the 1970s and 1980s, but it did not come into its own until the late 1980s, when for many practitioners and scholars it displaced the perspective of the World Bank, ECLAC, and other such organizations in the mainstream of development thinking and practice.

In the mainstream view, increased participation in the development process is seen as a primary responsibility of governments, which, in partnership with NGOs, are still viewed as the major executing agency for development. From the perspective of Another Development, however, participatory development is seen as a strategy to be implemented not from above and the outside but from below and within, that is, with the agency of community-based or grassroots social organizations. In this view, people need to be incorporated into the development process front and center and from the outset — in defining the problem, identifying possible solutions, and finally taking action. These scholars have been instrumental in the emergence of research techniques, such as participatory action research, that embodies this view. (On this see, in particular, Fals Borda, a long-time exponent of "action research.")

Participatory development (PD) is not a project but rather a process without a set time frame. The goal of PD is a decentralized, nonauthoritarian, and humanistic form of society that is environmentally sustainable and based on a sense of real community. A PD approach also accounts for, or at the very least acknowledges, the issues of power and privilege within communities or groups and also with any outsiders who may be part of the process. This form of development is thought to originate from the south and is viewed as transforming for both systems and participants. Participation in this context is or can be empowering when it takes into account the challenges of external structures, the agenda is not predetermined, and if it remains a radical concept. If it is simply a tool to implement predetermined objectives, participation is simply an insidious technique used to maintain a reformist agenda.

ECLAC (CEPAL): Participation as the Missing Link in the Development Process

No institution has been as central as ECLAC[2] in leading the opposition in Latin America to a neoliberal model of capitalist development and the search for an alternative form of development. For over fifty years ECLAC economists have debated neoliberal principles and policy prescriptions on the basis of a structuralist (and neostructuralist) model of the economy. However, this model in its various reformulations is predicated on the institutionality of the capitalist system —

private property in the means of production, the social relation of wage-labor, the market, and the state. The aim has been to give the capitalist development process a social dimension as well as a human face: "growth with equity" in an earlier formulation, "productive transformation with equity" in a more recent one (ECLAC 1990).

The key to the ECLAC model in its most recent neostructuralist formulation (Sunkel 1993) is the notion of participation as a "missing link" in the "productive transformation with equity chain" involved in the development process. "Equity," in this model, is required and can be achieved at two levels — access to society's productive resources and the distribution of the fruits of development. The aim is to broaden the social basis of the productive process — to incorporate as broad a social spectrum as possible, including the peasantry, indigenous communities, and the operators of enterprises in the informal sector that are entirely excluded from the development process in the neoliberal model.[3]

Chapters 2 and 3 elaborate on several critical variables of the ECLAC model, namely, the mechanism of popular participation and the process of institutional decentralization. And chapter 5 (Aquevedo on Chile) further elaborates on policies introduced by the *concertación* regime of Christian Democrats and Socialists in Chile in support of the ECLAC model. The key to this model is the notion that marginal producers and groups should be incorporated into the development process under existing conditions of small-scale production and that the people involved must actively participate in the process — and do so at its very center. This is the central point made by Albert Hirschman in his contribution toward development theory and practice in the region. It is also the theme of a book written by Matthias Stiefel and Marshall Wolfe (1994). The book summarizes a broad range of experience with popular participation in the region. In this connection, Stiefel and Wolfe, like Hirschman, point to the "declining state capacity to provide services and reduce income inequalities," accompanied by an equal reduction in "public confidence in the legitimacy of its efforts." When this trend is joined with the processes of political democratization, it is not surprising that the international community is "looking to 'participation' as a means of making their development projects function better, helping people cope, ... [and] as an indispensable dimension of the environmental policies . . . that can no longer be evaded or postponed" (Stiefel and Wolfe 1994, 19).

This point made by Stiefel and Wolfe is now widely accepted within the international development community as a fundamental principle with regard to both the implementation, assessment, and evaluation of development projects and the broader development process. In this connection, much of the recent literature has emphasized the multifaceted contribution that the productive incorporation of marginal groups can make to society (Friedmann 1992; Friedmann and Rangan 1993; Stiefel and Wolfe 1994). While very little has been done on specific strategies for sustainability in poor rural communities, it is clear that much of the experience in this regard recounted by practitioners with grassroots groups (for example, Glade and Reilly 1993) is consistent with the principles enunciated by theorists and analysts like Miguel Altieri (1987) and David Barkin (chapter 8, below). At issue in these studies is how to incorporate marginal groups and communities, particularly those that involve peasant producers and indigenous peoples. A lot more work and study are needed in this area (to identify the specific strategies that might work to ensure the sustainable development of marginal communities), but the overriding principle is clear enough: marginal groups and communities must be integrated into the larger (productive and political) processes of which they are a part.

David Korten and People-Centered Development

A major impetus to the search for an alternative form of development has been provided by the PCD (People-Centered Development) Forum. The PCD Forum traces its origins to March 1987, when more than a hundred members of NGOs and other development professionals from forty-two countries met in London for a symposium on "development alternatives."

The basic framework for the PCD Forum's approach, people-centered development, has been elaborated by David Korten, its founding member and president, on the basis of fourteen years of practical experience in Asia in exploring alternatives to the dominant model of state-led, free-market capitalist development. PCD seeks to provide an alternative to the production-centered development paradigm of the industrial era. The latter is still dominant, as evidenced by the enduring emphasis on increasing economic growth rates. From the perspective of PCD, the industrial-era strategy of maximizing production-throughput may have been appropriate and effective for its time, but it is now outmoded. Today's realities are of a high and increasing world population, hundreds of millions of people living in abject poverty, extreme disparities in the distribution of wealth and incomes, and increasing ecological degradation. New problems require new solutions, and PCD is a proposed framework to help seek those solutions.

From the perspective of PCD, economic growth is neither a prerequisite nor a necessary outcome of development. The standards of living of poor and disenfranchised people are to be improved not by increasing the rate of production but rather by changing production methods. This entails a shift, on the community level, away from specialization and integration into a world economy of diversity and self-reliance. It also entails the formation of smaller units, which are preferred not only because they are more conducive to the forging of human relationships but also because they are considered to be more efficient. A concomitant decentralization of political and economic systems is also required in order to enable individuals and communities to have more control over their lives. The success of these methods is measured in terms of human growth and well-being, equity, and sustainability.

The key to PCD is popular participation. In this, members of the PCD Forum not only pick up on ECLAC's argument for the need to incorporate marginal communities into the development process but also move beyond ECLAC in insisting on the need to place people at the center of this process. Participation here is seen as both a means for bringing about PCD and one of its goals. If decentralization is to be more than just the delegation of formal authority to lower levels, people must be able to participate in the decision-making processes that affect their lives. This entails more than just consultation; it requires the integration of people into real power structures. For this to occur, the initiative must come from below. In other words, the demands of community groups and civic organizations to have direct control over local resources and a voice in national policy debates must be met.

Ecological sustainability is another central tenet of PCD. The argument is that by creating a link between people's use of their resources and the consequences of that use, people will be a lot less likely to entertain destructive practices. Of course, people must have sufficient access to resources, knowledge, and appropriate technology if they are to avoid overexploiting local resources out of desperation. The assumption and experience of PCD are that given the opportunity people come up with diverse and innovative ways of solving local, specific problems and thereby complement the diversity that is inherent in nature and necessary for preserving its health.

DAWN (Development Alternatives for Women in a New Era) and the Issue of Gender and Development

The search for Another Development in the 1970s led to ideas about the need to incorporate women, members of diverse and disadvantaged or marginalized ethnic groups, and the poor generally into the development process, and to do so as active participants and not as victims. One of the first formulations of this view was advanced by Ester Boserup (1970) on the basis of a liberal feminist perspective — a perspective referred to as Women in Development (WID).[4] However, a more radical perspective was soon introduced. In this perspective the problems of underdevelopment and marginality are rooted in patriarchy, an oppressive system of male domination and female subordination that extends from the institutionalized structures of the world economy to the household (see, among others, Sen and Grown 1987; Beneria and Feldman 1992).[5] The solution to these problems, in the eyes of the many scholars and practitioners that share this perspective, is to build awareness and relations of solidarity among women as well as collective action against the oppressive elements of the system.

One of several significant theoretical and organizational responses to the widely felt need to incorporate women into the development process through the direct collective action of women themselves was DAWN. At the beginning and over the years, DAWN has provided a useful reference point for a network of organizational efforts that now extends across the region as well as important lines of ongoing research for feminist scholars (see, among others, Beneria and Feldman 1992; Bose and Acosta-Belén 1995).

Microenterprise Lending and Development
(Alleviation of Poverty at the Household Level)

In the 1980s, in the context of developments that were worldwide but particularly pronounced in Latin America, a number of organizations turned toward microenterprises in the informal sector of urban economies as potential agents of development. The impetus behind this turn in development theory and practice is not clear. As argued in chapter 3, it relates in part to the agenda of many governments to divest themselves from responsibilities for social programs and to downsize the state. Within this context a number of theorists and practitioners, notably (in the Latin American context) Hernán de Soto, a Peruvian economist and president of the Institute for Liberty and Democracy,[6] saw a new creative power in the efforts of many individuals and families to set up enterprises on the margins of the state; they further saw that, if channeled and promoted, this new creative power could become a major "engine of development" — to use a common metaphor. With references to ideas advanced by De Soto and others, governments and donor agencies (among others, the Carmeadow Foundation) all over the world initiated a major program of microenterprise lending, which soon became the strategy of choice for most international development agencies (Otero and Rhyne 1994).

The dominant trend toward microenterprise lending is based on the notion of solidarity lending, with reference to a highly successful experience of the Grameen Bank in Bangladesh. In this experience, a community group provides security for the loans taken out by individual entrepreneurs with ties of solidarity. The success of the Grameen Bank (a loan default rate lower than the norm for commercial loans) and other experiences with solidarity-based microenterprise lending have turned it into an important model of development.

A second and different model of microenterprise lending and entrepreneurship is associated with the practice of SEWA in Ahmedabad, India, both a cooperative and a union of unemployed women. Rather than relying on a solidarity group fomented by government and international donor support, SEWA has relied on a cooperative form of organization and a union of unemployed women entrepreneurs. The experience of SEWA has been exemplary, providing conditions and support that have enabled thousands of unemployed women to set up sustainable economic activities and enterprises. However, notwithstanding its success, SEWA has not provided the model for community-based microenterprise development in Latin America. Instead, the model for this development — for the broad range of experiences in the 1990s — has been provided by De Soto and the solidarity-lending approach toward the development (and formalization) of informal-sector enterprises.

How successful the approach has been is difficult to determine in that at the macro level little evidence has been provided. A number of studies by the ILO, however, suggest that the unstructured sector of relatively marginal economic activities and enterprises, together with its associated labor markets, has grown at the expense of more productive formal enterprises (International Labour Office 1996). This is due in part to the fact that the dominant neoliberal model of state-led but market-friendly development has been geared to (and benefited) a relatively small number of large capitalist enterprises in the region — about 10 percent of the total — that have exhibited a capacity to adjust to and insert themselves into the globalization process. Another category of enterprises, an estimated 35 percent of the total, that have productive capacity has been undermined by neoliberal policies that have pushed large numbers into bankruptcy. As for those enterprises operated in the informal sector or by peasants in rural society, at least half of all enterprises, they have been left to twist in the winds of neoliberal policy adopted by virtually all governments in the region.

Grassroots Sustainable Development

The concepts of sustainability and sustainable development emerged in various publications and forums in the 1970s and 1980s, most notably in several conferences organized by the United Nations Environmental Program (UNEP). With the publication of the Bruntland Report (UN Commission on the Environment and Development [UNCED], 1997) the issue of how to combine economic growth and environmental protection was placed at the center of the development agenda. As the UNCED saw it, the major agency for bringing about "sustainable development" was the concerted action of the world's national governments in support of Agenda 21, a plan of action arising out of the Rio Summit in 1992. However, by 1997 it had already become apparent that sustainable development could only be

achieved with community action to promote effective social development consistent with the requirements of ecosystem balance as well
as community-based resource management (Barkin 2000). To this
end a plethora of sustainable development projects were designed
and executed by nongovernmental and community-based organizations, with funding from the World Bank and bilateral aid agencies
in the rich industrialized countries of the Organization for Economic Cooperation and Development (OECD).[7] The range of such
projects implemented over the years is broad, but these projects have
tended to converge on the principles of ethnodevelopment, indigenous ecoknowledge, and community participation in project design
and resource management (Bromley 1994; Western and Wright
1994). In chapter 8, David Barkin addresses a key issue in these
projects — how to build sustainable communities on a grassroots
basis within the dominant neoliberal-policy and institutional context. This challenge is currently being taken up all over the region
by grassroots community-based organizations in the form of diverse
struggles and strategies for sustainable development. The theory of
this practice, however, is yet to be constructed, although Barkin in
his chapter in this volume and other writings does identify some of
its critical elements.

The Sustainable Livelihoods Approach (SLA)

International organizations involved in development set a target date
of 2015 for reducing by one-half the number of people living in extreme poverty, many of them in rural societies. At the turn of the new
millennium, it is apparent that this goal is not going to be achieved
by 2015. In fact, if anything, the number of those living in extreme
poverty has increased over the past several decades, as has the global
divide in incomes and living standards. The alleviation if not the reduction or eradication of extreme poverty, recognized by the World
Bank as early as 1974 as the major challenge confronting the world
community of development agencies and practitioners, was placed
front and center of the new development agenda set by these agencies in 1990 (see World Bank 1990). Nevertheless, despite a decade
of continued efforts and diverse strategies to deal with it, the problem of extreme poverty remains, as does that of relative poverty —
the growing number of those unable to meet their basic needs. In

response to this situation, and with reference to ideas advanced by Robert Chambers (1997), among others, the UK Department for Development (DFID), the United Nations Development Programme (UNDP), and the Society for International Development (SID) have begun to advocate a new "sustainable livelihoods approach" toward rural development.[8]

The essence of the sustainable livelihoods approach (SLA) is to place local and community-based development within the context of conditions created by "external" structures (levels of government, the private sector, etc.) and processes (policies, institutions, etc.). Within this context, the focus for analysis and action is on the impact of these structures and processes on the "livelihood assets" of the community — their capacity to generate financial, social, human, natural, and physical capital (Liamzon et al. 1996). Another concern of the SLA is to identify the forms of action that are capable of minimizing the negative effects of the external processes and transforming them. In this connection, attention has focused on "associations" — producer groups, cooperatives, and community-based organizations of various sorts. The reason for this focus is that analysis of many experiments with local development all over the world has led to the conclusion that such associations have the greatest potential for achieving collective or social empowerment, a process in which individuals and groups within a community have learned to interact with one another in a constructive manner, cooperate toward a common objective (identifying and addressing their problems), and undertake the collective action needed for social transformation and economic development. (On the various dimensions of SLA, the most recent formulation of Another Development, see, among others, Amalric and Banuri [1995]; Chambers [1997]; Liamzon et al. [1996]; and *Development* [1998].)

The Historical Context for Local and Community-Based Development in Latin America

Community and/or local development has a long history both in Latin America and elsewhere. In fact, it preceded by decades the search for Another Development initiated in 1974 by the Dag Hammarskjöld Foundation (see the journal *Development Dialogue*) and promoted by UNRISD and other international organizations such as SID. It also anticipated the concern with sustainable development expressed in UNCED and the Bruntland Report.

In the 1960s, a very particular model of community development was promoted in Latin America through the Alliance for Progress (AP) as a means of counteracting the effect of the Cuban Revolution. Under the auspices of the AP, the primary responsibility for the development project was given over to what later, in the 1980s, would be conceived of as "civil society," a conglomeration of community-based organizations that included churches, university groups, and the government-assisted and externally financed rural assistance extension programs that were at the center of the "community development movement" and its well-funded program for integrated rural development (IRD), the basic model for rural development in the 1970s. (On IRD see, among others, Honadle and Van Sant [1985].)

In the 1970s, in a different intellectual context — the basic needs and liberal reform approach, the major mainstream alternative presented to the radical demand for revolutionary change — various calls for Another Development emerged. At issue was a form of development that was people-led, human (small) in scale, participatory in form, and responsive to social mobilization from below. In this new context, community and local development became a matter of survival and achieving self-sufficiency, more than development per se. As for the political context, the major development in the decade was a movement to mobilize the working and middle classes, to incorporate them into the political process and increase their level of participation in the process of economic development. In this context the major agency for community development at the time was the state, a set of political institutions that was the captive instrument of the oligarchy and the bourgeoisie, an amalgam of commercial, financial, and industrial capitalists. One of the most significant political developments in this area was the military coup in 1973 led by Augusto Pinochet against the democratically elected socialist government of Salvador Allende and the subsequent seventeen years of military rule. Indeed, 1973 was also the turning point in the class war waged in Europe by capital against labor.[9] In Chile, the Pinochet regime launched what was regarded by one of the architects of the World Bank's Structural Adjustment Program as the "most radical, sweeping reforms in history." Not only did this regime pioneer the worldwide experiment with neoliberal reforms (liberalization, deregulation, and privatization), but it took specific measures to decentralize the government, reduce its role in the economy, and turn toward a more decentralized and community-based form of economic development. In this connection, Pinochet proposed "to teach the world a lesson in democracy." And indeed he has in that his experiments with institutional change came to be a major center of reference for the "structural" reforms that were introduced and widely implemented in the region and worldwide over the course of the next two decades.

The contribution of the Pinochet regime to the process of decentralized, community-based development was threefold. First, in 1976, barely two years into his dictatorial rule and administration, Pinochet set up the Corporation for Administrative Reform, which shifted certain functions from the central government to the regions and municipalities. The basis for this reform was set in the Declaration of Principles made in March 1974. It included the statement that "the essential point of the new establishment is the decentralization of power" — not just "political power" (to decide matters of general interest to the nation) but "social power" ("power for intermediate bodies of society to legitimately develop themselves in order to fulfill their own specific objectives"). Second, the regime promoted greater efficiency and effectiveness in policy implementation. In this connection, it was argued that the decentralization of sensitive social programs would allow the government to respond better and adapt its policies to differences in local realities as well as create avenues of popular participation in both the identification of needs and decisions as to how to allocate the resources directed toward communities. This approach and associated reforms became a model for the World Bank's partnership strategy pursued with much fanfare in the 1980s as well as the poverty-oriented New Social Policy (NSP) introduced by the Bolivian government in 1985 and by governments across the region since. (See chapter 2 for an elaboration of this NSP and chapter 4 on the case of Bolivia.) Third, local action by grassroots organizations, with NGO support, led to greater local control over decisions that affect people in their communities — to help them confront the conditions of a generalized crisis and meet their common needs (Razeto 1985; Teitleboom 1992).

In the 1980s, with reference to Chile's neoliberal experiment, the search for local and community-based development was widely promoted as the best alternative to the state-led or market-oriented approach advocated by governments, the World Bank, and other international organizations. The major agencies for this strategy were the myriad of local groups, voluntary associations, and NGOs formed in what was conceived of at the time as "the third sector." The theoretical context for the alternative development promoted by these organizations was what John Toye (1987) termed a "counterrevolution" in theory and practice — an approach that privileged the free market as the most efficient means of allocating resources across the system and bringing about economic development.

The political context for this counterdevelopment was formed by a number of discernible trends:

- a propensity toward crisis that was manifest in an incapacity to service external debts, rampant inflation, growing deficits on current accounts and government budgets, and a decline in levels of capital formation;

- a decapitalization of industry and the growth and the burgeoning of an informal sector composed of microenterprises that were characterized by low productivity, the lack of capital, irregularity in their operations, and the lack of social regulation;

- a process of structural adjustment, the liberalization of markets, deregulation of private-sector activity, and the privatization of state enterprises and public assets; and

- redemocratization, a process manifest in a widespread trend toward decentralization as well as the restoration of constitutional civilian regimes and the proliferation of NGOs, taken by international donors and governments as their strategic partners in the development process — as intermediaries with grassroots organizations and the poor.[10]

The 1990s saw another discernible shift in development thinking and practice, this time in the direction of consolidating the NEM of stabilization and structural adjustment measures. The problem with this model was that it tended to deepen the development gap and bore disproportionately on the poor and other vulnerable groups and categories of the population. To address this problem the model was redesigned so as to give structural adjustment a social dimension and the entire process a human face. (On this "new understanding," see International Monetary Fund 1992.)

ECLAC was one of a number of organizations to advance a model for this social development — social liberalism (ECLAC 1990). A key to this model was increased popular "participation," perceived as the "missing link" between "productive transformation" (technological conversion of the production apparatus so as to help it adjust to the changing requirements of the global economy) and "equity" (a more equitable access to society's productive resources). Another feature of this new model of social liberalism, oriented as it was above all toward the alleviation of poverty, was "the strengthening of civil society." Rather than relying on the NGOs to mediate with the grassroots and to execute development projects, attention was directed toward these grassroots organizations, most of them with highly informal organizations that lacked the institutional capacity that had been demanded of NGOs. The strengthening of civil society became the basis, if not the object, of a form of development that was not only market-friendly (based on a more balanced approach toward the role of the state and the market) but participatory and empowering. The major institutional requirement of this form of local and community-directed development was the decentralization of government services and increases in the responsibilities assumed by local governments — the municipalities. Chapters 3, 4, and 5 elaborate on the dynamics of this process, particularly as relates to the experience of Bolivia and Chile.

The Dynamics of Local or Community-Based Development

The Concept of Community

In his celebrated treatise, Ferdinand Tönnies (1963) makes a conceptual distinction between *Gemeinschaft* (community), where social relations are characterized by organic noncontractual social bonds and where individuals are bound together by a sense of mutual obligation and social identity, and *Gesellschaft* (society), where social relations are characterized by ties of external or formal association and where individuals are bound together only by convenience and a mutuality or rational calculation of shared interests. With this distinction, Tönnies gives another twist to a long tradition of sociological analysis and theory related to the theme of the loss of community under the impact of the forces of modernization, industry, and science — urbanism, industrialism, rationalism, secularism, materialism, commodification, and individualism.

In this tradition social analysis has become and remains very much divided between those who see reference to community as nostalgia for a past that cannot be revived or the projection of a utopian ideal and those who view it as an indispensable social condition of development. The history of development in the postwar period, at the levels of both theory and practice, reflects this division. At the level of practice (or policy prescription), community-based or community-directed development — the community development movement — has had a checkered but long history, waxing here, waning there, resurfacing or reasserting itself in different forms, places, and contexts. In each of the past five decades that constitute development as a field of study, both theory and practice have centered on the relative and corresponding roles of the market and the state, with different weights and values accorded to each. However, the concept of "community" has persisted throughout as a sideshow, and as such as a major center of reference for the by now ubiquitous and worldwide search for Another Development.

In the context of this search and the movement associated with it, the concept of community is intertwined with a series of other concepts such as "civil society," "the base," "local," and "popular participation" to form a consistent theoretical — and political — discourse in support of Another Development in one form or another. However, there are serious limitations to this discourse, which are discussed in various chapters below. One of them is that the persistent reference to the concept of a community serves to draw attention away from and ignore the internal class divisions and structural forces operating on individuals at this level, constraining their action in significant respects and ways. Chapter 2 explores this issue in some depth.

The term "local" is frequently used in the context of instituting a form of development that is people-led and participatory as well as in the context of the possibility of returning to preferable social forms in which communitarian values of the rural village are revived and revalidated and where the most diverse and heterogeneous social norms and cultural values are given free play. Here the local is counterposed to the global, a level of development in which there is no possibility for popular participation, no sense or spirit of community — a realm of objectivity where the structures and processes of an all-encompassing system rather than the thoughtful and purposeful actions of individuals can be seen to operate. This difference in context is crucial. The dynamics of change and development are radically different. While systems *function* or *operate* (on people and countries, depending on their position), individuals *act* and they can only do so effectively at a level where they can be capacitated and empowered, able to act collectively and generate the social forces needed to effect change and bring about the conditions of their development. The dynamics of these forces are explored in several chapters below.

Deconstructing the Discourse of Community-Based Local Development

Chapter 2 explores a critical dimension of the community development process missing in virtually all of the above schools of thought: the inner dynamics of forces generated by class divisions within human communities. In this sense the chapter provides a framework of ideas for an alternative analysis of the development process at the level of human communities. It is surprising how poorly the concept of community is defined and used both in the study of community development and in its practice. The concept of community implies a set of common understandings, social bonds of mutual obligation, as well as shared institutionalized practices. In this sense it is clearly more difficult to construct a "community" under some conditions than others. In the rural society a sense of community is more prevalent than in urban centers or cities, where a sense of community and, at times, a real operational "community" can be constructed at the level of neighborhood associations and local institutions. In many cases of community development, however, there is no real community — real or imagined. The term "community" in practice often denotes a bounded unit of people who relate simply to administrative or analytical convenience or geographical contiguity. In many cases, however, the people involved — or targeted by community development projects and programs — are divided along class lines and stratified along diverse dimensions. As a result, both in practice and in analysis, the notion of community not only is highly problematic but is difficult if not impossible to translate into either theory or practice. Chapters 2 and 3 here explore some dynamics of this problem.

Chapter 3 focuses on the regional (indeed worldwide) trend toward government decentralization. The bibliography of this volume illustrates the range of issues involved in an analysis of this trend. The trend itself is understood and presented as a mechanism for ensuring a more participatory process of economic development. Chapter 3 demonstrates that a number of conflicting (and converging) agendas are involved in this decentralization process. These agendas need to be — and are — deconstructed for their political meaning.

Chapters 4 to 7 provide a set of case studies into the diverse and complex dynamics of the development process associated with the search for an alternative form of development. In chapter 4, the focus is on a series of initiatives and institutional changes engineered by the Bolivian government to the twin objectives of reducing the conditions of extreme poverty and inducing a more participatory form of development. The two cornerstones of these policies were: (1) the institution, in 1986, of a New Social Policy (NSP), which, it has been argued, is "the most ambitious and far-reaching in Latin America" (Gleich 1999, 135); and (2) the promulgation, in 1994, of the Popular Participation Law and, in 1995, of the Administrative Decentralization Law. These two laws, together with the NSP, laid the foundation for a series of experiences both in Bolivia and elsewhere with popular participation in the development planning process and the decentralization of fiscal decision making. The highly successful — and ongoing (nine years to date) — experiment by the city government of Porte Alegre in Rio Grande do Sul, Brazil, with its "participatory budget-making process" to some extent can be traced back to these initiatives "from above" in Bolivia.[11]

Chapter 5 turns toward Chile and the efforts of the current democratic regime and the last democratic regime before it to institute a program of policy measures designed as a means of reducing and alleviating the poverty suffered by close to two out of five Chileans. The focus of these efforts is the Bio-Bio Region, one of the poorest areas in the country; the area has a high concentration of indigenous peoples and is on the margins of the country's second largest city and one of its major "growth poles." Once again, the major initiative involved in a series of efforts to institute a community-directed form of development is taken from within the government — "from above" as it were. This initiative is widely taken within the region as well as the world community of development practitioners as a model for other countries to follow. Thus the dynamics of its design and implementation warrant a close look. Eduardo Aquevedo, a sociologist working at the Universidad de Concepción, provides us with this close look, giving us in the process a glimpse into the dynamics of a government-initiated, decentralized program of community-directed, poverty-oriented development.

In chapter 6 the reader's attention is drawn to Costa Rica, which provides a context for exploring the current and dominant discourse on popular participation and participatory development. As observed by Arturo Escobar, a Colombian sociologist who writes in the emerging tradition of post–development/modernism, a lot of the pitfalls involved in efforts to institute a participatory form of development can be traced back to problems in the way development is conceived and written and thought about — that is, in the form of the discourse involved. Escobar (1997) here addresses a highly debatable issue that has been placed on the agenda by advocates of a poststructuralist (and postmodern) approach toward development. While she does not address this issue in terms framed by these analysts and theorists, Laura Macdonald raises serious questions about the NGO practice of participatory development as well as the discourse associated with it. One of the key points she makes is that in the context of a widespread naïveté with regards to NGOs as inherently participatory, the notion of "participatory development" should not be rejected but should be reclaimed.

In chapter 7 Aquiles Montoya turns toward the process of community-based participatory development in El Salvador. During the 1980s, the decade that gave rise to widespread and multifaceted experiments in local and community-based development all across the region, El Salvador was ravaged by a civil and class war that made community-based local development both difficult and necessary. In the 1990s, in the context of a peace accord signed by the warring sides, conditions for this form of development have changed in some respects, not in others. Montoya here reports on a large number of experiments with community-based development in these changing contexts — drawing conclusions about the process involved. One conclusion is that what are involved are not only issues of leadership and ideology, internal organization and external support, access to resources, agency, and a workable strategy, but an understanding of how external forces and structures impinge on the community. The chapters by David Barkin and Henry Veltmeyer make the same point. Unfortunately, it is difficult to identify a set of conditions that apply under diverse contexts. Nevertheless, Montoya presents the results of a comprehensive quantitative study of one hundred El Salvadorian peasant communities that have been practicing Community Economic Development (CED) for the past ten to fifteen years. This study considers a wide range of factors including, for example, land tenure, economic activity, infrastructure, environment, and outside financial support, that are critical to community-development efforts everywhere. With reference to these indicators, Montoya concludes that although these communities are succeeding in overcoming conditions of poverty and marginalization, "this situation must be consolidated in order to realize its potential and be reproduced on a larger scale." He presents seventeen concluding reflections.

In chapter 8, David Barkin addresses a critical issue involved in the process of community-based development: how to sustain, in environmental, social, and economic terms, the communities at the base of the development process — how to build sustainable communities. With regard to this complex issue, Barkin reviews both the theory and the practice in the context of developments in Mexico. His general conclusion is that the neoliberal model is ecologically unsustainable and militates against community development in rural areas. This model thus needs to be replaced by one that permits communities in rural areas "to receive support from the rest of the nation to implement an alternative regional development program."

On a community level, the new model would be characterized by diversity and self-sufficiency (as opposed to specialization and integration into the world market), ecological sustainability, autonomy, popular participation (in planning and implementation), and local control over local resources. Some of the strategies pursued by local communities in this regard and the mechanisms being developed by them are explored by Barkin in some of his recent work (Barkin 2000).

In the concluding chapter, Anthony O'Malley reflects on the possible or likely future of community-based development (CBD). In the first part of his essay, O'Malley provides a theoretical discursus on the concept of "community" — a series of reflections on the postmodernist discourse that in recent years has come to influence the way community development has been thought about and practiced. He traces out the long historical roots of the notion of community as it relates to the development process. In this connection, O'Malley counterposes the idealism and romanticism of the postmodernist approach to various realist forms of structural analysis that have dominated the study of development over the years.

O'Malley takes as a key issue how CBD is conceived and put into practice — as a means or as an end. Reflecting on the complex dynamics of the process involved, he concludes that CBD does have a future, but it is by no means guaranteed. Among other things, it requires an active construction that takes into account the structural and conjunctural conditions of its agency. In this connection, O'Malley, in the final section of his essay, turns back to, and expands on, several points made in chapter 2 vis-à-vis the intra- and intercommunity dynamics of class. Thus we come full circle, turning back to ideas advanced as a guiding thread for the various studies on community development presented in this volume.

Notes

1. Mondragón, located in Spain's Basque region, is the largest and most successful group of worker-owned companies. Annual sales are US $4.8 billion, and 39 percent of their industrial sales are exports. Over eighty highly productive co-ops, seventy of which are industrial, employ over twenty-nine thousand people producing a wide range of goods and services. In this democratically governed, integrated complex of high-tech firms, worker-owners benefit from wages and capital appreciation, job security, extensive technical education, and occupational retraining. One industrial company is Spain's largest producer of consumer durables (refrigerators, stoves, electrical appliances) and Spain's fifth largest manufacturer. The complex includes a large chain of supermarkets; agricultural, construction, and service co-ops; a community-development bank; a technical school; and a social service system.

2. References to publications of ECLAC are listed under its Spanish acronym (CEPAL) when written in Spanish.

3. Stiefel and Wolfe (1994). The neoliberal model is primarily oriented and geared toward those large-scale enterprises that are able to adjust well to changes in the world economy and able to insert themselves into the globalization process under competitive conditions, an estimated 15 percent of the total. It also incorporates a category of enterprises and production units deemed to have "productive capacity." Thus an estimated 50 percent of all enterprises and production units, including those in the peasant sector and the urban informal economy, are treated as inefficient and marginal, and as such are expected to be shaken out and disappear in the development process.

4. A contemporary extension of this perspective into Latin America can be found in Rao, Stuart, and Kelleher (1999).

5. Variations of this radical perspective led to a serious debate within the feminist movement, raising questions that have by no means been settled even into the twenty-first century. Among development practitioners and scholars the dominant formulation of this perspective was in terms of gender and development (GAD), according to which patriarchy permeates not only the institutionalized structures of the dominant capitalist system but relations between men and women at the level of the household. The ensuing debate and literature on this issue are too voluminous to cite.

6. This center (the Instituto para la Libertad y Desarrollo [ILD]) has had a long-standing relationship with the Washington-based Center for International Private Enterprise that shares ILD's right-wing ideology and its notion of the private sector as the solution to dilemmas of development.

7. The number and range of sustainable development projects implemented over the years are large and broad, although to date there is no systematic assessment of their outcomes and impacts. Nevertheless, the relevant literature is huge and growing. See, in particular, Weaver, Rock, and Kusterer (1996). Some elements of this literature provide a holistic approach toward sustainable development, a model based on an assessment and evaluation of diverse projects and an analysis of their contexts — social, cultural, and political. Other elements of the growing literature on sustainable development include mediation between

the grassroots and policy formation processes that in practice are often involved. On this, see Blauert and Zadek (1998).

8. The growth and spread of this approach among sociologists are reflected in the theme — "Sustainable Rural Livelihoods" — of the Tenth World Congress of Sociology in Rio de Janeiro, 30 July–5 August 2000.

9. The high point and last major offensive of world labor in its struggle for higher wages and better working conditions occurred in 1968. In 1973, in the midst of a systemic crisis, capital struck back and launched a counteroffensive that reached well into the last decade of the millennium. On the dynamics of this class war, see, among others, Crouch and Pizzorno (1978).

10. Not all NGOs can be viewed as intermediaries, mediators between grassroots and outside-funding and policy-making agencies. Some NGOs are government owned (GONGOs); others have a business interest (BINGOs); and many others work in the public interest (PINGOs). In this volume, however, the term NGO is used in a more restrictive sense to refer to intermediary-type organizations that are part of what used to be termed "the third sector" but that as of the 1990s in development discourse, both official and unofficial, have been viewed as part of "civil society." NGOs of this type, although often accommodated to the World Bank and serving as a partner institution, are generally part of the popular movement, which, in the current context of globalization, has become global in scope.

11. On this model experiment in participatory local development, see, in particular, Neaera Abers (2000).

The Dynamics of Community and Class

Henry Veltmeyer

The concept of "community" connotes a sharing not only of certain ways of doing things but of a sense of social identity — of belonging and mutual obligation. As it happens, these two conditions define membership in all social groups, sociologically speaking, no matter the size or type — from "the nation" to the smallest scattering of a rural population within a bounded geographic space. But to fully constitute a community, further conditions are needed. One condition is small size. Thus, while one might conceive of a disembodied virtual community formed on the basis of a network of relations formed through the Internet without boundaries across time and space, in fact the individuals so "grouped" do not constitute a *real* community. A real human community requires that members know and recognize each other and interact directly, conditions that do apply in small towns and rural communities across Latin America and elsewhere. However, these conditions are difficult to maintain, or even form, in the growing number of medium-sized and large urban centers and cities in which the majority and growing part of the population can be found today. The processes of urbanization are long-standing, but in the post–World War II context they have greatly accelerated, resulting in, by the end of the millennium, a society that today is largely urban. In fact, around 70 percent of Latin America's population today can be found in the region's urban centers or cities.

This urban-rural split is the first great social divide in Latin

American society. Other divisions arise out of differences in the social relations of production that are formed across this urban-rural
divide. In these terms it is possible to identify variations of the following "social structure." The first element of this structure is the
dominant class of individuals who own or control the means of social production. Traditionally this element of the population has been
viewed as a capitalist class in that it disposes of capital, the sum total
of society's financial resources and productive assets — and wealth.
This class, by and large, is concentrated in the large cities, but elements can be found in the smaller towns and even the countryside —
the agrarian capitalists. A second part of the class structure is composed of small landholders, independent producers, and operators
of small businesses in both the countryside and the cities and small
towns. French historians, as well as Marx, defined this element of
the population as a "petite bourgeoisie" — a class of small property owners or town dwellers. It is estimated that this class makes
up anywhere from 10 to 25 percent of the total population of Latin
America. A third element of the class structure can be loosely defined
as "the working class" in that it involves the direct producers of society's wealth. These persons — who can be differentiated according
to occupation and industry, form of remuneration (wages), and conditions of work — do the work that adds value and surplus value to
social production. This class takes many forms. In the urban centers
the population is divided into a formal and informal sector on the
basis of conditions of work, the type of enterprise to which they are
connected, and the form of remuneration: self-employment versus
employment for wages, the defining characteristic of the traditional
working class.

The Latin American Social Structure

At the structural level, a number of critical factors and characteristics
define the population in Latin American. One is spatial distribution
and location. In these terms, Table 2.1 distinguishes between two
groups, one located in the region's urban centers and the other in
the countryside — in the smaller communities and farms of rural
society. The table also points toward a fundamental change in the

TABLE 2.1

THE POPULATION OF LATIN AMERICA AND THE CARIBBEAN:
SOME BASIC DISTRIBUTIONS, 1994

	Population (1000s)		Percent Urban			Labor[a], Percent Female		
	No.	%	'70	'93	ch[b]	'70	'93	ch[b]
Argentina	33,875	7.5	78	87	(09)	25	28	(3)
Bolivia	7,238	1.6	41	59	(18)	21	26	(5)
Brazil	159,000	35.1	56	71	(15)	22	28	(6)
Colombia	34,545	7.6	57	72	(15)	21	22	(1)
Chile	14,026	3.1	75	84	(09)	22	29	(7)
Ecuador	11,226	2.1	45	57	(12)	16	19	(3)
Mexico	88,431	17.2	59	74	(15)	18	27	(9)
Peru	23,381	5.1	57	71	(14)	20	24	(4)
Paraguay	4,767	1.1	37	51	(14)	21	21	(0)
Uruguay	3,167	0.7	82	90	(08)	26	32	(6)
Venezuela	21,051	3.7	72	92	(20)	21	28	(7)
Belize	211	0.1						
Costa Rica	3,347	0.7						
Cuba	10,682							
Dominican Republic	7,769	1.7	40	63	(23)	11	16	(5)
El Salvador	5,641	1.2	39	45	(06)	20	25	(5)
Guatemala	10,322	1.9	36	41	(05)	13	17	(4)
Honduras	5,497	1.2						
Nicaragua	4,275	0.9						
Panama	2,583	0.6						
Caribbean-ES[c]	6,108	6.7						

Sources: (1) Population figures — Organization of American States 1994; (2) World Bank 1995b.

    a. The official labor force — that is, those registered as employed or seeking employment (employed/unemployed). In the Latin American context, this excludes large categories of workers, in particular women, who do not offer their labor for sale or whose labor is otherwise not accounted for.
    b. Percentage-point change.
    c. Includes English-speaking islands of the Caribbean (Trinidad & Tobago, Bahamas, Barbados, Dominica, Grenada, Jamaica, St. Lucia, St. Kitts, St. Vincent), Surinam, and Guyana.

urban-rural distribution of the population and, as of 1970, in the gender composition of the labor force.

    Table 2.1 not only identifies significant country-by-country variations in the urban-rural distribution of the population but highlights significant changes in the structure of this distribution over the past two and a half decades. In most cases, the shift of the population toward the urban centers has involved a change of at least ten percentage points, and this trend continues apace. Table 2.1 also

TABLE 2.2

THE STRUCTURE OF ECONOMIC ACTIVITY, SELECTED COUNTRIES,[a]
RANKED (OUT OF 132) IN REVERSE ORDER
OF PER CAPITA INCOME, 1994

		GDP (million $)	Percent Share	Percent Share of Total Production			
				Agriculture	Industry[b]	Manufacturing	Services[c]
49	Bolivia	6,760	0.5	16.4	25.7	13.8	48.4
63	Ecuador	14,718	1.1	12.6	39.8	19.0	47.7
67	Colombia	53,367	4.5	14.9	32.2	19.2	50.3
69	Peru	44,074	3.7	6.9	41.2	28.1	51.4
70	Paraguay	6,911	0.5	26.7	22.2	16.2	47.7
87	Venezuela	61,527	5.2	4.7	48.3	20.5	44.5
89	Brazil	412,747	34.9	10.5	33.1	25.2	53.7
94	Chile	40,248	3.4	9.1	40.7	19.9	38.8
96	Mexico	268,892	22.7	7.6	29.0	22.3	61.9
98	Uruguay	11,516	1.0	10.7	25.2	20.7	61.9
103	Argentina	266,005	22.5	6.5	41.5	26.1	56.8

Source: Organization of American States 1994. Selected data from Tables A-5, A-6, B.

a. Selected countries make up 84.9 percent of the region's population and 95.2 percent of the region's GDP. The biggest three economies (89, 96, 103) make up 59.8 percent of the population and 75 percent of the GDP.
b. Composed of mining, manufacturing, and construction.
c. Composed of commerce, transport/communications, finance, government, and others.

identifies a general trend toward the feminization of the labor force. This trend has accelerated over the past fifteen years, despite the fact that the vast majority of women enter the informal sector of the labor force, where their numbers are notoriously undercounted.

Even with the most limited demographic analysis, it is possible to identify clear patterns to these variations that correspond to differences in the social structure. To some degree this is reflected in other elements of the social structure, such as the distribution of economic activities (Table 2.2) and the distribution of income (Table 2.3). A cursory examination of these patterns, and the socioeconomic conditions to which they relate, suggests that the corresponding structures are interconnected to form a system.

Within the economic and social system in place throughout Latin America and elsewhere, income is a critically important determinant of the "life chances" of each individual and household. Most people require money or income to meet their basic needs, and the major

TABLE 2.3

DISTRIBUTION OF NATIONAL INCOME, BY TOP/BOTTOM QUINTILES
(1–2) AND TOP DECILE (3). SELECTED COUNTRIES, LISTED IN RANK
REVERSE ORDER BY PER CAPITA INCOME LEVELS, 1993

	GNP Per Capita		Income Distribution				Rural Population in Poverty
	% US	Int'l $	(1) L 20%	(2) H 20%	(3) H 10%	2/1	%
Bolivia	9.8	2,420	5.6	48.2	31.7	9.6	97
Colombia	22.2	5,490	3.6	55.8	39.5	15.5	45
Peru	13.0	3,220	4.9	51.4	35.4	10.5	75
Brazil	21.7	5,370	2.1	67.5	51.3	32.1	73
Chile	34.0	8,400	3.3	60.4	45.8	18.3	56
Mexico	27.5	6,810	4.1	55.9	39.5	13.6	51
Argentina	33.3	8,250	4.4	50.3		11.4	20

Source: World Bank 1995b. Figures break income earners into quintiles: (1) the lowest 20 percent; (2) the top 10 percent; and (3) the top decile.

source of this income is work, either for wages or a salary (employment) or on one's own account (self-employment) in the form of commodity production — the direct production of goods and services for sale. In every Latin American society, with the exception of Cuba, there exists a class of individuals who receive income in the form of rent or profit derived from ownership of property or some means of social production. Most people, however, have to work for a living. That is, they are part of the working class, dependent on the sale of their labor-power. Table 2.4 provides a graphic representation of the class structure of Latin American society and of the position of workers and producers within this structure.

The Dynamics of Class and Community

In describing the social organization of the population, the concepts of class and community are frequently counterposed. But in actuality class and community, their relations and dynamics, more often intersect. Relations of community solidarity are more easily forged in rural society, where, in fact, administrative boundaries (municipalities) are more likely to correspond to real or effective communities, that is, to relations of solidarity and a sense of mutual obligation

TABLE 2.4

THE LATIN AMERICAN CLASS STRUCTURE IN THE 1990s
(PERCENT DISTRIBUTION OF THE ECONOMICALLY ACTIVE
POPULATION)*

		Urban		Rural
I	Capitalist class	4		2
II	Middle class			
	Professional/bureaucratic	6		2
	Small business operators	10		4
	Independent producers			12
III	Working class			
	Formal sector	20	Proletariat (waged)	25
	Informal sector	60	Semiproletariat	20
IV	Peasants			35

Source: Calculations made on the basis of estimates and projections from data in World Bank 1996 and International Labour Office 1996.

*These rough estimates of the class distribution are based on official data on the economically active population, which includes those who are employed, those who are self-unemployed, and those seeking employment in the labor force.

among individuals. In these terms, in Latin America there are hundreds of thousands of essentially small rural "communities." In the urban centers, the term "community" does have an empirical referent, but it is not so easy to define and is very difficult to construct. Often it corresponds to relations formed among individuals in particular neighborhoods, where residence, as opposed to work, forms the basis of a sense or spirit of community. Clearly, a sense of community under these conditions has to contend with a multiplicity of relations and conditions that cut across the population within a neighborhood — and that divide them.

As for the countryside, a sense of community tends to persist and is relatively widespread, so much so that it can be used to define the population as a network of ties and relations that bind people together into various organic entities.

These rural communities constitute the basis of efforts by governments, nongovernmental organizations (NGOs), and outside agencies to induce a process of economic development on the basis of one project or another. We have here the major object of community-based or rural development. However, as Laura Macdonald suggests in chapter 6, below, the problem is not so simple in practice. In fact, the designation "a community" serves but to identify existing groups of individuals who happen to share a geographic proximity or administrative boundary or unit — a municipality. In actual fact, more often than not relations of solidarity — even the people's sense of community — do not define those so grouped. Different members of the community stand in different relationships to the means of production, some owning considerable property, some little, and others none at all, forced thereby to work for others in exchange for a living wage. In other words, the elements of the broader class structure are reproduced at the level of the community. And such communities are divided not only by class but by class conflict.

In this context, community-based development is difficult to realize in that any organization formed to this purpose, or project implemented, cannot encompass or represent the whole population or "the community." The issue becomes: What elements of the community are represented by or engaged in a particular project? Who represents the community in this context?

A revealing case study of the problems involved in connecting community to development is presented by the social anthropologist Gavin Smith (1989) in his case study of Huasicanchinos in Peru. What is most useful in Smith's analysis is his examination of the relationship between community and class, the Scylla and Charybdis of social analysis. In this analysis, Smith establishes the two concepts as complementary. He shows in exquisite detail that members of a community can unite in a common struggle even though the interests, aims, and objectives of the different classes that comprise it — and that connect it to the wider society — diverge. In the specific case of the struggle of the Huasicanchinos for land, a form of commonality was produced on the basis of a shared discourse and common or concerted action. But this did not mean that class differences were subsumed or replaced by community ties — that everyone was bound into an organic unity on the basis of social bonds and a sense of mutual obligation toward a common identity. Again and again Smith shows that divergent class interests both within and outside the community threaten to destroy the community and to undermine the commonality of its struggles (Smith 1989, 233).

In this situation, Smith provides an illuminating theoretical commentary on the process of social transformation within a community of peasants — a people who by and large share the same conditions of life and culture and thus more easily constitute a community. The same process can be found in different contexts and targeted as an object of analysis or of a development project.

Another case in point is the complex of peasant communities in Mexico, constituting some fourteen million people (around 15 percent of the population) who are spread across the country but concentrated in a large number of small communities, many of them highly marginalized.

The first thing that can be said about these marginal communities is that, strictly speaking, they do not constitute a community as such, which is to say, they can be internally differentiated — and divided — along class lines. Most of the population in these groups are "peasants" — caught up in the real and moral economy of small producers (of corn and beans), working land to which they might have individual title but in many cases share collectively within the *ejido* system. However, in the not atypical case of Chiapas, many peasant communities are formed by quite different and diverse ethnicities; over half the population has been proletarianized, that is, rendered landless and forced to work for the owners of large estates in the vicinity or further away, leading to a process of seasonal and sometimes permanent migration. The dynamics of this process are complex, under some conditions resulting in the formation of social movements for change and under others in a process of community development — the object of development activities (or projects) initiated with or without "participation" by government or outside agencies and executed, most often, by NGOs.

The problem, as we noted above, is that in neither theory nor practice is the connection of the community to the wider society, and to its economic and political systems, brought into a clear focus. This problem could be posed (and in the literature it often is) as a question of the penetration of economically and politically marginal and geographically remote (and often indigenous) communities by outside forces. The dynamics of this penetration also have a class dimension that needs to be analyzed. However, studies of these matters are not immune from the ambiguity and intellectual schizophrenia that characterize so many academic studies in this field when it comes to the marginal status and miserable state of so many traditional, indigenous communities.

On the one hand, many of these communities are geographically isolated as well as marginal in economic, social, and political terms, which has led many scholars to view the conditions of their marginality (deprivation, poverty) as the result of geographic isolation and to see those conditions as self-imposed rather than as the result of social and political exclusion, discrimination, and the nature of the relationship that these communities have with the broader society, its culture, and its economic and political institutions. In these terms, these scholars frequently evoke the need for these communities to overcome their isolation and to integrate into the wider society — to be incorporated into its institutionalized practices and structure. On the other hand, the conditions encompassed by the term "marginality" are correctly viewed as the product not of the marginal status of indigenous communities but of the specific form of their relationship with the broader "civil society" and the state, even the world economy.

Take the case of Chiapas, one of Mexico's richest states in terms of natural resources and one of the poorest in terms of the incidence of marginality, the objective conditions of which correspond to the large number of indigenous communities of peasant producers and the large size and distribution of the indigenous population. It has been estimated that at least 60 percent of these peasants are, in fact, *jornaleros* — wage-laborers for the large *hacendados* (ranchers and *caciques* who own most of the arable land, commercial operations, and productive resources in the region and control the political system). And a large number of peasants, dispossessed of their access to land, have migrated to the Lacandon forest in search of wage-labor in a petrochemical plant (the country's largest), a hydroelectric complex, oilfields, and logging operations. As Thomas Benjamin and others (Botz 1994) have documented, the conditions of this process (which Marx would have termed "primitive accumulation" — the dispossession of the producers from their means of production) have converted many indigenous peasant-producers into landless workers, a superexploited semiproletariat. The conditions and dynamics of this long historic process make it difficult to conceive of the "marginal" peasant community as isolated from the wider society, disconnected from its economic structure. Moreover, the largely self-subsistent base of the peasant economy, constructed within the institutional and legal framework of the *ejido* system of community landholding, is also part of Mexico's national economy. Not only does it serve to reproduce the incredibly cheap labor that so many *campesinos* are compelled to offer to the *hacendados* and capitalists across the country, but, as one consequence of Mexico's entry into NAFTA (North American Free Trade Agreement), it is also subject to unfair competition from US producers, competition that has crippled the local economy.

In view of NAFTA and other such regional arrangements, the complex of peasant communities, constituting the economic and cultural basis of Mexico's indigenous peoples and society, is very much a part of a national — indeed global — economy and deeply affected by its workings. Thus it is that Subcomandante Marcos, in the immediate wake of the Zapatista uprising, could speak of NAFTA as "a death sentence" for the indigenous people of Chiapas and the country. However, the uprising and the subsequent process of negotiations — and transition of the EZLN (Ejército Zapatista de Liberación Nacional) from an army of national liberation into a new political force — make it just as clear that there is a significant "political" dimension to the relationship that the country's indigenous peoples have with Mexican society.[1]

A central issue in the prolonged negotiation process is the need to fundamentally change the constitutionally defined (and politically effective) political relationship of the country's indigenous peoples to the government and to the state: to meet thereby the Zapatista movement's critical demands for "liberty, independence, and democracy — and social justice." At issue in these demands is the struggle of Mexico's indigenous peoples to escape the objectively given (and experienced) conditions of their exploitation and oppression — the relations of class that connect them to the outside and divide them internally. As for the "outside," it encompasses a solitude that reaches all the way from the local to the global — to the world economic system and its macrodynamics.

Notes

1. In Mexico, for example, at least 70 percent of the country's estimated fourteen million indigenous peoples live and, for the most part, work or produce for subsistence in what are officially characterized as "marginal zones," areas characterized by higher than average indexes of low income, malnutrition, illiteracy, child mortality, and lack of access to adequate housing, electricity, potable water, and other services. These zones encompass fifteen hundred municipalities across the country.

THREE

Decentralization and Local Development

Henry Veltmeyer

No concept is as central in the study of development, or as problematic in its application, as "participation," viewed from the most diverse theoretical perspectives as a critically important requirement of development. Over the years, the concept has been given diverse meanings and has been subject to numerous twists in practice. These twists reflect not only shifts in conception but changes in the real conditions that underlie and to some extent induce these shifts. In the context of conditions in the 1980s, the notion of participation or participatory development was closely linked to a widespread process of government decentralization and local community-based development.

Associated with this trend, providing for it a context of socioeconomic and political conditions, are the following: (1) the emergence of a neoconservative antistate ideology (expressed, among other places, in ideas of a minimalist state and the need to privatize the major means of social production); (2) a counterrevolution in development thinking and practice; and (3) the institution of a neoliberal model of structural adjustment. In these circumstances, the concept of participation has been linked to a global trend toward the decentralization of government and an associated search for a local or community-based form of development.

The purpose of this chapter is to analyze the dynamics of this decentralization process in terms of conditions found in Latin America. To this end, the chapter is organized into three sections. The first section traces the major twists and turns in the notion of participatory development. The second section examines the trend toward decentralization of government in the Latin American context. In this context it is argued that the impetus for the process relates to initiatives both from above (from within government itself) and from below (from pressures to democratize the political institutions of society and the relations between the state and civil society). The third section examines several dynamics of this twofold process, highlighting a number of findings that are summarized in the conclusion.

The Itinerary of a Concept

The concept of popular participation is deeply embedded in the theory of democracy, but in post–World War II development studies, one of the earliest formulations of the concept appeared in a 1964 study by the UN's Economic Commission for Latin America (ECLAC). At the time, the concept of participation as a necessary condition of development was somewhat anachronistic in that it did not have the slightest resonance or intellectual force. One reason for this was its formulation in the context of (1) capitalism's "golden age," an extended period of unprecedented high annual rates of growth in total output, and (2) the intellectual adjunct to this golden age — the grandiose formulas and optimistic prognosis for successful development associated with the theories of growth and modernization advanced by the grand theorists of the new discipline of economic development. It would be twenty-five years before ECLAC, the founder and principal expositor of the structuralist thinking that dominated the study of development, would return to this concept of participation. In the meantime the concept was given a systematic reformulation by exponents of Another Development — a form of development that depended on neither the functioning of the free market nor the agency of the state in regulating it.

This search for Another Development, announced publicly at a conference organized in 1974 by the Dag Hammarskjöld Foundation, signaled a very different and changed historical context. The world economic order installed at Bretton Woods in the wake of World War II had exhausted its limits, and the entire global capitalist system lapsed into a deep structural crisis. This crisis was manifest in (1) a general tendency toward declining rates of productivity growth; (2) stagnant growth in output; (3) an underlying "profitability crunch" (a declining rate of profit on invested capital); (4) the discovery (by the World Bank) that at least 800 million people in the "Third World" of sub-Saharan Africa, Asia, and Latin America were unable to meet even their basic needs; (5) the simultaneous emergence of mass unemployment and runaway inflation; and (6) the inability of the developmentalist (interventionist) state to deal with the problem of underdevelopment and poverty and of the actually existing state to cope and deal with the problems of unemployment and inflation.

The conditions of this changed context were reflected in development thinking — and practice — at a number of levels. First, the central concept of development was broadened and extended to include a specific and distinctly social dimension — health, education, social security, and welfare (meeting basic needs). In these terms, the concern for and goal of development were no longer just matters of economic (GNP per capita) growth but included the creation of social conditions, the meeting of basic needs, the alleviation if not the reduction or eradication of world poverty, and a more equitable distribution of the world's productive and economic resources — and the benefits of economic growth.

In this changed context, the concept of participation, or participatory development, had two major centers of reference. On the one hand, the reform-oriented liberal intellectuals who dominated the field as development consultants and planners, as well as the national governments and international organizations that employed them or contracted their services, generally took "participation" to mean the incorporation of the intended beneficiaries into the development process. Thus it was recognized that in terms of education and health, women were generally central agents in the development process but excluded from most of its benefits; and that in terms of both improved access to society's productive resources and increased wage employment, the participation of women was both liberating (from the shackles of tradition) and a necessary condition of their social development — a means of social capital formation. In this context, development was (and is) predicated not on changing the

system that produces its socioeconomic conditions but on changing the position of women (or of agricultural producers, the urban
poor, or other intended beneficiaries of the development process)
within the system — removing any barriers to their equal access or
opportunity.

On the other hand, participation was conceived as a source of
social empowerment, constituting and capacitating the objects of
the development process as active subjects, involving them in each
and every phase, including initial diagnosis and the determination of
the community's problems and needs.

Subsequently, in the 1980s and 1990s, these alternative approaches coalesced into an intellectual movement with certain
identifiable features and basic principles:

1. development as empowerment, the expansion of choice, the
   realization of a potential given to every human being in equal
   measure;

2. the need to go beyond the state and the market (the development agencies identified in the dominant development
   discourse) toward the community (the locus and key agency
   of the development process);

3. popular participation as the sine qua non of the development
   process, its goal, means, and agency (Goulet 1989; Rahman
   1993; Stiefel and Wolfe 1994);

4. that the necessary conditions of participatory development are
   that it be human in scale (small), local or community-based, and
   people-led (Max-Neef, Elizalde, and Hopenhayn 1965; Korten
   1987; Rahman 1991); and

5. that it requires both equity (a more equitable distribution of society's resources, that is, social transformation) and democracy,
   predicated on a fundamental change in the nature of the state
   and its relation to civil society.

Probably the most systematic formulation given to this concept
of participatory development was by the United Nations Research
Institute for Social Development (UNRISD), which organized and
sponsored a series of international forums and conferences on

its various dimensions (and the principles and possible conditions of its implementation) from 1979 to 1982. This formulation by UNRISD was a touchstone of various reformulations and experiences in the 1980s — in a radically changed context. The social base of this reformulation was a vast and growing complex of grassroots, community-based organizations (CBOs) and an international network of associated nongovernmental organizations (NGOs).

The 1980s provided another critical conjuncture of conditions that produced or led to what amounts to what John Toye (1987) terms a "counter-revolution" in development thinking and practice and an associated neoliberal model of structural adjustment and free-market reforms — the liberalization (of trade and the flow of capital), deregulation (of private activity), privatization (of the means of production and state enterprises), and downsizing/modernization of the state. The ideas behind this Structural Adjustment Program (SAP) were not new. Indeed, they had been around since the 1960s, and in the 1970s they informed the national policy of the military regimes in Chile and elsewhere in the Southern Cone of the continent. The SAP was also imposed by the IMF (International Monetary Fund) on the government of Jamaica and a number of governments in sub-Saharan Africa. But it was not until the economic and debt crisis of the early 1980s in the South, and the coincident emergence of a series of neoconservative regimes in the North, that the political conditions for its implementation were generated worldwide. In this context, regime after regime in Latin America and elsewhere in the South was constrained to adopt the SAP. By 1990, only four countries in Latin America had not done so, and these (Peru, Argentina, Brazil, Venezuela) would do so in the space of a few years — Peru in 1993, Argentina in 1994, Brazil in 1994, and Venezuela in 1996.

The 1980s in Latin America and elsewhere in the South were characterized by the contradictory development of (1) a debt crisis, the conditions of which included an excessive dependence on external financing, a hemorrhage of internal financial resources, and a decline in the rate of domestic capital formation and investment; and (2) a redemocratization process, the major conditions of which were the reinstitution of an elected civilian constitutional regime and the opening up of a space for the action of political parties at the national level and community-based organizations (CBOs) and

NGOs at the local and regional level. In this situation, SAPs were widely introduced with social, economic, and political impacts that have been extensively studied and documented. As for their economic impacts, the general pattern has been for the restoration of macroeconomic equilibrium (control of inflation, balanced accounts) without the economic reactivation, the restoration of sustainable economic growth, predicted by the theorists of structural adjustment.[1] At the social level, the most striking impact of SAPs has been the extension and deepening of social inequalities (and inequities) as regards access to productive resources and the distribution of income. Conditions of this inequality include (1) a dramatic deterioration in labor's share of national income and a corresponding increase in capital's share; (2) a dramatic fall in the real value (purchasing power) of wages; (3) the polarization of household income, with a dramatic increase in the number of low-income households and a decreasing share in total national income;[2] (4) the concentration of income in the form of capital and the private fortunes of a small number of billionaires; and (5) the growth and deepening of poverty, extending from 40 percent of the population in Latin America to 44 in 1989 and over 50 percent by 1993.[3] Politically the major impact of the SAP has been the generation of latent and manifest forms of social discontent, which have exploded in various waves of semispontaneous riots and protests, and the proliferation of diverse forms of resistance and opposition (Waldon and Seddon 1994; Veltmeyer and Petras 1997).

By 1989, at least four to six years into the SAP, in most cases the neoliberal program of structural (free-market) reforms reached its limits. For one thing, as indicated, the anticipated economic recovery and reactivation had not occurred. For another, the social inequalities generated by the SAP in turn generated a level and forms of social discontent that undermined the stability of the political regimes in the region and their neoliberal policies. And the redemocratization process expanded the political space for the mobilization of this discontent. Under these conditions (and based on a "new understanding as to the requirements of structural adjustment" [Salop 1992]), the IMF, the World Bank, and the IDB (Inter-American Development Bank), among other financial institutions, and the operating agencies of the UN system (including ECLAC) overhauled and redesigned the SAP, giving it a social dimension (a New Social Policy) and a "human face."

The new development strategy — "social liberalism," as it is referred to in the region — formulated in this context, and widely implemented in Latin America after 1989 with various permutations provided by ECLAC, has five basic characteristics, each a pillar of an associated theoretical model: (1) an emphasis on *participation,* that is, the incorporation of the targeted beneficiaries, in particular women and the poor; (2) *decentralization* of decision making related to the design and the financing of development programs and projects, sharing the authority and power of vital decisions with local governments and community-based institutions (*partnership*); (3) *targeting the poor* — prioritizing the problems and conditions of extreme poverty, alleviating and mitigating them with policies and projects financed with a special social investment fund;[4] (4) specific *policies related to health, education, and productive employment* — and, in a number of versions, small- and microenterprise development — with the aim of incorporating women and the poor into the development process, *empowering* them, and securing their active participation;[5] and (5) *structural reforms* (including the privatization of social services) that will provide an appropriate institutional framework for the New Social Policy and the process of social development involved.

The Latin American Experience of Decentralization: The Dynamics of a Democratization Process

The Context of Decentralization

If one were to sum up what the 1980s meant for Latin America it would be in terms of four assertions: (1) debt crisis, economic stagnation, and the decline of economic conditions for the majority of the population (in some cases deterioration to a level achieved in 1970); (2) the retrenchment of military and authoritarian regimes and their replacement with constitutional, democratically elected civilian regimes; (3) the widespread implementation of the SAP, an amalgam of stabilization and austerity measures (currency devaluation, anti-inflation) and "structural" economic reforms (outward orientation, liberalization, deregulation, privatization, downsizing) designed by the IMF and the World Bank; and (4) the refoundation of the capital-accumulation process based on a radical change in the capital-labor relationship and the associated class structure.

On the one hand, within the context of these objectively given conditions, one of the most notable developments in many Latin American countries was the formation and proliferation of a variety of highly participatory strategies — self-help projects, independence and reciprocity in production and exchange of products between the urban poor, the organization of communal soup kitchens and dining halls, and the provision of community housing and services (Razeto 1985). The development of this popular economy in the burgeoning informal sector, which functioned without the mechanisms of the formal market and the state and was responsible for virtually all the enterprise and employment generated in the 1980s, was a response of the urban poor to the economic and political conditions of the economic crisis (the inability of the formal economy to absorb them) and political dictatorship (the closing of a political space for the operation of their traditional political organizations). On the other hand, this development also reflected specific strategies pursued by governments, in the context of a generalized fiscal crisis, seeking to reduce the level of demand for their services and subsidies (Guerra Rodríguez 1994).

Whatever the connection, the growth and relative success of this popular economy coincided with government efforts to reduce and downsize the state and to privatize social services, as well as a neoconservative ideology that celebrated the resourcefulness and creative energies of individuals, whose agency was viewed as being superior to that of governments. The end result, as much a coincidence of interest and objective necessity as the effect of any consciously pursued strategy, was, as we have seen, a New Social Policy (NSP) implemented by virtually every government in the region. And behind this policy was a new institutionality that included a decentralization of government services and powers, in partnership with local governments and intermediary NGOs, designed in theory so as to increase the level of popular participation and local powers of decision making.

It had become a widely accepted matter of principle that the suc-

cess of development projects and programs depended on increasing
the level of popular participation — the empowerment of the beneficiaries to help them take a more active role in the process of their
own development (Blaikie 1985). Quite apart from this stated and
widely accepted principle (and even before the onset of a fiscal crisis), a number of governments in Latin America sought to increase
the level and forms of local participation, viewing it not so much
(or at all) as a means of empowering the people but as (1) a functional resource, a means of meeting social demands with limited and
declining government resources and capacity, and as (2) a means of
shoring up or establishing governments' legitimacy.[6] In this context,
various economic and social development strategies to decentralize
government, to change thereby the relation between the state and
civil society, were designed and experimented with across the world
and in most countries of Latin America. The Latin American experience will be briefly summed up and evaluated here, with particular
emphasis given to developments in Bolivia, Ecuador, and Mexico.

The political context for the movement to decentralize government in Latin America was constituted by a redemocratization
process that can be traced back to the retreat in Ecuador of the
armed forces to their barracks and the approval of a new constitution in 1979, a series of events that culminated in the victory of the
concertación democrático in Chile in 1989 (Blaikie 1985). In this
context, the dynamics of the broad-based movement to decentralize
the government operations of the nation-state were based, on the one
hand, on initiatives taken by the central government (and what in
Latin America is termed "the political class") and, on the other hand,
on pressures and demands "from below" — from groups organized
within civil society.

Development from Above

As for the initiatives "from above," the first by far (well in advance of the conditions that generally gave rise to the movement
toward decentralization) was taken by the government of Colombia, which decentralized a number of government departments and
transferred (or shared) a wide range of administrative responsibilities (from urban planning, housing, and education to utilities
and some infrastructure) as early as the 1960s. By 1978, the pro-

cess of administrative decentralization had advanced to the point of seriously undermining and weakening the workings of municipal governments, which had more or less been displaced by the decentralized agencies of the central government. As a result, the central government in 1978, for reasons that are not clear (in most cases, it is a question of either maintaining control, seeking efficiency or reduced costs, or securing legitimacy),[7] instituted a number of measures designed to reduce the "excessive centralism" of its decentralized agencies and to strengthen and capacitate responsible local governments. These measures included the transfer of a greater share of total public revenues toward local governments, resulting in what amounted to the most effectively decentralized system of government in the entire region, with up to 24 percent of public funds in control of local governments (versus 5 percent in Ecuador, 4 percent in Mexico, and a regional average today of below 10 percent).

In Ecuador, decentralization in the same form (administrative transfer, devolution of responsibility) was instituted in 1979 in the context of a newly approved democratic constitution and demands for autonomy and local self-government from a number of indigenous communities and regional organizations. In this context, the announced objectives of decentralization were the strengthening of democracy and the creation of an institutional framework appropriate to the implementation of an NSP targeted at the extreme social inequalities and high level of social exclusion (marginality) that characterized the economy and society (Stiefel and Wolfe 1994, 1988).

However, in attempting to implement its planned measures, the government encountered a series of obstacles, particularly in relation to the active participation of both local administrators and the targeted or intended beneficiaries. Although the issue needs further and closer study, a likely reason for this lack of participation was that the transfer of administrative responsibility and authority was not matched by the transfer of financial resources needed to exercise this authority and assume the transferred responsibilities. It was not until 1990, in the context of a major indigenous uprising and widespread push for local control over the extraction and exploitation of natural resources, and with the direct and active support of both the World Bank and the IDB (seeking to implement its NSP and partnership strategy), that the government took steps in the direction of strengthening local governments by the transfer of financial resources.

As in other such programs supported and funded by the World Bank, the results were meager, with little to no institutional strengthening, which in retrospect can be attributed to the fact that very few financial resources were transferred to local governments (in 1992 only 5 percent of total government revenues) and that the vast bulk of project funds (90 percent) was channeled into urban infrastructure, with little concern for institutional strengthening. Even the formation, in 1996, of a decentralizing committee and the preparation of the Decentralization and Deconcentration Law — which involved the active participation of over one thousand institutional representatives and was backed up by another indigenous uprising and its demand for "national" (ethnic) and regional autonomy — have done little to change the situation, despite a provision in the law for increasing the municipal share of public funds to around 8 percent (Carrion 1996, 142).

In Mexico, decentralization has been on and off the political agenda for years as of 1970, but it only came to occupy a critical part of government policy in the mid-1980s, with the advent of an administration committed to a neoliberal model of capitalist development. Under these conditions, decentralization took three forms: (1) strengthening of federalism via the sharing of responsibilities between the central and local governments;[8] (2) strengthening the institutional capacity (and political independence) of local governments via municipal reform in the form of transferring a larger share of financial resources to local and state governments (for local governments a tripling of their current share of 5 percent); and (3) promoting regional development via the incorporation of state and local governments in decisions relating to federal public investments within each locality — the institutional mechanisms of Los Convenios Unicos de Desarrollo and Programa Estratégica de Integración Regional — to address regional imbalances and prioritize medium-sized cities (Cabrero 1995).

As of 1989, with the advent of a new government by (the then-darling of the international financiers but now-disgraced) Carlos Salinas de Gortari, the strategy of administrative decentralization was supported and supplemented with Pronasol, an institutionalized form of the World Bank's NSP designed so as to incorporate into the development process the large number of the country's marginalized communities and poor municipalities.[9] However, despite this flurry of institutional measures and no end of political debate and discussions with representatives of local and state governments, as well as a host of initiatives and innovative experiments from these circles, Mexico today remains one of the most highly centralized governments in the region, attested to by the fact that only 3 to 4 percent of public funds are allocated to local municipal governments (Cabrero Mendozo 1995).

Development from Below

No country in the region illustrates as well as Bolivia the social dynamics of development from below with regards to the process of government decentralization. Bolivia provides a clear case both of the roles played by civil society in the process and of the difficulties and problems involved in the effort to institute local democracy in various forms.

Formal democracy was instituted in Bolivia in 1982 at the national level as the result of an intense, long struggle waged by a wide variety of civil and class organizations grouped within the powerful Central Obrera Boliviana (COB — Confederation of Bolivian Unionized Workers), indigenous peasant organizations and social movements, and regional civic corporate bodies (*comités cívicos departamentales* — which grouped together community-based organizations of civil society as well as provincial and municipal government authorities). Like the class-based organizations ranged within the COB, these civic committees, organized around the demands for regional control and autonomy, had been revitalized as a result of their struggle against the dictatorship of the central government and its internecine political conflicts. One of the major demands of these committees was precisely political-administrative decentralization, which was understood unambiguously as a means by marginal regions and communities of securing regional control over their resources — and a measure of autonomy. As a result, in Bolivia decentralization became the central axis of the redemocratization process — the movement in the 1980s of changing the relationship of the state to its civil society.

In this context, an intense political debate opened up, resulting in the preparation of up to twenty-two legislative projects. However, for want of consensus among the diverse factions of what in Bolivia is termed "the political class," none of these projects was translated into law until 1992, when the *comités cívicos,* the armed forces, the COB, and enough "politicians" came together to achieve Senate approval for the latest project. Nevertheless, the project was stalled in the Chamber of Deputies, in a political dispute that placed, on one side, the now-resonating demands of civil society for "democracy" (deepening of political reform) and, on the other, the "political class" and its party apparatus, seeking to preserve its traditional prerogatives of power and influence. It would take several years of debate before this impasse was broken with the passing of two complementary pieces of legislation: (1) the Popular Participation Law, which legislated the existence of *organizaciones teritoriales de base* (OTBs), which were allocated the authority — and corresponding revenues — to make decisions that relate to conditions that directly affect the local community or municipality;[10] and (2) the Administrative Decentralization Law, which constituted the institutional framework for "popular participation" and municipal autonomy, in particular a nexus between the national and local municipal governments — for the sharing of public service and accountability.

According to some, these two laws as combined and in their political conditions have created a contradictory and problematic situation for the proponents of local democracy and participatory development. On the one hand, the measures instituted with these two laws have transferred to the local governments responsibilities related to the meeting of social demands and the resolution of social conflicts while retaining for the central government effective control. The problem, according to some COB intellectuals, is that in theory decentralization involved "a process of transfer of responsibility and resources . . . to the . . . provinces, cantons, ayllus, and communities . . . so that the rural population, on the basis of its own efforts, can overcome its present situation of stagnation, and incorporate itself as an active force of national construction" (Aporto 1994, 53). However, in practice, by allocating the authority to make decisions and the financial resources that go with it to the municipality, a political-administrative unit of local government, the federal government has tended to undermine and weaken the authority and functioning of "the community," the social unit with which most Bolivians, and particularly the country's numerically important indigenous peoples, identify and to which they are fundamentally tied (Arrieta 1991; and Mayorga 1997).[11] On the other hand, the Popular Participation Law has opened up a political space for which the organizations of civil society have waged a long and hard struggle. In this context, the state is more permeable to social demands and closer in its decisions to local realities, which not only provides the national government a measure of legitimacy but provides the basis for better government as well as a degree and form of local participatory development. At the same time, the political reforms instituted by these two laws have had a demonstrated tendency to weaken traditional community-based or solidarity organizations and the functioning of unions that articulate interests beyond the merely local.

In this situation, a twofold political dynamic can be discerned. On the one hand, social movements of community-based civil organizations have managed to achieve a greater measure of "democracy," that is, political space to operate freely with more avenues for popular participation. On the other hand, in this process social movements of class-based organizations that seek social transformation rather than the extension of democracy and more freedom are weakened in their capacity to challenge the power structure and to effect change. In effect, the capacity of people to participate in policy-making decisions and to act politically becomes involuted and restricted to local issues, reversing the apparent gains made in democracy. As a result, the political left is placed in a quandary, unable to oppose a political development that opens up avenues of popular participation but that restricts the form and level of this participation, inhibiting the participatory democracy to which many, the "social left," are committed.

The Limits of Community-Based Participatory Development and Local Democracy

The UNRISD, the UNDP, and other operating agencies of the UN system in their conception of "human development"; the World Bank in its NSP; ECLAC in its model of *productive transformation with equity;* and the global network of NGOs and other proponents of Another Development all converge on the need for and centrality of popular participation in the process of development. In this intellectual context, despite enormous differences in conception as to the path to be taken toward such a participatory form of development, as well as questions as to its appropriate agency, these diverse approaches to national and community-based development have generally looked favorably upon the global trend toward decentralization of government and the associated change in the given relationship of the state to civil society. But our review of numerous studies of this experience shows that the rationale for such decentralization in most cases, and the dominant impulse behind it, is the search by national or central governments for either economic efficiencies in the provision of public services that they can no longer afford or increased legitimacy in the context of a redemocratization process and associated pressures from well-organized groups in a reconstituted civil society. However, notwithstanding this reality and the conservative (antichange) political forces ranged behind it, the consensus view (among the various proponents of participatory development who generally share the view of the need for change) is that decentralization has created — and creates — necessary conditions for a more human and participatory form of development as well as the political space for corresponding democratic politics. The institutional basis for such participatory development, in the context of decentralization, is the municipality, a political-administrative unit of local government that most closely corresponds to, or is close to, the "community," the social unit to which most people belong, with which they generally identify, and where they live their everyday lives.

In the context of the decentralization process, the municipality is generally regarded as a privileged space for democratic politics and participatory development. This is the case for the World Bank, concerned as it is with the design and targeting of enlightened government policy, a cost-effective implementation of its New Social Policy. It is the case for ECLAC, concerned as it is to find an organization that is constituted at a level and on a scale compatible with popular participation, allowing for an equitable form of development that is not likely or simply not possible at the level of the nation-state. And it applies to all those intellectuals and development practitioners involved in the ubiquitous search for Another Development who have turned to, and generally rely on, the protagonism of grassroots, community-based organizations.

In different ways these diverse organizations have ended up drawing a similar or the same picture of the decentralization process and its possibilities. However, our review of existing studies on this process indicates that there is something wrong with this picture. For one thing, it does not correspond with the facts, which appear to be as follows.

First, the municipality, the political-administrative unit targeted for strengthening and empowering, does not constitute a "community" — the social unit that most people belong to or identify with. In this connection, the advocates of democratic decentralization see the municipality as "the natural space where the community and government are brought together."[12] And indeed it is. However, they are brought together under conditions that serve the purpose of government (delegate and share responsibilities related to the provision of public services, cost-effective administration, down-the-line accountability and control, legitimacy, and regulation of social demands) and that tend to undermine and weaken — even destroy — the organizational and political capacity of traditional community- or class-based organizations, in the process weakening the ties of people to their increasingly fragmented communities.[13]

Second, the community as conceived in development discourse (as an organic unity bound together by social bonds, relations of mutual obligation, common interests, and shared social identity) does not seem to exist, except perhaps with respect to the small-scale societies constituted by the indigenous peoples in the Andean highlands of Peru, Bolivia, and Ecuador; in the Amazonian rain forests; or in Guatemala and the southeast of Mexico. The sociological and anthropological literature on this point is enormous, but it seems to have entirely escaped the attention of scholars and practitioners in the field of development.

What many of these studies tend to show is that most so-called communities are anything but communities and that, when examined closely, they tend to dissolve into diverse relations of power and conflict, with (1) a minority in control of the means of production and political authority — and power; (2) various middle strata dependent on petty production or public service within the locality or oriented toward, and dependent on, connections to the outside world (in terms of communications, culture, and often even with respect to economic activity or employment); and (3) large numbers of segmented and poorly organized low-income small producers, low-wage hunters and gatherers, and an underclass of landless or otherwise marginal workers, many of them forced to migrate in search of subsistence. As Gavin Smith (1989) has detailed and shown so convincingly in the case of one Peruvian community, the existence of class divisions and relations of conflict within a community (or territorial social unit, to use a more general and descriptive category) does not mean that at certain conjunctures, and for certain purposes and common interests, these people are incapable of coming together and forming fairly representative social and political organizations. They can and do. However, the construction of any community-based strategy or development program, or political organization, needs to take into account the conditions and social relations under which the "community" is constituted both in itself and in its connections with the outside world — the broader society. Thus, for example, in a World Bank institution-strengthening project designed to benefit a "community" in the outskirts or environs of Potosi, La Paz, or Cochabamba in Bolivia, it might be discovered that the effective if not intended beneficiaries are certain elements of the local oligarchy who do not favor the access of indigenous peoples and peasants to the municipal council of the city and who have no intention to share resources or political power with them.[14]

Third, a decentralized form of political development focused on the municipality, in the context of conditions in Latin America, more often than not seems to have the effect — if not the aim — of restricting the scope of political action to local issues, effectively incapacitating people from organizing for more fundamental change. In this context, for example, the political conditions needed to implement the ECLAC model of productive transformation with equity do not exist and are not available. As it happens, in the course of structural reforms implemented at the nation-state level over the past decade and a half, the productive apparatus of Latin America's economies indeed has been transformed. However, this transformation has been without equity, or, not to make too fine point of it, with considerable inequity — converting the ECLAC model into "a new fairy tale for the 1990s" (Guimarães 1989). Under the conditions created by the process of government decentralization, the capacity for people in the region to organize, be mobilized, and act in their collective interests beyond any purely local issue (such as building a school or clinic) has been undermined. And the development that has occurred in the process has been neither equitable, participatory, people-led, nor human.

Conclusions

Decentralization of government (policy making and administration) is viewed by ECLAC, the institution that more than any other has led the search for an alternative to neoliberal capitalism in Latin America, as a necessary condition of participatory development and as such the "missing link" in its proposed development model of productive transformation with equity. However, our review and brief analysis of existing studies allow us to conclude that ECLAC's solution — "development from within," as Osvaldo Sunkel (1991) defines it — is not supportive of the agenda set by the proponents of Another Development. Rather, it is supportive of the agenda pursued by the World Bank and other such institutions (of the "international financial community") and implemented by virtually every regime in Latin America. This is to say, it is a case of development "from above and the outside" rather than "from below." In this context we have found, and argued, that the participatory model in Latin America, as designed and implemented on the basis of government decentralization, has failed to shift power and control from the state to the people. As we see it, there are two dimensions to this failure. On the one hand, the model is constructed on the basis of, and with reference to, an administrative unit (the municipality) rather than the sense or existence of real communities. The connection between the two often is problematic if not nonexistent. On the other hand, the democratic impulse embedded in the decentralization project — and process — is very convoluted. As a project that is designed as much on "the outside" (by economists from the World Bank) as "the inside" (ECLAC economists) and implemented from above (as a government initiative), decentralization has resulted in a highly limited and ineffective form of democracy. The secret of local power (based on mechanisms of popular participation) is precisely that decision making and administrative capacity are localized — restricted to local issues. In this context, the process of (re)democratization and participatory development is hijacked, subordinated to the economic agenda and political goals of the existing neoliberal regimes. The capacity of people to participate in decisions relating to larger-than-local issues, and to effect change in nationwide structures, has become increasingly limited. In short, in the Latin American context decentralization has tended to limit rather than extend the institution of democracy. It is, we suggest, a question of myth and appearance over reality.

Notes

1. The evidence provided by the few systematic comparative studies initiated or conducted by the IMF is ambiguous. An internal study by the IMF comparing countries subject to SAP and those that are not found no systematic correlation beyond a general tendency for nonrecipient countries to perform better than recipient countries. In Latin America, the only country that has experienced a relatively sustained recovery of economic growth is Chile, but even here it was not until 1992 that Chile managed to recover the capacity lost in the deep recessions of 1974–75 and 1981–82. On this, see Collins and Lear (1995) and Leiva and Petras, with Veltmeyer (1994).

2. The statistics on this polarization are dramatic. Prior to the structural reforms of the 1980s, Latin America as a region exhibited the greatest income distribution disparities in the world — the ratio of income received by the top 20 percent of households on average being over ten times that of the poorest 20 percent and in a number of cases up to twenty-six times greater (in the case of Brazil), as compared to an average ratio of 4.5–6/1: for countries such as Taiwan or South Korea and the OECD (Organization for Economic Cooperation and Development) group, or for that matter sub-Saharan Africa (Veltmeyer 1997a, with World Bank data). But these disparities were extended and deepened, leading to an even greater polarization, in the 1980s and 1990s, the result being the sprouting of a handful of billionaires on the one pole and a massive number of people living in abject poverty on the other. On this polarization, see, among others, Lustig (1995); Morley (1995); and Vuskovic (1993).

3. ECLAC-UNDP; cited in *Latin American Special Reports* (SR-92–5), October 1992.

4. Modeled on Bolivia's Economic Emergency Fund set up in 1985, the NSP generally has taken the form of a social investment fund (SIF), financed primarily by the multilateral financial institutions and UN agencies, and, except

in the case of Chile, placed under the control of the president's office. After their inception in Bolivia, SIFs were set up in Mexico (Pronasol) and Chile (FOSIS) in 1989–90 and soon thereafter in virtually every country in the region. These SIFs were implemented within the framework of the World Bank's new model for social policy based on three principles: (1) targeting the poor, (2) privatization of social services, and (3) decentralization (partnership with local governments and NGOs).

5. As pointed out by Friedmann (1992), the concept of "empowerment," central to Another Development, has been appropriated by the World Bank and the UN operating agencies as a critical element of their discourse. Indeed even Ronald Reagan used the term, quite emptying it of its intrinsic meaning as given it by the search for Another Development.

6. In the Latin American context even authoritarian governments could and did view "popular participation" as a means of legitimating their exercise of power, permitting controlled expression of popular sentiments while eliminating at the same time independent channels of organization and representation. Thus Pinochet in the late 1970s and early 1980s instituted a national circle of women's clubs and neighborhood associations controlled by appointed mayors and municipal authorities. And in Mexico, the government has orchestrated a series of tripartite pacts with unions and entrepreneurs, accommodating the union movement to the government's antilabor austerity measures on the basis of and with the participation of workers themselves.

7. Although Zamosc (1986), among others who have studied and reported on these developments in Colombia, does not establish the dynamics of the process, it is likely that various regional, if not local, government organizations and organizations of civil society generated pressure and demand for these changes. However, it is equally probable that the World Bank and the IDB, as in neighboring Ecuador and Venezuela, and in both Bolivia and Chile, were directly involved in pushing the new strategy of partnership with local governments and intermediary institutions. The issue needs further close study.

8. In this respect see the Ley Organica de la Administración Publica Federal, the Ley de Planificación, the Programa de Descentralización de la Administración Pública Federal; and in 1993 the Convenios Unicos de Desarrollo.

9. It is estimated by INEGI (Instituto Nacional de Estadística, Geografía e Informática — the National Statistics Institute) that there exist fifteen hundred or so such communities with a high marginality index and characterized by a high incidence of extreme poverty. This includes over fifteen hundred municipalities (58 percent of the total number), encompassing twenty-four million people — and 78 percent of the country's indigenous peoples (Sedesol, *Regiones Prioritarias; La Jornada*, 11 November 1996, 23). Together with FOSIS in Chile, the now-abandoned Pronasol has been considered a model of the NSP in Latin America. For an evaluation of its impacts, see Laurell (1994).

10. Within a year of the law's promulgation, 10,500 OTBs had been legally recognized. The critical issue, as with the 1979 constitution in Peru, is the legal recognition of traditionally constituted forms of organization and communities as OTBs for the purpose of municipalization of local power. In Peru, the 1979 constitution at least recognized the existence of peasant and indigenous com-

munities (the new 1993 constitution makes no reference to them whatsoever), allowing them to participate as such in the regional assemblies. Unfortunately, real power was not placed or did not reside in these assemblies but in the regional councils, in which these communities did not participate. Thus, as in Bolivia, through one means or another the power of decision making, and the purse, is channeled into political units where the central government is able to meet — and control — the community (Marcos 1994).

11. For a similar argument with respect to Peru see Marcos (1996).

12. The Mexican Association of Municipalities, in a public campaign co-ordinated with the Association of Presidents of Democratic Municipalities, addressed a letter (newspaper ad) to the Chamber of Federal Deputies meant to convince the legislature if not the executive to implement the protocol agreement laid out in the document "20 Contracts for Democracy" signed by the government (*La Jornada,* 5 December 1996, 40). One article of the agreement was to increase the municipalities' share of public funds from its current level of 4 to 20 percent.

13. This point is argued, with substantial evidence, by Mayorga (1997), among others, in Bolivia, and Marcos (1994, 1996), in the case of Peru.

14. In this context, Arrieta (1991) notes that it is easier for an Aymaran like Victor Hugo Cárdenas to sit next to the president, as vice-president, in a cabinet meeting than for an indigenous person to sit in a *consejo municipal de pueblo.*

FOUR

The State and Participatory Development in Bolivia

Henry Veltmeyer and Juan Tellez

The past two decades have witnessed a fundamental change and an epoch-defining transformation in the form of social and economic organization around the world. A defining feature of these changes is the formation and global extension of a capitalist production system and the free flow of goods, services, and capital, as well as information, on a global scale. One source and driving force of this process is the evolution of new computer-based technologies that have drastically shortened the transportation and communication circuits of the production process, laying the foundations thereby of a new post-Fordist regime of accumulation and corresponding mode of regulation. Another source is what the International Labour Office (ILO), among other international organizations and international financial institutions, has identified as a new "institutional and policy framework," based on economic liberalization, which has facilitated the free movement of capital and trade in goods and services within a deregulated environment and the privatization of the means of production and associated economic enterprises. In a number of contexts, the new institutional and policy framework for this process has taken the form of the Structural Adjustment Program (SAP), a package of policy measures and associated institutional or "structural" changes designed by the economists of the World Bank and associated multilateral financial agencies such as the International Monetary Fund (IMF). The SAP, pioneered in the 1970s by the Pinochet military regime in Chile, was experimented with by several other governments under military rule (Argentina, Uruguay), and in the 1980s it was implemented by Mexico, Bolivia, and a number of other countries under conditions of a regionwide debt crisis. With the onset of the 1990s, virtually every country in the region had either adopted the SAP or would soon succumb to pressures to do so. In the space of a few years those countries that had been slow to adopt or fully implement it (Peru, Venezuela, Argentina, and Brazil) came around to participate in the "the bold revolution" that was sweeping the world, adopting a package of policy measures and institutional reforms based on a neoclassical theory and neoliberal vision of a world market freed from government intervention, the anticipated means of producing an optimum of economic and social development.

The neoliberal reform agenda includes, among other features, the following: (1) a series of short-term stabilization measures, fiscal austerity and currency devaluation, designed to establish *macroeconomic stability* (in terms of accounts and prices) and to promote exports; (2) market *liberalization,* the freeing of trade and capital flows among and within nations; (3) *deregulation* of the private sector, seen as the driving force of the economic system; (4) *privatization* of the means of production, reversing the nationalization of industry that marked previous decades and devolving state enterprises to the private sector; and (5) *modernization* of the state, downsizing its operations and reducing its economic role to the provision of support for the market, the motor of the development process, and the private sector, its conductor and driving force.

The implementation of this agenda and the associated adjustment process have taken different forms in different countries, as have the dynamics of resistance and other political responses to the agenda. On one level it is possible to identify clear and obvious patterns in the development of this process, with reference to structurally determined limits to the degree of variation in the experience of different countries. To this extent, the postmodernist perspective on the contextuality, specificity, and radical subjectivity of experience has little relevance, less than the class perspective it has sought to displace.[1] However, on another level there appears to be considerable variability in the experience of different countries with the reform process, based on conditions that are specific to each. In the light of this complexity, analysis of the development and reform process should take into account both structural and conjunctural factors, as well as those that are societally specific. In this context, and to this purpose, this chapter provides a case study of the reform process as it has unfolded in Bolivia, a country whose development over the past fifteen years in a number of respects can be taken as symptomatic, illuminating the nature of the reform process experienced by so many countries all over the world — particularly in Latin America.

Military Dictatorship, the New Oligarchy, and the Historic Struggle for Democracy (1971–85): The Historic Context of Reform

In 1971, Hugo Banzer's military regime took power, two years after the destruction of the second guerrilla movement in Bolivia and the defeat of a ten-month experiment of the Popular Assembly under the government of J. J. Torrez, who attempted to implement a social-popular revolution based on an organization of popular political forces. The 1970s were characterized by the struggle between Banzer's tyrannical regime and the dynamic popular resistance led by the powerful Confederation of Bolivian Unionized Workers (COB), which challenged the military regime on the basis of clandestine organizing.[2] In this regard, the 1970s were a continuation of the social and political dynamics of a dual power that can be traced back to the national revolution in 1952.

In the 1970s the newly formed oligarchy found its political expression in the alliance of military forces led by Banzer, the MNR, FSB, and active political support from the United States. These actors were at the hub of the political bloc that designed and monitored Bolivia's development, representing the common interests of the new oligarchy and foreign investors in the profitable exploitation of Bolivia's abundant natural resources.

In this context, the implementation of the government's development plans and its allocation of resources required and involved the use of brutal military intervention, the abuse of civil rights, and the repression of the organizations that had formed in the popular sector of Bolivia's civil society. In order to impose the economic development strategy of the new oligarchy, Banzer established a ruthless police-state apparatus that was set to rule the country with an iron hand and without a velvet glove. In 1974, Banzer abolished by decree the legal existence of unions, and the decree was followed by brutal repression of unions and community leaders. According to the Human Rights Commission, between 1971 and 1978 the regime was responsible for the disappearance and assassination of 10,400 individuals, who were mostly connected to these organizations as well as the democratic political parties, although Banzer and his military comrades also turned against their erstwhile political allies, the MNR and FSB, whose leaders and activists were similarly persecuted. Banzer's regime judged that the forces at its disposal were sufficient for managing the government of Bolivia without the help of any political party or allies except the United States and without the backing of the international financial institutions.

In this context Banzer's authoritarian regime turned its attention toward four strategic areas: (1) La Gran Mineria, dominated by the mining bourgeoisie in the highlands; (2) the agroexport economy dominated by the bourgeoisie in the lowlands; (3) the financial sector and its bourgeoisie; and (4) the caste of military officers concentrated in La Paz. These four sectors characterized Bolivia's "new oligarchy," the major beneficiaries of government policies and the country's development process. During Banzer's regime this oligarchy had easy access to long-term credit, obtained extraordinary contracts for infrastructure development, and exported their earnings to banks in the United States and Europe.

Bolivia's development under Banzer's regime was based on three factors: (1) the unprecedented increase of the external debt (the external debt increased from 1.5 to 4.1 billion dollars); (2) the super-exploitation of labor (not only were wages frozen but as in colonial times the army drafted youth aged eighteen years and older, and as part of their military service they had to work the sugarcane harvest); and (3) the favorable prices of mining commodities in international markets (the price of a pound of tin increased up to $7.10 when Bolivia was exporting twenty-eight thousand metric tons per year, and as a result of measures taken by OPEC Bolivia benefited from a rapid increase in the price of oil). These were the economic bases for the Banzer regime's strategy of development.

Notwithstanding Banzer's policy of repression, popular organizations strengthened their will to shape a society in which there was social justice and fought to regain democracy in Bolivia.[3] Political party leaders on the left and the unions, particularly those in the mining sector, survived the turbulence of the time. In fact, in the process of organizing the masses and mobilizing the forces of opposition and resistance, the popular movement continued to strengthen, leading to the formation of a historic popular bloc. Without precedence and with considerable courage, the union and grassroots organizations used innovative forms of organizing and mobilizing the popular-democratic social forces of opposition, resistance, and alternative development. These forces organized with the powerful COB, despite the efforts of the regime and its US backers to undermine them, and, working from the basis of a clandestine leadership, they maintained a strong resistance to the regime's economic development strategy. Throughout the seven years of military rule, the COB gave the military dictator no rest or respite. Worse (for the regime), although clandestine, the COB expanded its membership to incorporate regional civic movements and new social organizations that were demanding the return of democracy, the freedom of civil rights, and local control of regional development. In fact, it was under Banzer's authoritarian regime that a push emerged for regional autonomy and decentralization, key dimensions of a popular-democratic and participatory form of development. It was in this same political context that Bolivia experienced a resurgent indigenous movement under the influence of the Túpac Katari Revolutionary Movement of National Liberation, one of whose leaders would be incorporated into — coopted by, according to some — the neoliberal regime of Sánchez de Lozada formed in 1993.

A series of powerful labor strikes in 1974 and 1976, commanded by a clandestine leadership, was a demonstration of the vibrant force of the popular movement led by the powerful miner's unions within the COB. The movement shook the military regime and forced Banzer and his comrades to mobilize the armed forces across the country.

In 1978, democracy (if not paradise) was regained in Bolivia as a result of a massive national-popular mobilization initiated by four women from the mining centers (among them Domitila Chungara) and capitalized on by the powerful COB. At this conjuncture, under the weight of the forces accumulated in the popular sector, and despite the unconditional support of international financial institutions, the Banzer regime was unable to contain the massive movement of Bolivia's historic popular bloc. The hunger strike of four women turned into thousands of hunger strikes organized around over 150 pickets across the country. This struggle was coordinated with a wave of massive popular demonstrations from one end of the country to another. As a result, Banzer was defeated. He had no choice but to resign and call for general elections. Given the longtime domination of the political process by the military, for many Bolivians the institution of national elections was an unprecedented and new experience.

The 1978 national elections were dominated by the Democratic United Front (UDP)[4] led by Hernán Siles Suazo, who had a clear advantage over the other presidential candidates. The predominance and electoral victory of the left were largely due to almost two decades of undemocratic political practices in Bolivia and the triumph of the popular movement over Banzer's military regime. However, the results of these first elections were never announced, interrupted as they were by another military coup in which the ballots were confiscated. The new military officer in charge of this operation was Juan Pereda, Banzer's minister of state. In fact, this military sabotage of the election process was nothing else but an *auto-golpe militar* designed to expand the military's control over Bolivia's society and prevent the return to government of the democratic left. Nevertheless, the COB once again mobilized the forces of resistance and opposition in the struggle to reestablish democracy and call for a second round of national elections.

Between 1978 and 1982 Bolivia experienced what many Bolivians regard as the most disgraceful political experience in its contemporary history. In three years of political carnival the presidential palace was occupied by no less than seven military officials. The rapid changes of military officers were largely as a response to the popular movement's pressure to restore democracy in Bolivia. This pressure was exerted in a context of widespread political instability and of severe economic crisis, which in turn provoked an unparalleled social turmoil and conditions of nongovernability, leading to a wild succession of military regimes and eventually the road toward structural adjustment.

In 1982, with the triumph of the UDP, led by Siles Suazo, who ascended to power on the basis of strong support from the working class and its organization within the COB, Bolivia regained a measure of liberal democracy, creating conditions for a political opening and struggle that led to the end of almost two decades of military rule. Thus did Bolivia, together with Ecuador, pioneer a regionwide redemocratization process, which in the space of ten years saw the negotiated retreat of the generals to their barracks and the installation everywhere of a civilian regime.

However, for the UDP government in Bolivia, this democratic transition took place in a context of the country's worst-ever economic crisis marked by (1) the collapse of La Gran Mineria, which accounted for the bulk of export revenues and formed the basis of the most militant sector of the working class; (2) an appreciable decline in productive capacity and activity — in 1981–82, at the worst point, these were down by 7 percent and continued to decline until 1985; (3) fiscal accounts in serious deficit, the product of several decades of maladministration, excessive spending, and the extraction of rents; (4) a high level of external indebtedness that in terms of servicing requirements placed severe constraints on the capital available for productive investment, resulting in one of the lowest levels of capital formation in the entire region — from an annual average of 22 percent from 1975 to 1979 down to 11 percent from 1980 to 1984 and only 7 percent in 1985, the year in which Bolivia's economic crisis peaked; (5) astronomical rates of inflation, which in October 1984 climbed to an astonishing 25,000 percent (down to 11,000 percent in 1985); (6) a level of external debts that on a per capita basis exceeded that of Mexico or Brazil; and (7) an economic crisis that in its depth has been exceeded only by Chile in 1982.

The conjuncture of this economic and political crisis generated the conditions of a neoliberal counterrevolution initiated by the regime of Victor Paz Estensoro, an old-guard leader of the MNR who was elevated by the electorate to state power in 1985.

In the immediate context of economic and political crisis, the dynamics of political change unfolded in two directions. On the one hand, the COB, controlled by the radical left expressed through the DRU (Dirección Revolucionaria Unitaria), sought to radicalize the democratic process toward a socialist program for development. To this end, the COB mobilized the popular masses with a platform based on the *salario mínimo vital con escala mobil* (a minimum wage on a flexible scale adjusted to inflation). However, given a rate of inflation that reached 25,000 percent, it was clearly unrealistic to expect that wage increases would be pegged at that rate. In this context, the COB's platform had more of a political than an economic purpose. And the COB succeeded in capturing the desire of the masses to have the economic and political injustices changed once and for all (which meant among other things the overthrow of Siles Suazo). In this context the radical left perceived the center left represented by the Siles Suazo–UDP government as the enemy, the major obstacle in the struggle to create a socialist society, and called for a general strike of workers accompanied by a blockade of roads and streets and massive demonstrations.

On the other hand, the conservative political parties, including the MNR, the FSB, and Banzer's party, the ADN (Alianza Democrática Nacionalista), took advantage of social and political turmoil and entrenched themselves in the parliament so as to thwart Siles Suazo's attempts to resolve the crisis through the stabilization of the economy and the introduction of social reforms. At the same time, the Siles Suazo government had to contend with one of its most serious political problems: opposition from the new oligarchy, which by then had developed ties with the emergent narcotraffic sector, which had penetrated the military ranks and the right-wing political parties. In addition, the IMF and World Bank exercised enormous pressure with regards to service payments on the debts accumulated by the UDP and the preceding military regimes.

In the conjuncture of these diverse political developments, both internal and external pressures made it impossible for the UDP to implement a popular strategy of development with innovative initiatives, particularly with regards to local and regional development strategies in which municipal governments and indigenous communities would play a larger role in the decision-making process. The UDP's efforts to introduce popular economic reforms resulted in an explosion of social unrest, which in early 1985 forced Siles Suazo to resign from his term as president and issue a call for national elections.

The 1985 elections brought to state power the MNR, which in the aftermath of the 1952 revolution had been forced by the popular masses to implement a program of land reform, mine nationalization, and universal voting. Ironically, in the context of mid-1980s, the same MNR charted a course for Bolivia in exactly the opposite direction, namely, the implementation of neoliberal policies of privatization and liberalization designed to support the private sector as opposed to the state as the major agent of the development process. These policies, together with corresponding institutional reforms, gave an entirely different political foundation to the development process in Bolivia.

Stabilization and Democracy: The Making of a New Economic Policy — Victor Paz Estensoro, 1985–89

Origins and Implementation of the NEP

Under conditions of a fragile democracy and the heightened expectations and mobilized demands of an electorate freed from military rule, the depth and severity of the economic crisis experienced by Bolivia from 1980 to 1985 eroded the capacity of the political class to govern the country. The conditions that led to a widespread demand for political order and economic stability explain in part the urgency of and need for the economic stabilization and adjustment measures implemented by Paz Estensoro's government. The transition from a military regime to a civilian-constitutional regime characterized by economic crisis, social unrest, and political instability was after all the most important issue to be resolved by the newly elected government in 1985. In September of that year the New Economic Policy (NEP) was launched by Decree 21060, which was extended by the subsequent regimes formed and headed by Jaime Paz Zamora (1989–93) and Gonzalo Sánchez de Lozada (1993–97). Decree 21060 was not only a policy for economic reform. It became the new ideological and philosophical framework to redefine Bolivia's future economic, social, and political activities.

The NEP, however, was not the result of endogenous thinking, as the MNR would like Bolivians to believe. As in Chile, some ten years earlier, it was drafted by the "Chicago Boys," a group of economists trained in the United States (at the University of Chicago and Harvard) and working closely with US advisers.[5] In fact, the MNR's economic team, led by Sánchez de Lozada, at the time minister of finance, held seminars and training workshops facilitated by Jeffrey Sachs and his team.

The exponents of the NEP argued that the chief purpose of the reforms entailed by it was to bring hyperinflation under control and to provide an effective framework for reducing the fiscal deficit and liberalizing foreign exchange with the purpose of reducing expenditures and increasing revenues. Thus it was presented as a series of stabilization measures. However, Decree 21060 also set up the basis for a long-term structural reform — the implementation of the World Bank's SAP. In this context, Decree 21060 was used to justify the imposition of a new regressive tax system, the privatization of public enterprises, liberalization of trade barriers, and the deregulation of labor standards and foreign investment.

The major obstacle to the government's instituting the NEP was the COB and its capacity of mobilizing the forces of popular opposition and resistance. In order to create the political conditions for the implementation of the NEP, it was imperative for the Estensoro regime and subsequent regimes to undermine the power of the COB. A prerequisite for the success of the neoliberal model was a high level of governability, a confidence in one ruling agent in charge of government. In this regard, the COB in its capacity and role as a competing power was an impediment and threat to the regime and its commitment in the NEP to a neoliberal strategy for national development based on the New Economic Model (NEM). Thus, the Estensoro regime sought to undermine the sociopolitical power of the COB and its role in representing the popular bloc and further sought to confine the COB's role to a *gremialist* or union organization.

Within the framework of the NEP, the space occupied for so long by the COB was reassigned to the political parties. To this end the strategy of the MNR was to dismantle the hitherto powerful (or "glorious") FSTMB (Federación Sindical de Trabajadores Mineros de Bolivia), the cornerstone of the COB in the previous fifty years of Bolivia's history. The most effective measure in this regard was to close the state-owned enterprises in the mining sector. Before effecting such a closure, the MNR laid-off over twenty-five thousand mine workers (out of thirty-two thousand), thus weakening the power of the COB.

However, Paz Estensoro did not have carte blanche in the implementation of this strategy. In the first place, he encountered an energetic popular movement of resistance to his policies. In mid-1986, the Por la Vida protest, led by the COB and headed by the miners' unions, marched from Oruro to La Paz. To stop and break-up the march, the government had to mobilize seven highly armed military units as well as the air force, dictate a state of emergency abrogating civil rights and banning unions, and subsequently persecute the union and political leaders who continued to mobilize acts of resistance to the NEP.

The problem — and irony (from the oppositionist perspective of the forces represented in the popular movement) — is that despite the repression, in the subsequent national elections the right-wing parties that were aligned with the regime and supportive of its NEP were re-elected by popular vote.[6] In fact, the Paz Estensoro regime, like most of the democratic regimes established elsewhere in the region in the 1980s, enjoyed an appreciable margin of political and electoral support based, above all, on its capacity to maintain macroeconomic stability. However, this support was by no means an indicator of the level of satisfaction with the regime's capacity to meet public expectations and demands; rather it reflected the psychological trauma and economic concerns associated with hyperinflation — as well as the excesses of retreating or displaced military regimes. A clear indication of this situation in Bolivia was the surprising electoral turnabout from 1979 and 1980, when a center-left coalition headed by Siles Suazo was given an electoral majority, as well as 1982, when this coalition came to political power, to 1985, when the electorate turned to the ex-dictator Hugo Banzer, followed closely by the conservative caudillo Paz Estensoro.

Both Banzer and Estensoro advanced very similar proposals for a new program of economic policies, which is why their subsequent alliance caused no surprise. Nor did the NEP, introduced in 1985 and extended by the two subsequent regimes, cause much if any surprise, except perhaps with regard to the capacity of each regime to generate sufficient political support for a severe shock treatment applied to a weakened Bolivian economy and for the most radical program of structural adjustments and economic reforms of its day — and since. Only Chile in the previous decade, and Argentina and Peru in the next, can be compared to Bolivia as regards to the level of severity and the scope of adjustment made to the economy and the changes wrought in society in so short a time frame.

The NEP was implemented in three phases (stabilization, privatization, and capitalization), each corresponding to a change in political regimes and associated dynamics of popular resistance and opposition. The first phase of the NEP was implemented by the government of Victor Paz Estensoro under Decree 21060. It took the form of orthodox policy measures such as the reduction of government spending, the abolition of subsidies, and the dismissal of public employees; restriction of the money supply (to reduce consumption and thus inflation) and devaluation of the currency — up to 93 percent (to promote exports); liberalization of product and capital markets and flows; deregulation of private activity (to release the productive forces of the private sector); and the privatization of state-owned enterprises. These stabilization and adjustment measures were supplemented by various heterodox measures with regard to the servicing of the external debt (through renegotiations with the Club of Rome) and the reorganization of the tax regime, as well as a series of reforms designed to reduce the size of government and the role of the state in the economy — reforms that the officials of the World Bank, the IMF, and the IDB insisted upon (Laserna 1995a, 49).

Social Impacts of the 1985–87 SAP

The effects of the stabilization and adjustment program have been striking. The mass firing of workers in the militant mining sector (up to 60 percent of the total) was highly visible, executed as much for political as economic reasons (as explained earlier), and problematic insofar as the central role of the miners in the popular class struggle.[7] Measures to reduce the fiscal deficit had an equally visible negative impact on the urban middle class and its various strata. But despite protests from various sectors of organized workers, the stabilization measures did lead to some recovery of average real wages and per capita incomes. In 1987, per capita incomes increased by 2.1 percent in relation to the decline of 4.40 percent in 1982 and 6.50 percent in 1983 (Iriarte 1996). Yet, although by 1987 Bolivia's economy began slowly to grow by 2.10 percent, or even 4.1 percent in 1991, the growth rate was insufficient to permit a recovery of the losses sustained in the years of economic crisis. For instance, after twelve years of structural adjustment, Bolivia had not yet recovered the level of per capita income achieved in 1977.

Nor has the SAP-induced economic growth led to an improvement in the level, form, and conditions of employment. On the contrary, in the period of structural adjustment, the informal sector has grown without precedent, and overall employment conditions have been negative for the labor force. Indeed, one of the clearest changes wrought by the NEP has been in the structure and conditions of employment and in the associated structure of the capital-labor relation, the most critical element of the capitalist production system in place.[8] On this point, all available studies, including those conducted by the ILO and research centers such as CEDLA, agree that 90 percent of all jobs generated in the process of structural adjustment since 1985 — and this includes an estimated average of fifty thousand jobs a year in the most recent (1992-95) phase — have been restricted to the informal sector. This means that government policies targeting unemployment and job creation have not had the expected results, despite their aggressive programs and initiatives. Rather, employment growth in the informal sector represents the response to these policies by individuals who are compelled to seek jobs on their own account, to set up their own enterprises, and to either accept jobs of low pay and poor working conditions or offer their services or labor under conditions of economic insecurity, without legal protection. In this regard, although the officially defined rate of unemployment has been somewhat reduced, the dramatic expansion of the informal sector both in Bolivia and elsewhere in the region is a clear indication of a generalized tendency toward the casualization and informalization of employment and a change in the conditions of employment. The latter are marked by lack of legal protection, increasing insecurity and uncertainty, as well as dramatic growth of what Karl Marx in a different and earlier context defined as an industrial army — that is, a reserve pool of surplus labor visible in its effects on the disciplining of labor and the weakening of its organization, its capacity to negotiate, and its flexibility (labor loses its mobility and becomes available at lower rates and in worse conditions).

These shifts also reflect changes in a structural tendency toward the recomposition and concentration of capital, and an associated reduction in the share of labor in national income and in value added in the process of production. In this regard, the share of labor has been reduced from 36.5 percent in 1970 to under 26.9 in 1985 (ECLAC, various years). With respect to value added in manufacturing, the share of wages and salaries (remuneration of labor) was reduced from 43 to 26 percent in the same period (World Bank 1990).

Another revealing area vis-à-vis the impacts of the 1985–initiated SAP or the NEP is that of social development, encompassing education and health, as well as social services and welfare. A surprising feature of the measures taken in this area is that despite the clear reduction of spending, the major indicators exhibited a general tendency toward improvement. For example, by 1989, several years before the initiation of the so-called war on poverty waged in the form of the Bolivian Social Strategy, both infant/maternal mortality and illiteracy rates had been reduced, as had the percentage of the population (if not the absolute number) in extreme poverty (CONAPSO 1991; De Soto and Schmiedheiny 1991; CID-COTESU 1993; ILDIS-CEDLA 1995). In the same context, the rate of schooling, vaccination coverage, and communal services had also increased and continued to do so in subsequent years.

One explanation for these advances in social development in the context of decreased spending levels is the greater efficiency of new methods for administering a reduced level of social services, and the agency of community-based organizations in the provision of these services.

So can be explained the gradual improvement in the social conditions experienced in Chile and elsewhere in the 1980s in a general context of cutbacks in social welfare and service spending. Generally, and in the specific case of Bolivia, such cutbacks were not reflected in the social development statistics precisely because community-based social organizations, and NGOs of various sorts, stepped into the breach and supplied these services on a self-help or community basis.

A similar development was noted in Mexico after the devastating earthquake of 1985, to which the civil society responded much more effectively than did the state. In Bolivia also there is considerable evidence of a dynamic civil society responding with stepped-up activity and organization to the economic and fiscal crisis and to the austerity and adjustment measures of the government. Indeed, indications are that the response of civil society has been considerably more effective than the NSP in allowing for, if not actually producing, the social advances made in the past decade.

The Paz Zamora Regime (1989–92) and the New Social Policy (NSP)

The second cycle of economic reforms under the NEP was implemented in 1989–93, a period in which the New Social Policy (NSP) was implemented by the government of Jaime Paz Zamora. Together with FOSIS in Chile and Pronasol in Mexico, Bolivia's NSP (in the form of the Fondo Social de Emergencia [FSE]) would come to constitute a model emulated by other countries in the region. Paz Zamora's economic reforms focused on the restoration of confidence in the economy and the creation of opportunities for private investments, which remained at a low of 4 percent of GNP. Corresponding measures included the further compression of wage-rates, already subject to control by the government (in violation of its free-market principles); the institution of a new mining code and the Privatization Law of 1991; and further downsizing of the state apparatus and reduction in the number of public employees — by an estimated 10 percent. Also, both exports and imports were further liberalized, with duties on capital goods reduced to a low of 5 percent.

These reforms instituted from 1989 to 1993 under the NEP[9] were accompanied by an aggressive short-term job creation program, which the government would have preferred to show as a strategy to reduce the official unemployment rate. But to some extent the problem of unemployment persisted. Yet in its five years of operation, the FSE created an average of twenty thousand jobs a month via the financing of three thousand projects, with a total investment of close to $200 million.[10] Almost 50 percent of these funds were contributed by international donors, the treasury general contributing only 15 percent.

For Paz Zamora, the FSE was a relative success, given the socio-economic conditions it created for short-term relief of the worst effects of the economic crisis and the subsequent structural adjustment. As a result of this assessment, the FSE was turned into a permanent government program and created the Fondo de Inversion Social (FIS), which became a model for the World Bank's "new understanding" of the need to redesign the SAP in the war against poverty (Salop 1992) and as such was emulated by other countries in the region. As formulated in Bolivia and elsewhere, the FIS served as a mechanism for channeling (1) external resources as well as mobilizing local ones; (2) dynamizing reduced public investments in education and health; and (3) implementing the government's new Estrategia Boliviana Social (EBS), which was announced in September 1991 and implemented a year later. However, the most critically important feature of the FIS was the conversion of a public spending program into one based on social investment, that is, with social development viewed as a matter of social investment rather than spending of public funds.

Bolivia's new social strategy, which in other contexts has been identified as a New Social Policy (NSP), was institutionalized by Decree 22964 in September 1992. The strategy declared a radical antipoverty program as a national priority. In design the strategy identified four critical components or institutional pillars: (1) targeting (*focalización*) the poor — communities characterized by a high incidence of marginality and poverty; (2) partnership with local governments and intermediary nongovernmental organizations (NGOs); (3) a decentralized, participatory form of community-based development; and (4) an approach to what the UNDP has come to call "integrated human development."[11]

The policies adopted by the government were designed to give the adjustment process a human face and a social dimension — to mitigate its negative impacts and "extraordinarily high social costs" (to quote from an Inter-American Bank memo). The debate in civil society was about to what extent the grassroots organizations and NGOs should participate in such programs such as the FIS, managed within a neoliberal policy and institutional framework. At issue in this debate were various questions of political principle as well as the risk of government co-optation, of being used by the government to advance its agenda.

As for "targeting" the poor, the new policy orientation not only reflected the World Bank's "new understanding" about the need for an NSP (SAP with a human face) but conformed to the government's perceived need for more efficient use of limited and reduced resources[12] and its ideological orientation toward a minimalist non-interventionist state, its economic role reduced to the provision of basic infrastructure and those conditions that would establish the market as the motor of the development process and the private sector as its driving force.[13]

As elsewhere, Bolivia's NSP, and particularly the FIS, was instituted in response to the manifest deficiency in the design of the SAP and the underlying problems of poverty that, by most accounts, were both extended and exacerbated in (and by) the neoliberal reform process. In Bolivia, one of the poorest countries in the region, with over 70 percent of the population officially classified as poor (up to 93 percent in the rural sector), the problem was particularly serious. According to an account given by the World Bank, the problem of poverty in Bolivia, affecting principally small-scale indigenous peasant producers, is deeply rooted in traditional economic and social structures and the corresponding policies of an inefficient, populist, and interventionist state. However, a number of other studies, including ones conducted by the UNDP, clearly show that Bolivia has its share of the new poor, with reference to problems generated by the economic crisis and the neoliberal reform process of the 1980s (World Bank 1990).

In response to these problems and underlying conditions, and to their politically destabilizing effects, the economists of the World Bank, the UNDP, and other operating agencies of the UN system redesigned the SAP, to give it a human face and to create the conditions for what the ECLAC has defined as productive transformation with equity and the UNDP as human development. The key to this redesigned model of structural adjustment was what the executive director of the IDB among others has termed Bolivia's social development as a case of social liberalism. This definition entails a new relationship of the state to civil society, a change institutionalized through a series of reforms implemented by the Sánchez Lozada regime.

The Sánchez de Lozada Regime (1993–97) and the Plan for All

In 1993, the Bolivian electorate elevated to power a regime fiercely committed to the deepening of the neoliberal reforms initiated in 1985. The regime was headed by the US-educated mining magnate Gonzalo Sánchez de Lozada of the MNR, one of the architects of the 1985 Decree 21060, and the vice-president was the Aymara leader Victor Hugo Cárdenas, head of the MRTKL (Túpac Katari Revolutionary Movement of National Liberation), who once embraced a Marxist and indigenous multicultural ideology characterized by the belief in and demand for cultural and national indigenous autonomy. The regime was supported by the populist caudillo Max Fernández, founder and head of the Unión Cívica de Solidaridad (UCS),[14] as well as the Movimiento Bolivia Libre (MBL), the largest center-left party in the political spectrum, which eight years before had characterized Decree 21060 as a Pinochetazo against the people of Bolivia.

The centerpiece of the Lozada government was the Plan de Todos (Plan for All), a program that featured three major policies enacted by law and constitutional change: (1) popular participation; (2) decentralization; and (3) capitalization. The plan further included an initiative to privatize the country's six strategic state-owned enterprises: the national power corporation; the telecommunication company; the Bolivian airline; the railway corporation; the national oil corporation; and the mining refinery of Vinto. The privatization of these companies was to be accompanied by a new pension reform based on the Chilean model (as a mechanism of domestic capital formation) and a reorganization of the government apparatus in the executive branch. These policies, enacted into law within a year of the regime's inception, both deepened and completed the neoliberal reform process initiated in 1985, expanding existing opportunities for domestic and foreign forms of private capital. Apart from creating an institutional framework for the new economic and social policy, these reforms were explicitly designed to modify the organization and functioning of the government and in the process to change the relationship of the state to civil society — and to the economy.[15]

Reorganization of Executive Power

The reforms instituted by the government in the executive branch consisted of the reorganization of executive authority and power under Law 1493 in September 1993. The government reform aimed to reduce the cost of government expenditures and to facilitate decision making at the local grassroots level. To this end, the number of ministries was reduced to a maximum of twelve, including three superministries in the field of development: (1) economic development (with a secretariat of industry, commerce, tourism, energy, mining, and transport and communications); (2) human development (with a secretariat for education, health, housing, urban development, ethnic affairs, gender and intergenerational affairs, rural development, culture and sports, and, most important, coordinating social investments and spending — the operation of the SIF); and (3) sustainable development (with secretaries of planning and environment, popular participation, and territorial affairs).

This reorganization of executive power and the administrative apparatus was a clear response to the international debate and consensus at the time on issues of national development, governability, and sustainability. Similarly, it indicated the government's opening toward and positive response to the recommendations issued at numerous international forums organized by ECLAC, the UNDP, as well as the World Bank, about the need to increase institutional capacity to coordinate economic, social, and environmental policies — and to do so with efficiency and popular participation, which could only occur through a process of decentralization of power.

This reorganization of the executive, however, proved less effective and more difficult than anticipated; indeed it generated more problems than it solved. For example, the new organization of the executive distorted a clear line of communication that had previously helped in handling political and economic problems. Hitherto peasant organizations could directly approach the Ministry of Agriculture, which had been responsible for peasant affairs. Now these affairs were divided among four secretariats, each located in a different government department — rural development, agriculture, natural resources, and alternative development. The peasant organizations thus not only had to connect to the government at a lower level in the decision-making hierarchy but had to do so in a form that inevitably led to interdepartmental conflicts and a complicated system of institutional negotiation and that prevented an effective or efficient response to the concerns and demands of the peasants.

Constitutional Change

In August 1994, the government passed the Constitutional Reform Law. Although it introduced a number of democratic reforms such as the right to vote at age eighteen, the creation of a constitutional tribunal, and direct elections of deputies by district, the government failed to secure greater flexibility in constitutional reform procedures. Given that these procedures are based on the 1967 constitution, which visualized and provided for a strong executive and an active role of the state in the economy, reform of these procedures was a priority for the government. The government had hoped to take advantage of its legislative majority to introduce the flexibility that would allow it to accelerate measures to liberalize and privatize the economy. However, the fear that the MNR might or could abuse its consequent power to change the constitution prevented its allies from joining forces, and so the reform failed.

The Decentralization Law

On 28 June 1995, Bolivia's Decentralization Law was approved in the midst of challenges and frustrations. In the 1980s, Bolivia, together with other countries in the region (and indeed the world), experienced diverse pressures to decentralize the administrative and political structures/institutions of government. In a number of contexts, the proposals toward decentralization came from the government itself, concerned as it was, under widespread conditions of a generalized fiscal (as well as economic) crisis, with the provision of services that it could no longer afford. In these circumstances, the World Bank, the IDB, the UNDP, and ECLAC (this Latin American regional institution has led the intellectual battle against neoliberalism and the search for an alternative form of development) became players in the political and economic processes that were unfolding. According to several analysts, decentralization is the missing link in the process of productive transformation with equity. The De-centralization Law in the context of Bolivia created the institutional basis for popular participation in the process of development.

In other contexts, however, the major impulse and demand for de-centralization and participatory development (and democracy) came from below — from the popular sectors of civil society. In the case of Bolivia, as explained earlier, the demand for decentralization was at the core of the left-wing political platform. Indeed it was a cen-tral concept in the resistance against Banzer's military regime. The Regional Civic Movement in particular embraced this approach. Further, it was the Siles Suazo–UDP government that supported a municipalization process in which the government would delegate to the local level the implementation of services and the administra-tion of the infrastructure. But in the context of the MNR, the chief reason for such moves was that the government could no longer af-ford to sponsor the programs and contain the popular struggle for local government and regional autonomy. Under these conditions, the Decentralization Law, enacted in 1995, provided a crucial link in the government's Plan de Todos and its neoliberal program of structural adjustment to the economy and society.

The Popular Participation Law (PPL) and Municipalization

The government of Sánchez de Lozada introduced one of the most profound institutional reforms in contemporary Bolivia: the Popu-lar Participation Law (PPL), passed in April 1994. First, within the government's decentralization strategy, the law extended the juris-diction of local municipal governments — hitherto restricted to the urban radius — to rural areas that had been in effect and for the most part governed by indigenous and traditional organizations lacking both legal authority and any public resources. Second, the law trans-ferred decision-making authority and administrative responsibility for the infrastructure related to education, health, and local roads to the municipality, and to this purpose allocated by law 20 percent of the public purse to the municipal government level, as well as authorizing municipalities to collect directly taxes on property and vehicles.

There is some question here as to the underlying political dynam-ics involved in the institution of the PPL. On the one hand, the PPL is consistent with the government's decentralization agenda and the associated strategy, promoted by the World Bank, of relying on local governments and social organizations for the implementation of its development projects, and popular participation in decision making related to such projects. On the other hand, in the prelude to the PPL, the government had to confront some of the largest mobilizations of indigenous people over the last forty years. In the political context of these and other such mobilizations, and of the demand for recognition of the indigenous people's own social and economic organizations, autonomy, and local control, many Bolivians, including the government itself, in the form of the Ministry for Sustainable Development, viewed the PPL essentially as a response to the popular struggle and pressure for change (Medina 1995; Melgar Rojas 1995; and Molina 1997).

Without further study of these conflicting — or in this case, complementary — dynamics, the PPL could reasonably be viewed as a form of development "from above" (initiated from within the state apparatus) and "from below" (the result of a popular social movement). In any case, by a number of accounts it has expanded the political space for independent action and local control by community-based organizations that have been legally recognized in the process as organizaciones teritoriales de base (OTBs).

The label "popular participation" derives from the fact that in addition to councils and municipal boards, the law made provision for the formation in each municipality of *comités de vigilancia* elected directly by representatives of OTBs — neighborhood associations, agrarian syndicates, and other forms of legally recognized local (community-based) organizations. Within a year of the law's promulgation, over 10,500 OTBs were recognized, creating thereby a mechanism for popular participation in governmental decision making.

The PPL provides an institutional basis for the government's strategy to advance and deepen the reform process — to implement its new economic and social policies.[16] In effect, it constitutes the government's response to the call by ECLAC, the UNDP, and even the World Bank for a participatory form of integrated and human development that (in ECLAC's formulation) can lead to productive transformation with equity. However, the government's new policies also provoked serious political divisions and debate.

At issue was the charge from certain political quarters that the PPL and the constitution of OTBs were designed to (1) sow confusion within the popular movement[17] and (2) serve the government as a means of weakening community-based or sectoral organizations such as labor and peasant unions in terms of their capacity to represent their constituencies and press their demands for change (Molina 1997). In effect, critics have charged, apart from the effort to undermine and weaken the popular movement, there tends to be a disjunction between the community as a social unit and the municipality as a political-administrative unit — and between local economies and municipal revenues.[18] In sharing its decision-making power with the municipalities (with the simultaneous weakening of its intermediary organizations), the central government has effectively increased its degree of control while providing new opportunities for co-optation. In addition, the new institutionality limits the political actions of popular organizations to strictly local issues, incapacitating them in dealing with larger issues and in effecting change of structures that extend beyond the local community.[19]

Toward a Conclusion: Revisiting the Question of Democracy

The transition toward democracy in Bolivia has been characterized above all by the search for a new economic, social, and institutional order. At the beginning of the 1980s, in a context of economic and political crisis, the idea of democracy was a central reference point of political mobilization by the Frente Amplio, a broad front of social and political forces of opposition, but the Frente lacked a clearly defined institutional profile — a concept of its institutional requirements. Each political party and social organization engaged in the battle for democracy had a different view, and vantage point, even a different concept of democracy. But, notwithstanding this ideological diversity, there was a general consensus as to the need to reform and modernize the state. Prior to this point, most of the divergence had to do not with the role of the state as such but with political conflicts over the social division of its revenues and resources (*el patrimonio corparativo*) and the pattern of public spending. But this was changed by certain economic realities such as the virtual bankruptcy of the mining enterprise, a rate of inflation that eroded the little remaining purchasing power of wages, and a destabilizing fiscal deficit in the context of a huge and growing debt burden and widespread economic insecurity. In the context of these conditions and the associated political chaos, demands for change focused on the need to alter the function and organization of government — and of the relationship of the state to the economy and civil society. That is, ideas about institutional reform and the modernization of the state, implicit in the proposals advanced by the civic associations for regional autonomy and local government, were given a new impetus and put on the political agenda and gained widespread support from different political circles.

The reconstruction of the state, and its relation to civil society, thus became the focal point of a complex intellectual and political struggle that has engaged the most diverse social and political forces. At issue in this struggle were diverse and conflicting conceptions of democracy as an end in itself and as the necessary basis for instituting one political project or another. On the one hand, officials of the existing regime in Bolivia and elsewhere in the region (see comments on 6 January 1997 by Ernesto Zedillo, president of Mexico, on Mexico's new federalism) view decentralization, and the associated or resulting increase in social participation, as the most effective, indeed only, means of ensuring governability and "good governance." In this regard, decentralization and popular participation are seen as two aspects of a single process, the convergence of the state (decentralization) and civil society (participation). In the same connection, decentralization is seen as the missing link in the chain of productive transformation-equity-sustainability (Boisier et al. 1992, 58–60), and national governments are seen as active agents of the process, able to develop a participatory culture within civil society as well as adjust the state apparatus to participation via the democratic decentralization of power.[20]

As for the diverse critics and opponents of the neoliberal model, they generally agreed on the need to democratize the relationship of the state to civil society — and to create a participatory form of development and democracy that will foster the political conditions of an effective movement for social change and the institution of an alternative model of economic and social development.[21]

But which conception and set of political forces will win out — that is, find the political means of its institutionalization — is not clear. Both supporters and opponents of the neoliberal regime in the current context are able to muster a range of social and political forces in the ongoing struggle for economic and social development. To establish the precise correlation of forces and the possible or likely outcome at this crossroads of Bolivia's history will require a much closer analysis of the dynamics of this political process. This is the challenge faced by engaged social analysts of the reform process in Bolivia and elsewhere in the region.

Notes

1. Postmodernism as an intellectual perspective on the development process can be traced back to a long tradition of idealist critiques of science and the possibility and validity of a structural form of analysis. On the most recent counterpoint in this debate (poststructuralism versus Marxism) within the field of development, see, among others, Schuurman (1993).

2. The emergence and formation of a social movement and struggle for democracy, and the associated process, are treated in a number of studies. As to the social forces and actors involved, see various studies in Laserna (1985). The institutionalization of democracy is treated well in studies compiled by Mayorga (1987). Also see Calderón and Laserna (1983, 1990), Lazarte (1988), Velasco (1985), and Zavaleta (1974).

3. On these and related issues, see the works cited in the previous note, including the following: various studies in Laserna (1985); Calderón and Laserna (1983, 1990); Lazarte (1988); Velasco (1985); and Zavaleta (1974).

4. The UDP was formed with three main political forces: the MIR (Movimiento de la Izquierda Revolucionaria), a party that was born embracing a neo-Marxist approach that combined class analysis with the national-popular legacy and context of Bolivia; the MNRI (Movimiento Nastionalista Revolucionario de Izquierda), led by Siles Suazo, who was one of the leaders of the 1952 national revolution; and the PCB (Partido Comunista de Bolivia), which had a strong connection to Moscow. Other smaller parties and leaders were part of this left coalition.

5. On the NEM that underlies the NEP and policies now adopted by virtually every government in the region, see, among others, Bulmer-Thomas (1996).

6. The experience of Mexico, which has raised the same question (see Lustig, 1995), suggests that the relative weakness of the political response, particularly among the working classes, can also be explained in part by the conditions of economic and social restructuring reflected in the growth of an informal sector in the region's urban centers and a popular economy requiring of households a survival strategy with or without reduced recourse to services provided by the state.

7. As to this centrality — namely, the presence of at least ten thousand miners in the streets of La Paz in 1985 in protest of the *paquetazo* — and the vanguard role of the tin miners in the COB, see, among others, Lazarte (1988) and Toranzo Roca and Arrieta (1989), who can be counted among the few economists or sociologists who have attempted to evaluate the political impact of the change in the Latin American working class wrought by the economic reform process.

8. It was estimated by COB intellectuals that by 1994 the NEP had brought about the destruction of at least 150,000 jobs in the private sector, on top of the tens of thousands of jobs lost in the public sector by decree, privatization, and mass firings (*Informe R*, 16 December 1994, 27). The expulsion of twenty thousand and more workers from COMIBOL (Corporación Minera de Bolivia — Mining Corporation of Bolivia) resulted in a massive transformation of miners into farmers, mostly in the growing of coca, reflected in dramatic growth of coca production (now estimated to encompass 6 percent of the GNP and from 60 to 70 percent of exports) and the militancy of the *cocaleros* in the current struggle against the government's neoliberal NEP and what the major federation of *cocaleros* together with the COB regard as an antiworker state.

9. For a neoliberal or officialist perspective on the NEP, see Sachs and Morales (1988). A more critical perspective is provided by Aguirre et al. (1990).

10. The key feature of these jobs so created, a fact generally ignored in the evaluations commissioned by the government, is that they are generally short-term and that any more permanent job-generation is in the informal sector, which, it is estimated, accounts for 90 percent of all the jobs generated in the process of structural adjustment (PREALC 1991).

11. The influence of ECLAC and UNDP thinking in the design of the NSP, in the search for an integrated form of human development, is clear in the protocol of Bolivia's Plan de Todos announced in 1993, which identified four main pillars of Bolivia's national development strategy: economic growth, social equity, environmental protection, and democracy. On the ECLAC model in this regard, see, among others, Boisier et al. (1992) and Veltmeyer and Petras (2000).

12. See the Ministry of Finance and Economic Development (Morales 1994, 59) on the reduction of social-program spending from 1987 to 1992 by the government from 32.7 to 23.6 percent of the national budget.

13. This ideological orientation is derived from the participation of the president and his economic team in US educational and other institutions that promote this neoliberal ideology, practice it in other contexts, and enforce compliance in countries like Bolivia on the basis of the mechanism of access to international development finance and the renegotiation of the external debt.

14. This electoral support was later translated into what commentators have termed a cheap alliance based on a governability pact between the MNR and UCS signed in June 1993 and revised in March 1994 (see *Informe R*, 27 May 1994).

15. As formulated by Samuel Doria Medina, minister of planning, at a meeting in Paris of the World Bank Consultants Group for Bolivia, "it is necessary to privatize . . . as quickly as possible, and to redefine the role of the state . . . so that the government of Bolivia can accomplish its aims." In the same context,

Medina added, "the private sector must be charged with the responsibility for production, while the state should only provide for improving infrastructure, development of the social sector, and protection of the environment" (*Informe R*, December 17, 1991).

16. The key PPL components can be summarized as follows: (1) Recognition of Bolivia as a multiethnic country. For the first time in Bolivia's history the indigenous communities were acknowledged constitutionally as existing social entities. This constitutes a major step toward change in Bolivia's stratified and racist society. (2) The role of municipalities and local governments. The PPL defines the fundamental role of municipal governments in their administrative and development tasks, conferring on them new attributes including the management of health, basic community services, education, culture, sports and recreation, and infrastructure. (3) The distribution of government resources. Before the PPL, municipalities received 10 percent of domestic revenue, from which 85 percent was allocated to urban municipalities in three main cities. With the PPL, municipalities received 20 percent of domestic revenues, distributed on a population-density basis. This allocation of financial resources through the PPL has been a major change, particularly for those municipalities that have been neglected in national development strategies. Municipalities now had to learn how to prepare strategic plans, to develop accounting systems for community development, and to build their own capacities. (4) Structures for people's participation. This was perhaps the most relevant component of the PPL regarding local development. The PPL encouraged the formation of OTBs, which are composed of existing organizations in communities (unions, NGOs, indigenous and traditional authorities, civic organizations, etc.). The chief role of the OTBs is to exercise control over the strategic planning process and over the implementation and evaluation of municipalities' activities and development plans. To this end, the OTBs are instructed to establish the *comités de vigilancia* to pay close attention to the municipal government's budget and activities. As such, they are required to ensure that the strategic plans are culturally and ethnically sensitive, environmentally sound, and inclusive of women's participation.

17. The PPL was a clear response to the demand for autonomy, local government, and ethnocultural identity advanced over years of struggles by a broad social movement of peasants and indigenous peoples as well as a struggle for regional autonomy waged by a movement of civic committees. In its legislation in the areas of popular participation and integrated alternative development and associated policies, the government has effectively appropriated the language and discourse of the popular movement, outflanking and undermining it in the process, as well as creating an environment of confusion and disorganization. For example, in the wake of the PPL and the constitution of OTBs, a number of community representatives at the local-government level concluded that the era and need for unions were over and that the communities were beneficiaries of the coparticipation process set up, rather than the political and economic interests associated with the local government (see *Informe R*, 16 December 1994, 6–7).

18. As for the question of local economies versus municipal revenues, there are a number of issues involved, including the fact that revenues are allocated ac-

cording to population and that in many cases people reside in and are members of different communities than those where they work or engage in economic activity, creating in some cases an enormous disjunction between the resource requirements of certain economies and the revenue-generating capacities of the relevant municipalities.

19. According to Carlos Hugo Molino, national secretary for popular participation, in his commentary on a conference presentation by Juan Enrique Vega on popular participation and democratic governability, the opposition to the PPL from across the social and political spectrum — he identifies four major interlocutors: the political class; the syndicates; the civic associations, many of which, he notes, are absolutely conservative and oligarchic; and the intellectuals (as well as NGOs, the church, and the armed forces, each with a stake in raging political debates on the issue) — has to do with the fact that the move to institute popular participation, and to enact enabling legislation to decentralize government, is essentially a government initiative, which naturally provokes skepticism and opposition in the fear that the capacity of each organization to represent its constituency will be eroded and displaced. The most trenchant criticisms of the PPL, however, come from the left, with regard both to the unions and to the political class. The left, nevertheless, is in a bind (if not politically disoriented and caught off-guard by the government's move) in that it is difficult to oppose a law that to some extent responds to a long popular struggle for participatory democracy, regional autonomy, and local control — and that opens up a political space for popular-sector organizations. The debate — and struggle — continues.

20. In this idea advanced by various ECLAC economists, popular or social participation is seen as another form of creating power and, as such, with respect to real versus formal participation, cannot be understood or implemented without decentralization, which is a policy designed to "stimulate participation within a counter-hegemonic matrix and constitutes the principal lever of . . . local development initiatives . . . facilitating change . . . [and] promoting sustainability" (Boisier et al. 1992, 53).

21. As noted by a number of contributors to *Informe R,* a fortnightly report on political developments in the popular and labor movement in Bolivia put out by CEDOIN (Centro de Documentación e Información Nacional), in its ideological and political struggle with the popular and labor movements, the Bolivian government (like its consulting organizations such as the World Bank) consciously and effectively appropriated the ideological discourse of popular participation. The effect, if not the intent, has been to disorient and weaken the popular movement.

FIVE

Poverty and Local Development in the Bio-Bio Region of Chile

Eduardo Aquevedo Soto

In this chapter we synthesize a number of the more important conclusions of a research project carried out in 1995 and 1996 under the working title of "The Social Morphology of Poverty in the Bio-Bio Region." The discussion is divided into four parts. The first part attempts to identify the essential features of the new development model instituted in Chile as a result of the military coup of 1973, focusing on those aspects of the model connected to the production and reproduction of poverty. The changing dynamic of the labor force as a constitutive element of the neoliberal model is especially important. The second part looks at the socioeconomy of the Bio-Bio Region (Region VIII), a locale in which this new model has been implemented with particular thoroughness. The simultaneous appearance in this region of highly successful export activity and the highest incidence of poverty and indigence in a long time cannot simply be seen as a coincidence. The documented exceedingly high social costs associated with growth and regional competitiveness invite us to look at the patterns of accumulation and policies of regulation that dominate on the regional level, with particular emphasis on the role of development actors (particularly, large corporations) and the responsibilities of public institutions.

The third part is an exploration of the problem of poverty in this region. Using the macrolevel analyses from the preceding sections, we will look at the three matrices of poverty and its reproduction. The first relates to the socioeconomic disequilibria that antedate the current model and that we shall call "cumulative traditional poverty." The second deals with the restructuring undergone during the late 1970s and for most of the 1980s. This restructuring considerably aggravated the traditional forms of poverty and produced unprecedented, new short-term forms. The third matrix involves chronically high levels of unemployment in the region that, when combined with the deregulation and flexibility of the labor market, have made employment more volatile and have created new forms of poverty. At the end of the third section, we will discuss the social policies of the *concertación* government.

In the fourth and final part we suggest a number of hypotheses for local and regional development, drawing attention to the sociopolitical and cultural aspects favorable to conferring a better bargaining position on local or regional governments, particularly as regards small and medium-sized businesses (SMSBs) and the creation of an "endogenous" form of development.

I. Chile's New Development Model

The military coup of 1973 abruptly closed a stage of capitalist development in Chile, one based principally on the production of industrial goods for the internal market within a framework of public regulation of economic and social activity. This regulation favored primarily the industrial and financial sectors but also tended to benefit important segments of the middle and lower, or popular, classes (for example, in the form of social spending on health, education, and transport). This capitalist development model was in many respects inefficient, especially regarding production, and resulted in high levels of socioeconomic inequality and other forms of social exclusion (Fajnzylber 1983; Vuskovic 1975). Thus it was that beginning in the 1960s and ending with the coup of 1973, there was increasing criticism of this model from both the popular class and local businessmen. In a sense, then, the government of Salvador Allende and his Popular Unity Party can be understood as a frustrated attempt at a serious reform of this development model. In any case, the social and political debacle of 1973, in our opinion, was both a manifestation and a consequence of the contradictions of this model. It was also a demonstration of the social and political limits of permissible transformation or replacement of this model with another alternative model of development.

A New Development Model

Starting in 1973, a new development model was implemented in Chile. It was based on neoliberal ideas and was considerably different from the model it replaced. Policies of accumulation clustered around the production of primary goods for and external market supported by an accompanying deregulation and privatization of socioeconomic activity to the benefit of the local businessmen and transnationals. The market was taken to be the central, or only, regulator of all activities, in the first instance those in the economy, but subsequently extending to and embracing social, political, and cultural activities.

For capital, the implementation of this model signified an extraordinary increase in spatial mobility and opportunities to centralize and integrate, thus allowing increasing levels of monopoly, large transfers of income from labor to capital, modernization of technological and organizational dimensions of important segments of production, significant decreases in the costs of production and a concomitant increase in surplus and accumulation, an increased level of internationalization (transnationalization, denationalization), and, finally, the export of this accumulation and a greater dependence (subordination, integration) with respect to the world's major economics.

For labor, in contrast, the implementation of this new model has meant a broader application of Taylorism within firms, that is to say, an intensification of the rhythm of work and a reinforcement of the "despotism of the firm." It has meant the introduction of extreme flexibility and segmentation of the labor market, an expansion of precarious employment or underemployment and the subsequent loss of negotiating leverage, and a considerable weakening of labor's participation in the distribution of national income. Finally, it has meant a serious fall in real incomes, particularly in the form of the minimum wage, throughout the period 1973–89. All this has resulted in increased productivity of labor, but also in an increased level of brutality in the exploitation of workers.

Among the above features, three are decisive and form the pillars of the new model. These are (1) the manner in which the Chilean economy has become both dynamically and peripherally inserted in the world market by means of the increased export of what are essentially primary products; (2) the generalization of market mechanisms through privatization, reprivatization, state and fiscal reforms, liberalization, deregulation, central bank autonomy, and economic "opening," all at the expense of public intervention and regulation; and (3) the expansion of Taylorism in the workforce and its emphasis on the strategy of labor flexibility. This last feature, as Fernando Leiva and R. Agacino have emphasized for the Chilean case (Leiva and Agacino 1995), far from being an effect of the new model, is one of its central strategies.

The Economic Model and Labor Flexibility

There is already an extensive literature on the first two of the above-mentioned three decisive features. But the specific feature of labor flexibility, and its decisive connection with poverty and the weakening of unions, has been less studied in Chile, although there have been some excellent initial studies. For the purposes of the present study we may divide up the phenomenon of flexibility into three general areas:

1. *The number of wage earners* — flexibility allows a company to be more adaptive by varying its workforce and/or working hours to meet its particular exigencies and also allows companies to dispense with the obligations formerly imposed by collective agreements, especially regarding the costs of employment and unemployment. Associated results are the removal of compensation, subcontracting, and an increase in temporary work and work done in the home.

2. *Wages* — flexibility calls into question or rejects outright systems for indexing wages, a minimum wage, and other policies associated with employment. On the contrary, wage increases are now associated with productivity, and wage negotiations are decentralized.

3. *Labor functionality* — flexibility has come to mean that owners can reorganize the work process itself by seeking to employ

multiskilled workers, thus ensuring or at least making possible internal workplace mobility and the expansion of tasks required of each worker. This implies substantial investment in workforce training and is a basic feature of what may be called "proactive flexibility" (Leborgne and Lipietz 1992), but this implication is still far from being universally accepted by the dominant entrepreneurial sector in Chile and Latin America.

We are not suggesting here a total rejection or even resistance to flexibility in any form within the labor market. On the one hand, we are questioning the purely regressive and "reactive" forms of flexibility whose object seems to be the structural weakening of the negotiating capacity of workers and the subsequent precariousness of their social and economic conditions. On the other hand, a dynamic or "proactive" flexibility in the labor market increasingly appears to be a necessity given new types of production and will thus be a necessary component of any alternative development strategy or model of current importance.

Flexibility in these three areas — in the Chilean case, especially the first two — allows owners to reduce wage costs, to intensify the rhythm of work, and, above all, to impose obstacles to forms of union, social, and ultimately political resistance by means of the fragmentation of the labor sector produced by this strategy. The precariousness of employment must thus be looked upon as a direct consequence of the strategy of flexibilization.

In Chile's case, this strategy was initiated almost simultaneously with the formation of the military dictatorship beginning with the proscription of strikes and democratic election of union officials. Between 1978 and 1979, a series of decrees — Decree Laws Numbers 2200, 2756, and 2758 — were passed that fundamentally transformed the labor legislation in force since 1931. These decrees established as fundamental the employer's right to fire an employee at will, while at the same time they limited and weakened the ability of workers to organize and obstructed union actions. Further changes were introduced during the crisis of 1982–83 (Decree Law Number 18134) that sought to make wage levels even more flexible, and this was followed in 1987 by the promulgation of the new Labor Code and its Provisional Reform. These changes redefined the individual work contract, union organization, collective bargaining, arbitration, and the contracting out of labor, and generally served to deepen the process of deregulation and flexibilization begun a decade earlier (González 1996).

The labor reforms initiated by the *concertación* government during 1990–94, though they sought to moderate the legislation established during the previous period, were not in fact a serious revision of the flexibilization strategy. This resulted in a definitive consolidation and legitimization of the fundamental features of this strategy and gave the imprimatur to a general ascendancy of owners over employees by legally sanctioning the unprotected character of the latter in relation to the former. Thus, Pablo González, perhaps somewhat euphemistically, has suggested that "the philosophy inspiring the changes of [President] Aylwin's administration might be characterized as the social legitimization of a flexible and dynamic labor market" (González 1996).

The concrete results of the flexibilization process in Chile have been low rates of unionization and a consequent loss of negotiating ability, the extreme segmentation of the labor market, the increasing precariousness of employment, and the slow unequal evolution of real wages with a concomitant significant deterioration among the poorest sectors in the distribution of income. This new structural state of affairs in the Chilean labor market, fostered in many important respects by flexibilization policies, has been the formative matrix for the reproduction of poverty and social exclusion so evident during the last two decades (Leiva and Agacino 1995).

The Two Faces of the Economic Model: Dynamism and Exclusion

The institution of this development model and the profound structural transformations it has implied have substantially modified the functional dynamic of Chilean capitalism. Since the end of the 1980s up to the present, this process has revealed two fundamental developments:

1. An important macroeconomic dynamism and strong international competitiveness. This has resulted in the cycle of solid growth that began in 1984 and continues today. This expansion

has a strongly structural basis as evidenced by export activities as well as the considerable growth in both local and foreign investment since the end of the 1980s. This structural basis involves:

a. a drastic reduction of the global costs of production, especially wages, as we have indicated in the strong contraction of real earnings in Chile during the period 1973–89, a contraction that has seen only a slow and unequal recuperation;

b. growth in labor productivity by virtue of the generalization of Taylorist methods and the increase in labor flexibility;

c. an increase in the efficiency of capital by means of the technological and organizational modernization of nuclei of production oriented toward exportation; and

d. a broad ideological consensus created by the country's dominant groups over the past three decades regarding the currently dominant economic model. This consensus was achieved to a large extent over the years thanks to systematic terror and various forms of cultural and ideological manipulation and has resulted in a weakened capacity for social, political, ideological, or labor resistance among those social sectors most affected by the dominant economic orientation. Under these conditions, and as long as they remain unaltered, there can be no unsolvable social or political obstacles to the Chilean economy continuing its expansive phase into the near future.

2. The fundamentally exclusionary, inequitable, and predatory character of the economic growth generated by this model, a feature that is inherent in the model itself. This results in the reproduction of high levels of poverty and indigence, on the one hand, and extreme wealth, on the other. It also results in the regressive and scandalous tendencies in the distribution of incomes and the inequalities and disequilibria within and among regions, as well as the systematic and massive exploitation of

the country's natural resources accompanied by an accelerated deterioration of the environment.

II. The Bio-Bio Region: The Problems with Outward-Oriented Development

A good example of how this economic development model works in Chile is the current socioeconomic situation in the Bio-Bio Region (Region VIII), where conditions have been aggravated by the fact that the region is in a subordinate position to the process of capital accumulation in the rest of the country. At the end of the 1970s, the region began to undergo a process of restructuring that changed important aspects of its social and productive profile. We now direct our attention to these aspects and their consequences.

Although the Bio-Bio Region has great economic potential — a virtue that has resulted in its often being considered an alternative pole of development vis-à-vis the Metropolitan Region centered on Santiago (UNDP 1996) — and although, even amid the aforementioned restructuring processes, the region nonetheless has managed to maintain its essentially industrial character, the region still has experienced a decline, and even destruction, of specific traditional segments of the agricultural, mining, and manufacturing sectors as these processes have fostered the emergence once again of a dynamic export-oriented sector based on primary products secured from fishery and forestry resources. Regional exports have increased from US $411 million in 1983 to US $2.592 billion in 1995, going from 10.7 percent to 16.3 percent of total national exports.

The region's industrial base has a long history founded upon the production of iron and steel, metal products, petroleum refining, chemical products, food, shoes, and textiles. In 1990, the industrial sectors contributed around 40 percent to the gross regional product and thus cannot be considered a mere "flash in the pan." At the same time, the region's contribution to the country's total industrial production has varied between 19.5 percent and 22.1 percent for the period 1985 to 1990 (Antinao 1997). A few industrial areas such as textiles, glass, and china have felt the ill effects of restructuring production over the past number of years; yet these are beginning to experience a recovery after upgrades to their technology.

However, even given its indisputable position in the national economy, generating as it does about one-tenth of the national product
and a sixth of national exports (almost a quarter if we exclude cop-
per), thus placing it second only to the Metropolitan Region, the
last twenty years have seen it become one of the worst performing
regions in the country. There has been low growth, mediocre levels
of competition when compared to the national scale, scarce or nonexistent contributions by the big transnational corporations to its
development, high levels of unemployment, poverty, and indigence,
a high level of concentration of incomes, and, generally speaking,
low indexes of "human development." The foregoing serve to indicate that the dominant development model at the regional level,
which we could characterize as export-oriented and neo-Taylorist,
has introduced structural disequilibria and instabilities. Let us take
a look at the more decisive of these latter.

Low Economic Growth and Weak Regional Competitiveness

Of first importance is the fact that, leaving aside certain sectoral
dynamics, the rates of accumulation and growth in the regional
economy are notoriously mediocre. While the nation as a whole experienced a rate of growth of 6.5 percent between 1986 and 1992,
the region only experienced 4.18 percent (Antinao 1997). This tendency for the region to underperform vis-à-vis the national average
continued into the period 1992 to 1996, and is clear from the slow
but constant decline in the region's contribution to the GNP: 11.8
percent in 1960; 11.68 percent in 1985; 10.65 percent in 1990; 10.3
percent in 1992; and 9.79 percent in 1995.

These low growth rates can be explained as due to the comparatively low levels of investment, particularly public and foreign
investment (UNDP 1996). In a recent study, Rodrigo Saldías showed
that between 1990 and 1995 aggregate foreign investment in Region VIII (the official administrative name for the Bio-Bio Region)
represented only 1.9 percent of the total invested in all the regions, a
datum that may be compared and contrasted to Region I with 11.4
percent, Region II with 25.3 percent, Region III with 10 percent,
Region IV with 2.7 percent, and Region VII with 2 percent (Saldías
1997). Moreover, the aggregate investment in Region VIII has been

concentrated in specific sectors, principally forestry and energy, and in specific geographic locales, all of which tends to foment the essentially heterogeneous production of the region. These data — along with others related to the outlook for regional income, regional production, industrial and nonindustrial exports, and development — have been characterized by UNDP as "overall an extremely negative economic outlook for Region VIII," describing it as the second most unstable region in the country with poor indicators such as per capita income, growth in the regional product, and public and foreign investment (UNDP 1996, 180).

UNDP's aggregate parameter of "overall economic outlook," when crossed with other factors such as companies, persons, institutions, infrastructure, science, and technology, has allowed it to construct a so-called competitiveness indicator for the various regions of the country. According to this indicator, Region VIII is only performing well in the cross-tabulated areas of entrepreneurial performance and science and technology. It performs poorly in the areas of human resources and institutions such as municipal budgets, public expenditure, and regional autonomy, together with the aforementioned overall economic outlook.

Large Corporations, Transnationalization, and Outward-Oriented Development

Another decisive element for understanding the heterogeneity and disequilibria of Region VIII's socioeconomy has been the role of large corporations, particularly those that are principally transnational in character. With respect to this role, the work of S. Boisier and V. Silva has been of singular importance (Boisier and Silva 1990), and they indicate a combination of data and tendencies that are important to note.

1. In Region VIII there are fourteen incorporated companies operating within the industrial sector, all of which may be categorized as large companies in terms of their number of employees. The smallest employs 121 persons while the largest employs 6,489 persons, and taken together they employ a total of 21,826 persons, which is equivalent to about 68 percent of the total regional employment in the manufacturing sector and about 82 percent of industrial employment in the category of "large corporations" (fifty or more persons). Two

of these corporations are parastatal, and of the remaining twelve, five are financed by regional or national capital.

2. Of 238 regional industrial firms, 77.2 percent are concentrated in traditional sectors such as food, shoes, coal, steel, and petrochemicals, while only 8.4 percent, or twenty-six, are in newer sectors such as informatics and capital goods.

3. Of these firms 43 percent have achieved medium-level technologies such as computerization of accounting, inventory control, and some measure of automation of the production process, while only 5.2 percent have incorporated, even if only partially, technologies such as computer-designed and -controlled production.

4. There is a significant relation between the larger employee size of the corporations and the establishment of the head office in Santiago, the national capital. In spite of the fact that only 10 percent of the region's companies have a head office in Santiago, this percentage increases to 25 percent for those companies with one hundred or more employees and to 50 percent for those with more than two hundred employees. Of the thirteen most important corporations, only one has its head office in Concepción, the principal city of Region VIII.

5. Of the thirteen largest corporations representing 64 percent of regional industrial employment, two are parastatals, while of the eleven private ones only five are made up of national capital, and of these five, only one is made up of local capital. The remaining six private corporations — Celulosa Arauco & Constitución, Cía. Cervecerías Unidas, Cía. Siderúgica Huachipato, Forestal Carampangue, Forestal Colcura, and Wood Products and Synthetics — have considerable amounts of foreign capital, the majority being in fact controlled by transnationals.

6. Foreign capital in the publicly traded corporations of the region's manufacturing sector amounts to some 50 percent. Among these corporations, seven employ almost half of the labor force of the combined total for all fourteen corporations, which represents 31 percent of the total employment for the region's industrial firms.

7. The transnationalization of the regional economy is quantitatively and structurally important, since the seven corporations controlled by foreign capital comprise the total sugar and steel production of Chile, the largest, diversified forestry product and cellulose manufacturer in the country (this latter being the third most

important export corporation in Chile), and an important percentage of the national production of beer, other beverages, forestry products, panels, and glued wood products.

This tendency toward the transnationalization of the regional economy and the increasing importance of the large corporation is a principal feature of the ruling development model and is a tendency that has, despite certain changes in the composition of the corporate structure, become accentuated and deepened over the past six years. There can be little doubt that it has had serious consequences for the region's socioeconomic development, quite different from the potential impacts secured by developing strictly regional companies and SMSBs.

One of the most important of these consequences, and quite apart from the fact that decisions and administration issue from businesses based in Santiago, is the fact that *the greater part of the surplus generated in the region, particularly by exporting companies, is not locally reinvested,* while their contribution to regional development via taxes is insignificant. This is connected with the fact that, given their importance, influence, and available resources, the large corporations pursue investment strategies oriented solely toward profitability, something that usually does not coincide with the objectives and pursuit of a sustainable and balanced regional development.

Under such circumstances, there can be little solid expectation that such large corporations, particularly those that are principally transnational in character, will contribute in any effective manner to regional development. Rather, in view of their nature and interests, such corporations in fact *cannot* support the endogenous development of production, and without this latter there can be no conceivable, real development. This latter implies (1) significant rates of reinvestment; (2) the creation of forward linkages that will intensify industrialization, diversify production, and promote increasing amounts of value-added; (3) a growing and dynamic articulation between small and large businesses, with the large corporations committed to production projects over the long term; (4) permanent growth in workforce training and skill acquisition; and (5) a dynamic relationship between business and regional universities regarding training and scientific research that will promote technological innovation and the recycling and/or formation of technical personnel.

Endogenous development consists of not only socioeconomic and technological variables such as the foregoing but also political variables. Specifically, it implies the existence of sociopolitical forces and local/regional powers that are truly committed to a strategy of locally focused accumulation and regional development. The large transnational corporation *cannot* "play the game" of endogenous development for the simple reason that its basic interests and centers of decision making lie outside the region, in some cases even outside the country. Thus, its natural tendency is to generate or promote extralocal investment of accumulation and, in consequence, subordinate local production to centers of interest external to the region. International experience has suggested that there are exceptions to this, namely, that large corporation can "play the game" if there already exists a relatively solid socioeconomic, technological, and institutional context that favors endogenous development.

The UNDP has observed that "if an important fraction of the owners of the factors of production reside in the Metropolitan Region — or if further stages of value addition are located there — this Region will in fact be the 'winner' in a development strategy based on export promotion" (UNDP 1996, 96). This is precisely what has happened to Region VIII.

High Levels of Unemployment, Social Deprivation, and Poverty

The low levels of accumulation and overall growth of Region VIII, as indicated above, as well as the transfer of surplus outside the region, together with the consequent heterogeneity and structural disequilibria alluded to in the foregoing, all result inevitably in (1) elevated rates of unemployment; (2) a segmented, flexible, and precarious labor market; (3) high levels of poverty and indigence; and (4)) serious income inequalities. These latter are some of the conditions produced by the neo-Taylorist character of the dominant development model in the region and are worthy of a closer look.

High unemployment has become a permanent reality in the region over the last twenty years, reaching over 20 percent of the economically active population during the period 1976 to 1985. In the second half of the 1980s and the beginning of the 1990s, unemployment fell drastically to 5.3 percent in 1990 and 5.5 percent in 1992. However, as of 1993 the regional unemployment rate climbed sharply upward, exceeding 7 and even 8 percent between 1993 and 1996. In the first quarter of 1996 the unemployment rate reached 8.3 percent, compared with a national average of 4 percent.

Poverty and indigence will be examined in a separate section and in greater detail later on, but we point out now that a national socioeconomic survey generated every other year by the Ministry of Planning and Cooperation and the Department of Economics at the University of Chile indicates that for 1992 and 1994, Region VIII had the highest rate of poverty in the country at 46.6 percent and 40.3 percent respectively for the years surveyed. For the same years, indigence affected 16.8 percent and 13.8 percent respectively of the region's inhabitants. By the mid-1990s, the region had the same poverty rate that the country had in 1987.

Poverty and indigence are two of the most important indicators that allow us, using UNDP methodology, to assess the level of "human development" of a country, region, or community. If these indicators are combined with other associated indicators such as population, average pupil age, literacy, infant morality, average household income, and so on, the communities with comparatively lower human development in Chile are to be found in Regions VII and VIII. Of the thirty-five worst communities in the country classified according to the Human Development Index, thirty are to be found in these same regions, with twenty in Bio-Bio (VIII) and ten in Maule (VII). In contrast, of the thirty communities classified as the best, none belongs to Region VIII, and if we look at the fifty communities classified as having the greatest human development, only two are to be found in the Bio-Bio Region.

The twenty communities with the lowest regional indexes in this regard are Ranquil, Contulmo, Quilaco, Ninhue, Tirúa, Portezuelo, Coihueco, Cobquecura, Lebu, Quillón, Florida, Pemuco, Trehuaco, Curanilahue, Mulchén, Hualqui, Cabrero, Santa Juana, Quilleco, and Lota. In the national ranking of 199 communities studied, Lota was 168 and Ranquil 199, this last being the community with the least human development in the country and a long way from Vitacura, which ranked in first place. The ten communities in Region VIII that ranked as having the best human development were Concepción at 32, Talcahuano at 46, Chillán at 63, Laja at 80, Los Angeles at 101, Yungay at 105, Penco at 115, Tomé at 122, Coronel at 124, and Antuco at 126. All these communities came in at rankings not only distant from first-place Vitacura but also distant from all the communities of Greater Santiago. Only Concepción, Talcahuano, Chillán, and Laja fall within the 100 best of the communities studied.

The regressive distribution of incomes is another manifestation of the unsustainable structural disequilibria generated by the dominant development model in Region VIII. In 1995, the National Statistics Institute (NSI) published the results of its "Supplemental Survey on Incomes" carried out on households and persons between 1990 and 1993, and the following year the NSI provided data on regional incomes by analyzing the results of this survey. According to this data, the Bio-Bio Region was behind at least eight other regions for the period surveyed, and the per capita income was less than 80 percent of the national average, with the exception of 1991, when it reached 87.5 percent. However, in 1992 incomes fell to 76.2 percent and in 1993 to only 65.7 percent of the average national income. The differences at the regional level are even more disturbing: in 1991, the Bio-Bio Region's best year, the regional incomes stood at only 69 percent of per capita income in the Metropolitan Region, and in 1993, the Bio-Bio Region's per capita income was only 48.3 percent of the capital region's income.

The regions that have lagged behind Region VIII — Regions IV, VII, IX, and X — have experienced sharp rises in income levels, and the possibility cannot be discounted that they may pass Region VIII in forthcoming years. Region VII is the only region in the country for which the average income of the employed fell between 1992 and 1993.

If we take all these elements together, elements that provide us with a picture of the social reality of Region VIII and the results of a neo-Taylorist agenda and reproduction of the labor force, we cannot but agree with the negative outlook of the UNDP study regarding the human resource situation in the region, especially with reference to the incidence of poverty, educational conditions, sanitation, and the characteristics and levels of employment, among others.

Weak Public and Institutional Regulation

Given the ambit of the region's complex reality as presented above, we observe that empowered public institutions, especially regional and local governments, have played up to the present at least the role of "accompanist" to the dynamics of the dominant model, dynamics created by the most influential actors in the region, the transnationals. This role has become evident in (1) the lack of any design strategies that would effectively indicate a direction to be taken for an increasing "endogenization" of regional development; (2) the consequent infrequent public interventions in the form of expenditures and investment; (3) the miserable budgets for the great majority of municipalities; (4) the weak support given to the establishment of connections and synergies between companies, universities, and the region's communities and to the development of associated "regional technological networks" (Boisier and Silva, 1990); (5) the weak and insufficient promotion of SMSBs, particularly regional firms; and (6) the fragile autonomy advocated by regional and local governments when confronted with central authority, be this due to institutional and cultural centralism, dominant development strategies, financial and human resources, or power relations.

The case of Region VIII, the Bio-Bio, as outlined in the foregoing, suggests two essential strategies: first, to create a block of social, political, and cultural forces that would include regional and local governments and would be committed to effective strategies for regional development; and, second, to pursue a process of decentralization, which implies greater institutional initiatives as well as increases in available resources at the regional and local levels principally via control or acquisition of a significant part of locally generated surplus.

III. Poverty in Region VIII: Dimensions and Tendencies

Even though the population of Region VIII declined between 1987 and 1996, it still tended to generate exceptionally high levels of poverty when compared to national averages and has been in this critical situation most likely since the beginning of the 1980s. This region and Regions VII and IX together have the highest indexes of poverty and indigence in the country and are far beyond national averages.

According to MIDEPLAN (Ministry of Planning and Cooperation) data, in 1987 some 57 percent of the population of Region VIII were below the poverty line, and 26.1 percent, or slightly less than 380,000 people, were classified as indigent. In 1990, poverty levels dropped to 48.2 percent and indigence to 17.8 percent. The CASEN survey of 1992 indicated a drop in poverty in the Bio-Bio Region for 1987, but at the same time it confirmed the central tendency, namely, that for 1992, poverty affected 46.6 percent of the population while indigence affected some 16.8 percent. According to this data, the region has maintained its position as the poorest in the country since 1990, with poverty rates fourteen points beyond the national average of 32.6 percent. The rate of regional indigence is almost double the national average of 8.6 percent. In terms of population, in 1992 poverty affected 808,186 people and indigence 291,363.

The CASEN survey for 1994 indicated that 40.3 percent of the total regional population were classified as poor and 13.8 percent indigent, data that rank Region VIII as the nation's second poorest, only marginally better than the lowest, Region VII, with 40.5 percent. This situation becomes even clearer if we use the survey's data to compare Region VIII with other poor communities in the country. Of the ten poorest communities in the country, six are in Region VIII; of the twenty-five poorest, seventeen are in the region; and of the fifty-five poorest, thirty-one are in the region. Moreover, of the region's forty-nine communities, seventeen have poverty levels above 50 percent while forty-eight of the forty-nine communities have poverty rates above the national average of 28.5 percent; forty-seven of the total communities have levels of indigence above the national average.

The most recent CASEN survey, from 1996, indicates that in the Bio-Bio Region 33.9 percent of the people fall within the category of poor, and 10.5 percent are indigent, thus maintaining its place as the second-poorest region in the country (only ahead of Region IX at 36.5 percent), registering more than ten points above national poverty levels and with a rate of indigence twice that of the national average. Such official data suggest that while there has been a constant reduction in poverty in the region, from 57 percent in 1987 to 33.9 percent in 1996, there has nonetheless been no movement in the region's position as one of the three poorest regions in the country, and this despite its decisive geographic participation in the GNP of about 10 percent in 1996, although this appears to be declining or stagnating. In spite of this reduction, however, the evolution of poverty in the region constitutes a generalized, massive, and persistent process such that, according to CASEN data, only three communities in 1992 — Contulmo, Florida, and Concepción — were below national poverty averages, and in 1994 there were only two such communities, Concepción and Laja. There is no CASEN information of this type for 1996.

The CASEN survey for 1992 shows poverty figures far beyond the already elevated regional average of 45.5 percent for the majority of the region's communities (thirty-two out of forty-nine). Of the forty-nine communities comprising the region, twenty-four have poverty levels above 50 percent, while some have even higher levels.

The 1994 CASEN survey reveals three basic facts: first, that of the region's forty-nine communities, thirty-eight fall above the regional poverty level of 40.3 percent; second, that seventeen communities continue to show poverty levels in excess of 50 percent; and, third, that even though the regional poverty rate declined from 45.5 to 40.3 percent, poverty actually *increased* in twenty-one communities. According to unofficial sources, the 1996 CASEN survey indicates that this persistent poverty in principally *rural* communities will continue.

The variations in community levels of poverty show that regional indexes of poverty cannot capture the microreality within such communities and that the community level of poverty often surpasses regional levels and reaches alarming proportions. The explanations of this reality are no doubt complex, and we will be referring to some of these below, but we mention at this point that it is not inconsequential to this situation that the limited investments and other resources destined for socioeconomic development are usually targeted at the larger communities, especially the region's leading towns, while the greater number of peripheral communities, particularly the rural and urban/mining communities, have seen a much smaller relative share of new resources such as infrastructure and investment, and, thus, have seen constant or deteriorating conditions of poverty. We can see in these facts the reproduction of the center-periphery relations so evident at the national and international level, which in the case of Region VIII are played out against the backdrop of, on the one hand, the low reinvestment rate of regional surplus and its concomitant poor rate of accumulation and growth and, on the other hand, the problems associated with regulation and the public orientation toward a process of development.

Region VIII Poverty: Origins and Causes

Poverty in Region VIII is, as we have indicated, heterogeneous and has a close connection with the structural heterogeneity of the region. This latter is the outcome of a lengthy social and economic history marked by the decline, succession, and substitution and/or superposition of diverse structures of production and patterns of accumulation. This has changed from the strictly primary resource extraction of the nineteenth century, based principally on mining and traditional agriculture, to industrial manufacture focused on an internal market at the beginning of the twentieth century, and finally a return to primary resource extraction that has emerged during the last few decades. All these structures of production, some in decline and others dynamic, continue to coexist in the same geographic area in various forms of articulation and disarticulation with the new and dominant regional development model. To each of these structures of production there corresponds a structure of social relations, especially regarding labor and income. It is these latter social dimensions that we feel are most closely connected to the poverty in the region.

We are obliged to mention yet again that the high rate of poverty in the region cannot be disassociated from particular features of the new development model that has come to dominate in the Bio-Bio, among which we can point to low rates of accumulation and growth that are themselves a result of a lack of endogenous capacities, extraregional investment, and the peripheral role the region plays in the national system of production. These features in turn point to deregulated and flexible labor markets and the application of neo-Taylorist methods within the labor force. This combination of causes derived from the new development model explains, so it seems to us, the region's lack of ability to articulate in a dynamic way a diversity of productive activities, to promote the opportune restructuring of necessary forms of production, and, generally speaking, to generate growth and dynamic equilibria within the regional economic system. Thus the so-called historically high rates of unemployment and increasing precariousness of work, which together are constitutive of the region's poverty and indigence, may be seen as really logical outcomes of the presence and functioning of the currently dominant development model.

In this context, the production and reproduction of these levels of poverty have their origin in three primary, convergent realities: first, in the structure and relations of production that antedated the current development model; second, in the restructuring, or destructuring, of production in the region during the 1980s; and, third, in the new dynamic resulting from the imposition of deregulated and flexible labor markets in the region, with the consequent high rates of unemployment and underemployment. Let us look briefly at each of these.

Relations of Production Antedating the Current Model. In the Bio-Bio Region, the newer forms of poverty are combined with more traditional forms. The latter have their origin in structures of primary resource production, in particular subsistence agriculture, farming, coal mining, and so on, which were fully formed in the nineteenth century and whose activities gave shape to the current administrative boundaries of the region's provinces of Ñuble, Arauco, Bio-Bio, and Concepción. Such traditional poverty arising from agromining also arose within the context of the substitution model that was dominant for the better part of the twentieth century.

One of the main characteristics of this agromining dynamic was the employment of abundant, unskilled labor for meager wages. Given the focus of this production on primary resources, work conditions and the overall reproduction of the labor force were both precarious. This sort of work was perfectly compatible, for example, with the fact that until the 1940s education and public hygiene were inaccessible for the majority of the people. Thus, the accumulation based upon the structure of production arising from primary resource exportation functioned with (1) low technological inputs from capital, (2) generally low levels of productivity, (3) extreme levels of unemployment, (4) extensive use of unskilled labor, and

(5) extremely low wages or even only a "semiwage." The population most closely connected to these types of productive activities — particularly, coal miners, tenant farmers, and sharecroppers — existed in conditions of extreme poverty. That poverty must be understood to be a part of what made accumulation in the region, and even the country, possible.

It is in these socioeconomic sectors that we find the formation of the first "armies" of poor and indigent people in Region VIII. Such "traditional" poverty, which is in large measure a form of structurally induced poverty, and which can be seen today in the communities of San Ignacio, Trehuaco, Portezuelo, Quillón, Contulmo, Tirúa, Ñiquén, Lota, and Curanilahue, has a long historical connection with agromining activities. As long as such a structure of production is in place and remains stable, such poverty will be considered "normal." However, when the structure of production becomes unstable, as it has become over the past few decades, then the reproduction of poverty becomes unstable and the situation critical as attention is focused elsewhere in the labor market, for example, toward industry. It is no coincidence that the highest levels of poverty, unemployment, and indigence are to be found in precisely those areas whose productive activities are centered on agromining.

The agromining sector has, in fact, been in decline since the 1930s, as its activities were overtaken by the industrial substitution structure of production. Thus, a new form of poverty emerged that was integrally related to the more "traditional" form, arising out of the new process of industrialization and merging with it. One of the most important features of this process was the migration of peasants to the new urban centers — principally Talcahuano, Concepción, Penco, Tomé, and Los Angeles — in pursuit of work. These migrants had no training and usually found no stable employment in the new sectors of production; they thus became a population of semiemployed or permanently unemployed persons residing in the outlying areas of the new urban centers. An important component of this situation was the occasional, underemployed worker who often worked fourteen-hour days for miserable wages in low-productivity industrial activities. These workers made up the vast world of the marginal and the poor of the 1960s and were highly visible in areas surrounding the communities of Concepción, Talcahuano, Penco, and Tomé.

At the root of these new forms of poverty are the dynamics of substitution production and the type of accumulation associated with it. We are speaking here of a predominantly urban poverty that was a product of the disequilibria, contradictions, and structural distortions of the development model of this epoch, a model that was already entering crisis conditions at the beginning of the 1960s.

Even though there is little quantitative data concerning these earlier forms of heterogeneous poverty in the Bio-Bio Region, there is little reason to suspect that it would be any lower than poverty levels in the rest of the country, and these latter figures stood at 17 percent of all households in 1969 and at 28.5 percent of the population in 1970.

The Restructuring of Production and New Forms of Poverty. As Chile's economy was opened up to international markets and foreign trade, the crisis affecting the primary-resource sectors (agromining) of the region was intensified, as were the problems associated with industrial-import substitution activities. The ensuing process of "destructuring" and withdrawal of protection consequent upon this opening caused a fall in production with a concomitant fall in employment. As the crisis in traditional forms of agriculture became more aggravated, the flow of migrants to more economically dynamic areas became accelerated, augmenting in these locales the already large population of "floating," underemployed persons. The critical point in this process emerged between 1981 and 1983 when the country entered a severe depression occasioned by the serious distortions produced by the application of monetarist policies and deregulation during the preceding period. The enormous levels of unemployment this crisis produced in the region, sometimes exceeding 30 percent, had effects still evident today in various communities.

To these processes of disorganized production we must add others concerned with restructuring and rationalization. In order to recover the lost competitiveness in the traditional and manufacturing sectors, labor inputs were considerably reduced and certain dimensions of production were modernized by the introduction of technologies. At the same time, and with a view to the general improvement of productivity, entrepreneurs made an effort to intensify and broaden the application of Taylorist and flexibility models to the labor force. All this had the classic effect of contributing to an increase in the population of unemployed and underemployed and to the severe compression of real wages.

Alongside this train of events there emerged new foci of production (principally forestry and fishing) and a dynamic tertiary sector (retailing and financial services) associated with these. Not only do theses activities require less labor inputs, but such labor as is required is precarious in nature, usually subcontracted and temporary, and offers poor wages.

Gathered under the rubric of the destructuring and restructuring of production, such explanations serve in large measure to further our understanding of poverty in the communities mentioned above, all of which have been shaken to a greater or lesser extent by crises, transformations, and the restructuring of forms of production. As we have pointed out repeatedly, the indexes of poverty and indigence in the majority of these communities are directly associated with, and are exacerbated by, the logic and requirements of the new development model as this operates over populations already experiencing more "traditional" forms of poverty.

High Unemployment, Labor Flexibility, and "Poverty Employment." High unemployment has been a reality in the Bio-Bio Region for the past twenty years. For the ten consecutive years between 1976 and 1985, the average annual real unemployment rate was more than 20 percent of the labor force. In particularly critical years, unemployment went beyond 25 percent and even reached 30 percent (Antinao 1997). In the second half of the 1980s and the entire 1990s, the unemployment situation improved significantly, with rates lowering to almost national averages: in 1990, the rate had declined to 5.3 percent, and at the end of 1992 it stood at 5.5 percent.

However, beginning with 1993 the rate began to climb once again, moving upward to 7 and even 8 percent in 1993–95 and settling at 7.4 percent in 1996, one point higher than the national average. We have to recall that we are speaking of regional averages here, and that there are many communities, especially the poorest ones, that exceeded these averages. For example, in 1992, when national growth stood at 11 percent and national unemployment at 4.4 percent, there were eighteen communities in Region VIII with unemployment rates above 7 percent and twelve that exceeded 10 percent, among which could be found San Rosendo with 20.5 percent and Lota with 23.1 percent.

Along with such chronic rates of unemployment, we see the rise after the 1980s of that type of employment we have described as "precarious," that is to say, employment created under policy regimes of deregulation and labor flexibility. These latter policies are coincident with what might be called "poverty employment" within practically all the communities in the region, that is, employment principally temporary in nature, with low levels of remuneration, and with practically no protection, the greater part of which maintains those so employed at or below the poverty level. According to 1992 data, workers in this category — the "employed poor" — constituted 45.5 percent of the national labor force (Agacino 1995); we would suggest that the percentage for the Bio-Bio Region was even higher since "poverty employment" is typical of the two new poles of economic dynamism in Region VIII, forestry and fishing, in which subcontracting and temporary work are the norms. Although this type of employment also has become notorious in agriculture, manufacturing, and construction, it is in the communities in which forestry activities have become dominant, such as San Rosendo and Portezuelo, that the highest levels of poverty may be found, levels that are directly connected with precarious employment or classical unemployment.

Poverty: A Heterogeneous Phenomenon

Above all else, poverty in the Bio-Bio Region is extremely heterogeneous, that is to say, a product of quite diverse socioeconomic and cultural processes. Consequently, it cannot be understood simply as a static economic or monetary problem of material privation or underconsumption, but rather must be understood as principally a process of cumulative handicaps, a progressive rupture and degradation of a combination of linkages, textures, and social relations in the midst of which specific social sectors find themselves inserted. Poverty must be understood, then, as a dynamic, multidimensional process at once economic, social, and cultural. Thus it is that we find in the same community traditional forms of poverty side by side with those of more recent origin that issue from the newer sort of precarious employment, and each of these will conform to a different logic.

Although they obey different logics, we find that these are linked together in a trajectory along which converge simultaneously deprivations that are mainly economic (chronic un- and under-employment, insufficient incomes), social (educational deprivation, poor health, poor housing, delinquency, uprooted family life), and cultural (loss of identity, a crisis in values) (Gazier 1996; Paugam 1996). This multidimensional poverty affects those social groups who are most vulnerable and induces in them a weakening of so-cial bonds and the disorganization of social relations on the micro and macro level. This sort of social rupture has, alas, been little stud-ied, although it has, without doubt, serious consequences for those involved, especially the young. Much of the recent anomie, depoliti-cization, discrediting of politics and parties, gratuitous and irrational violence, and so on, may be attributed to a serious deterioration in social bonds caused by the continuation of high levels of poverty.

The Official Strategy: Problems and Perspectives

The insufficiencies of the current strategies used to combat poverty on the national level and in the Bio-Bio Region are a product of an er-roneous understanding of the social effects of the currently dominant growth model, a product of faults in targeting, and a consequence of weak support for initiatives in endogenous development. As the data from the 1994 CASEN survey showed, the region is stuck or even losing ground in the struggle against poverty, and this in turn points to the impotence of official policies.

This insufficiency is derived from various important weaknesses of official policy, especially at the regional level. As is well known, this policy has been a synthesis of two principal objectives: first, an attempt to secure sustained economic growth through the creation of productive employment and fiscal equilibrium; and, second, the implementation of universal and specifically targeted social policies. These objectives are thought to enable the poor to integrate them-selves into the labor market and the general development process. However, as we have said, this policy is weak in certain important respects, and we will mention briefly three aspects of this weakness.

First, there is a problem with the correlation between economic growth, on the one hand, and employment and incomes, on the other. Even though it can be shown that for the particular period 1987–92 economic expansion had a positive impact on employment and incomes, and thus had a direct bearing on the reduction of poverty, the situation gets worse from then on. That is, after this period relatively similar rates of growth have a decreasing effect on the absorption or reduction of poverty levels, a fact that suggests that because the growth model operates on the basis of a deregulated and flexible labor market and thus causes precarious conditions of employment, the model itself has now become a factor in the reproduction of poverty. Put another way, current strategies for poverty reduction stumble over the new characteristics of the labor market, characteristics that are themselves requirements of the New Economic Model. In addition, this model produces a pattern of strikingly unequal, regressive, and concentrated income distribution, something that not only perpetuates social inequalities but also conspires against the reduction of levels of poverty and social exclusion. This is as much as to say that an effective strategy for combating poverty would entail substantial modifications to current policies on employment, wages, income distribution, and labor legislation. Such changes, to speak frankly, would be tantamount to abandoning the currently reigning model for one that is socially and environmentally more sustainable.

Second, there is a generally segmented, unbalanced, and uncoordinated character to the targeting of programs. This is as much as to ignore the essentially multidimensional and heterogeneous character of poverty as this touches upon its social, economic, and cultural dimensions; this heterogeneity calls, on the contrary, for policies that are integrated and balanced. A notorious example of this unbalanced approach, with reference to the targeted area of production (such as coalfields), is the manifestly insufficient support of the government for zones of "extreme urgency," in the vain hope that investment initiatives from the private sector will appear. In this case, the neoliberal dogma of government "noninterference" in production not only aggravates a serious social situation but also contributes to the continuation of poverty. In fact, it is the zones that have been abandoned the most by the public sector — the rural zones — that are precisely the ones showing the highest levels of persistent poverty. In addition, as Dagmar Raczynski has pointed out (Raczynski 1995), there exists a juxtaposition of initiatives that will come to nothing in the absence of additional initiatives, as, for example, in the case of the lack of articulation between the so-called Plan for All (see the chapter above on Bolivia) and the FOSIS programs, and between these latter two and municipal programs.

Third, and what is probably most decisive, current strategies provide very weak support for what should be the most important element in the struggle against poverty, namely, a strengthening of the dynamics and processes conducive to endogenous, local development, based upon the strengthening of social organization, the articulation of the various agents for development (municipalities, companies, universities, unions, and so on), and the strengthening of the technical and organizational capacities of the municipalities. A true policy of decentralization should at least point in this direction in order to become an effective strategy for regional development.

The Question of Local Development

The assignment of the role of "agents of development" exclusively to the municipalities has its origins in the administrative reform introduced by the military regime in 1974 through Decree Law Number 573, which sought to decentralize the state. This decree divided the country into politico-administrative regions, and these regions into provinces, and the provinces into communities (*comunas*). According to the decree, municipalities were part of this decentralization, not only territorially but also functionally, and they were given executive powers, responsibilities for the delivery of services, and other enlargements of their mandate. These initiatives were given final form in Decree Law Number 1289 of 1976, which designated the municipalities specifically as territorial entities that were functionally decentralized and whose objectives were the satisfaction of local necessities and the promotion of the development of the community.

This process of decentralization and "municipalization" of the state brought about by the military regime was studied, examined, and criticized a number of years ago (Rodríguez and Velásquez 1994). It was pointed out, for example, that even though the municipalities had their powers enlarged, these powers were concentrated in the hands of a single authority, the mayor, who held his or her position not by popular will but by appointment from the nation's top authority. Also criticized was the lack of resources, or the inequitable distribution of resources, such that most municipalities were left with limited capacities regarding investment, the fostering of production, and technical and organizational training. Criticism also fell on the strong dependency created between the municipality and the central governing apparatus regarding the orientation of development policies. The experience of the great majority of the communities of the Bio-Bio Region shows these criticisms to be completely valid.

If the above-mentioned reform did indeed open up new spaces for local initiatives, it did so with no pretensions to fostering democratic local development, nor did it seek to foster any sort of endogenous local development. Democracy was only introduced in 1996 with the popular election of mayors in the various communities. In many respects, then, the work has just begun regarding (1) community organization and participation in a "civil society" that still lies atomized and without structure, and (2) the creation of a real sense of citizenship through the development of viable instruments for social communication and information. Such conditions of local democracy form an important prerequisite for solid local development (Sachs 1981).

Beside the question of democracy, a form of local development that was largely endogenous was far from the expectations and calculations of the creators of this package of administrative reforms. In effect, the reform implied no transfer of real power from the central state apparatus to the municipality, nor did it seek to provide adequate and equitable financial and/or technical resources for the development of production, and least of all did it provide support for the configuration of elements necessary for fostering systems of local production (Garofoli 1992). Under these conditions, the great majority of communities and municipalities were impotent when confronted with the problems of poverty. Only a few can show real indexes of local development, and such communities are precisely those that for geopolitical and social reasons — for example, being a provincial capital or a regional center — have a greater relative control over significant amounts of the social surplus.

Public policies of devolution that really seek to be efficient should stimulate these communities, especially the poor, to take in hand the promotion and articulation of all possible instruments and initiatives conducive to a local and sustainable endogenous development by channeling through the municipalities the tools, training, and resources that would further this aim. If we compare the experiences of the communities of the Bio-Bio Region with what has happened internationally regarding local and regional development, a number of basic lessons and hypotheses come to the fore, and we would like to provide at least an outline of these.

First, in the current context in which large transnationals and the general process of globalization play the central roles, the possibility of effective local and regional development has come to depend more and more on existing social, political, and cultural conditions. With specific reference to the process of decentralization, such development will depend on the formation and consolidation of social and political blocs at the local and regional level. These groups would, through democratic local elections, empower local and regional authorities to have some real negotiating capacity vis-à-vis the central government. This in turn depends on the ability of local authorities to capture or control an important part of the locally produced surplus and use this surplus on public expenditures and investment.

Second, given the foregoing, local and regional powers should foster increasing rates of economic growth through direct investment, be this public (in the initial stages) or private (through SMSBs). Such directing of public investment in the initial stages is absolutely indispensable for the creation of infrastructure and basic services (health, education, transport, and so on) as well as improvements in production. This investment is particularly necessary during a period of restructuring or reconversion of productive processes.

Third, local and/or regional authorities committed to development will give priority to the formation of a large and dynamic network of SMSBs that are firmly rooted in the local area. The participation of large corporations must be made conditional upon (1) an assurance of an acceptable rate of reinvestment of locally generated surplus, and (2) an acceptance of established social and environmental norms as these have been set out locally or nationally.

Fourth, real local or regional development implies a rejection or at least a significant diminution of the functionally peripheral role of the locality or region, which in turn implies that production processes must become locally centered or "endogenized." This is only possible with a reinvestment of local surpluses, as we suggested above, together with the creation of forward linkages, the diversification of production, increases in value-added production, growth of the SMSBs, the involvement of large corporations in long-term projects, the training of a skilled workforce, and, finally, the fostering of a dynamic relationship between the private sector and regional technical universities that would promote technological innovation and the creation, or retraining, of technical personnel.

SIX

NGOs and the Discourse of Participatory Development in Costa Rica

Laura Macdonald

In both the North and the South, skepticism about the capacity and willingness of state agencies and international organizations to address people's needs has become widespread across the political spectrum. Emphasis on the role of civil society, new social movements, participation, and participatory action research among students and practitioners of development reflects this antistatist perspective. However, insufficient critical attention has been paid to the equally problematic character of many "nonstate actors." Many have pointed to international nongovernmental organizations (NGOs) as practitioners of another type of development work in which grassroots participation flourishes, so that the poor are able to define what they receive and how NGOs are thus presented, and present themselves, as an alternative model to the hegemonic ideology and methodology of the official "aid regime."[1] Judith Tendler refers to this belief of NGOs in their own superior participatory qualities as one of their "articles of faith" (Tendler 1982).[2]

Because of their small-scale, grassroots, "people-to-people" character, then, NGO projects are frequently viewed as highly participatory phenomena, almost by definition. For example, Robin Poulton (1988, 4) outlines a simple equation, which purports to represent the "NGO model of the eighties": basic needs + participatory development = community development.

Poulton also offers a typical description of the merits of the NGO model as opposed to development strategies adopted by state actors:

> Against "top-down" urban-designed projects, NGOs are using participatory "bottom-up" methods which pass decision-making progressively to the people. Against the centralized models of bureaucracy, NGOs decentralize responsibility to local groups and community associations. Against a short-term project approach, the NGO methodology is evolutionary and long-term. Building self-reliant village organizations is a long, slow process: but they are and will be organizations of the people, which can work for developing people. (Poulton 1988, 32)

There is some merit to this argument. Most NGO projects *do* involve some form of citizen participation; official agencies have been prompted to include more forms of participation in their development work because of the NGO example; and some NGOs are indeed very committed to giving Third World peoples control over their own process of development. However, to characterize NGO assistance as an inherently more participatory alternative to other forms of aid overlooks the fact that most NGOs are dependent on state funding, are heavily influenced by (as well as influencing) official development bodies, and developed historically as a useful complement to official development assistance. NGO agents thus have more autonomy than most agents of bilateral or multilateral programs, but this autonomy is limited. The rosy picture of NGOs also ignores the fact that participation is a contested concept that has many different meanings and possible outcomes. In order to explore these issues, this chapter will discuss the various approaches to participation adopted in three NGO projects in Costa Rica in the late 1980s. These cases illustrate the problematic nature of participation and suggest some of the factors that need to be taken into account when attempting to implement it. I argue that the degree and form of participation promoted by NGOs will vary depending on the following factors: (1) the NGO approach to participation; (2) the influence of international actors (either state donors or international NGOs); and (3) the nature of linkages between the NGO and local groups or social movements. While these different elements may in practice be combined in diverse ways, two main ideal types of NGOs can be identified in the context of Central America:

1. "Mainstream NGOs," often associated in Central America with the United States Agency for International Development (USAID). These are characterized by

   - *institutional participation,* in which beneficiaries' participation is valued primarily for its contribution to the efficient implementation of a project; participants do not have real control over the design or evaluation of a project. In the current period, this has often gone hand-in-hand with programs complementary to Structural Adjustment Programs;

   - *foreign agency paternalism,* in which international NGOs and/or state donors control most important decisions and act to co-opt local leadership. The type of project implemented often conforms to the interests of the donor rather than the perceived needs of the recipients;

   - *limited local linkages,* in which local contacts are largely limited to state agencies and alliances with autonomous social movements are absent.

2. "Progressive NGOs" are characterized by

   - *an explicitly political strategy of empowerment,* involving not only greater control by community members at the local level but also their involvement in broader social movements seeking increased political participation by excluded groups in national decision-making processes;

   - *relative autonomy of the local NGO,* in which the international NGO respects the superior capacity of Third World partners to respond to local demands as well as the need to build a strong civil society over the long run;

   - *links with social movements* that are seen as a necessary element in building counterhegemonic movements in order to challenge the existing distribution of power and resources.

The progressive NGOs must compete with the mainstream NGOs both for external financing and for influence over the political allegiances and economic choices of the popular classes. However, the conflict between the two ideal types is not as clear-cut as a black-and-white portrayal might suggest. NGOs are complex and multifaceted organizations, full of contradictions that emerge from the interaction between, on the one hand, the (often-confused) ideology and methodology of the NGO and its donor(s) and, on the other hand, the reality that they confront in the field. In order to avoid over-simplification, I have therefore included an analysis of what I call a "contradictory" NGO, funded by USAID but displaying some autonomy from the donor and some elements of "progressive" practice. The case studies also illustrate that even the most progressive NGOs have, in many instances, failed to address the specific problem of women's participation.

The case studies were undertaken in Costa Rica, a country with a long and enviable record of democratic development and social welfare, although the existing economic and political model is currently under attack. The limitations encountered in the case studies point, therefore, to the serious problems encountered by NGOs attempting to promote participation even in the apparently most benevolent situations.

NGOs and Participation

Given the reservations expressed by many liberal democratic theories about the viability of systems based on widespread political participation,[3] and the shortage of genuinely participatory institutions in Western societies (apart from the vote), it is somewhat surprising that participation is now almost universally hailed as a key element in a successful development strategy. For example, Moeen Qureshi, a senior vice-president of the World Bank, stated in 1991:

> The World Bank has learned from its experience of development that popular participation is important to the success of projects economically, environmentally and socially. Our most important lesson has been that participation and empowerment involve questions of efficiency, as well as being desirable in their own right. (Quoted in Denham 1992, 5)

Underlying this apparent unanimity, however, are some unstated differences about what participation actually means and how it is to be achieved.

Most serious analyses of the concept have pointed out that there are many types of practices that are labeled participatory, many of which are in fact manipulative or merely illusive.[4] It must be recognized that any authentic approach to participation must respect the traditions and desires of the "target population" and must involve the substantial transfer of power to that population. Since any form of assistance involves complex power relations between donor and recipient, implementing authentic participation has been an illusive goal for NGOs. Some skeptical voices have emerged about the motives behind the apparent embrace of the concept of participation by Western actors. According to Rajni Kothari, "The more the economics of development and the politics of development are kept out of reach of the masses, the more they [the masses] are asked to 'participate' in them" (Kothari 1984, 541). Kothari has a similarly skeptical view of NGOs. He claims that world capitalism and international organizations such as the World Bank and UNDP are discovering in NGOs "a most effective instrument for promoting their interest in penetrating Third World economies and particularly their rural interiors which neither private industries nor government bureaucracies were capable of doing" (Kothari 1986, 2178).[5] In fact, Qureshi, from the World Bank, has stated that one of the difficult goals that the World Bank–NGO collaboration can help achieve is the implementation of "sensitive and successful adjustment programs" (see International Bank for Reconstruction and Development 1989, 5).

Observers of NGOs have discerned the gradual evolution of international nongovernmental assistance to the Third World through various stages, which can be associated with different approaches to the issue of participation.[6] Northern NGOs first emerged as the result of humanistic attempts to mitigate the effects of both poverty and warfare. Their precursors were the Christian missionary societies that offered food, medicine, and other services as well as religious inculcation to "heathens" in far-flung lands. These missions played an important role in the official legitimization of colonialism. Some would argue that the NGOs, their modern-day equivalents, perform a more sophisticated version of the same function.[7] Many important NGOs retain a religious identification, and although most of the major churches have rejected the heavy-handed religious inculcation of the past, fundamentalist Christian sects continue to adopt this approach.

Like the official "aid regime," many NGOs trace their direct origins to the North American response to the needs of postwar Europe. Some of the largest agencies — OXFAM, CARE, Catholic Relief Services, Church World Service, and Lutheran World Relief — were formed to provide relief and assist the reconstruction of Europe. Subsequently, they devoted their attentions to emergency situations in other parts of the world, including the partition of India, the flight of Arab refugees from Palestine in 1948, the Korean War, and starvation in Bihar in 1951 (OECD 1988, 18–19).

In the beginning, then, NGOs (like official development agencies) defined their role as limited to providing material relief to address short-term needs. However, also like the aid provided by official development agencies, early NGO assistance was not politically neutral. NGO development in Latin America had its roots in the Catholic Church's fear of social unrest and the Communist threat, as well as spreading Protestantism.[8] Gradually, European and North American NGOs tied to the church began channeling funds to both Catholic and Protestant groups in Latin America (FAO-FFHC 1987, 100–105). The church, the most powerful organization in Latin American civil society, thus played a crucial role in the formation of NGOs and their linkages with international NGOs.

The emergent Latin American organizations, like their foreign counterparts, focused on relief and service activities designed to contribute to political stability as well as alleviate poverty. Because dominant approaches to development theory in both the North and the South emphasized industrialization, capital formation, and construction of infrastructure as the keys to overcoming underdevelopment, participation by the poor was not viewed as necessary or even desirable. As in the modernization approach, indigenous values were seen as dysfunctional; the goal of missionaries was therefore to spread Western values rather than to encourage local participation.

NGO assistance was thus initially provided as charity, and recipients were treated as objects rather than subjects of the process. This charity and relief approach has certainly not disappeared. Food-for-work schemes, for example, are a common form of coerced participation implemented by NGOs. By the 1960s, however, the inability of charity to overcome underdevelopment gave rise to new strategies, which began to explicitly address the need for the poor to participate in development programs. This shift was related to the gradual consolidation of a basic-needs approach within the official aid agencies. A volume prepared for the International Labor Office (ILO) makes this connection between participation and basic needs:

> It can be argued that broad-based participation, in particular — but not exclusively — at the local level, has an important role to play in the successful implementation of a basic-needs strategy. The validity of this argument hinges mainly on the potential of popular participation to contribute both to the generation and articulation of effective demand for mass consumption goods and essential services on a sustainable basis and to the operation of an efficient system of supply-management; i.e., the production and delivery of basic-needs goods and services. (Lisk 1985, 82)[9]

This version of participation has a strongly instrumentalist and technocratic character — that is, participation is desirable in order to create effective demand and efficient implementation of the international organization's basic-needs strategy, not to increase popular power.

There was, however, substantial resistance to the implementation of a basic-needs approach on the part of both international organizations like the World Bank and Third World states. As a result, the buck was passed to NGOs to become the main agents of this form of participatory grassroots development. While there was thus some change in the rhetoric of bilateral and multilateral aid agencies, there was little change in their actual practice. Latin American theorists referred to the models adopted in the 1960s and 1970s as "developmentalism." In the developmentalist approach, the state, private industry, and international donor agencies play the leading role in national development, but NGOs can play a complementary, though subordinate, role at the local level in overcoming local inertia.

As a result of this assigning of an important, but marginal, role to local participation, most state development agencies from the North established formal mechanisms for cooperation with NGOs during the 1960s and 1970s. Government funding of NGOs considerably increased their resources and scope. However, as we will see below, the acceptance of government funding often places real limitations upon the action of NGOs, although the constraints may be either subtle or blatant, depending on the government involved (Lissner 1977). The main form of operation is development "projects" that support self-reliance at the local level and promote the incorporation of "marginal" populations into the national economy. Participation by the target group is seen as a cheaper and more efficient way of ensuring project success (defined in technical and economic terms) and thus requires greater organization of the beneficiary community.

The emergence of a Women in Development (WID) approach within development studies in the 1970s led to awareness that attempts to increase community participation often exclude women. During the United Nations Decade for Women (1976–85), many NGOs (as well as state donors) put greater emphasis on the effects of development programs on women, recognizing that previous approaches often had unintentional detrimental effects on women. Gender-blind approaches tend to ignore the factors (such as domestic responsibilities, lack of self-confidence, domination of organizations by men, and male control over women in the family) that limit women's participation. However, according to Sally Yudelman, NGO projects specifically targeted to benefit women have not attempted to increase women's access to education and training, credit and land, nor challenged women and men's domestic roles:

> The developmentalist approach is still dominant among Northern NGOs. However, the hegemony of developmentalism was gradually undermined by attacks from divergent forces during the late 1960s and the 1970s. On the one hand, in the North, some international NGOs, still frustrated by their inability to attack the root causes of poverty and underdevelopment, began to recognize that community development projects could only benefit a few favored communities, and that the success of local development efforts was frequently undermined by broader national and international forces. At the same time, dependency theory gained popularity — among some Latin American and Northern NGOs. Dependistas rejected modernization theory's dualist conception of Latin American societies and claimed that "backwardness" was the result of the systematic exploitation of the periphery by the core since colonial times. Some Northern agencies began to include development education and lobbying among their activities in order to influence the policies of the North which had a negative effect upon the South.

Further, changes occurring in the Catholic Church, inspired by Vatican II and the Medellín meeting of the Latin American Bishops' Conference, and the coming to power of military juntas in many countries of the Southern Cone led to new approaches to participation. Significant sectors of the Latin American church attempted to transform the church in order to push for social reforms. The so-called popular church, often in opposition to the conservative church hierarchy, began to organize the poor in Christian base communities (*comunidades eclesiales de base*). By encouraging the poor to critically reflect on the nature and causes of their oppression, these church reformers hoped to stimulate organized political action. According to Chilean NGO leader Rodrigo Engaña, the result was the establishment of new "paradigms" among Latin American NGOs, signified by ideas like "conscientization," "popular education," and "support to organizational processes": "In this conception were combined Freireian ideas about cultural action, Marxist ideas about society and the state, and the visions of the dependistas about the relations between developed and underdeveloped countries" (cited in Landim 1988, 9).

While these new approaches to NGO activity were an important step away from instrumental conceptions of participation toward wrestling with the critical issue of empowerment of the poor, they were not without potential pitfalls. As Majid Rahnema points out, Paolo Freire underlines the inability of the oppressed to understand their situation, but he does not recognize that the perceptions of the conscientizers are also distorted:

> The assumption that there are such important differences in the levels of consciousness of the participants creates an almost unsolvable problem for the author's proposed dialogical action. The exercise is intended to be a learning experience for all. However, it implies that the participants are not really equal and, therefore, the persons with "primitive" or "semi-transitive" consciousness have to learn from the few with a "critically transitive consciousness" before being able to make any meaningful contribution to the debate. (Rahnema 1990, 207–8)

Despite the best intentions and the most participatory techniques, these new-style NGO efforts may thus retain substantial elements of paternalism. Consciousness-raising techniques may also become ends in themselves, without leading to effective strategies for change.

NGOs and Participation in Costa Rica

The NGOs examined in Costa Rica confronted all of these dilemmas of participation and development. Unlike most Third World countries, the democratic context in Costa Rica means that individuals are free to participate in politics without excessive fear of repression. However, the legacy of a paternalistic, interventionist state has meant, paradoxically, that participation has occurred in forms that are directed from above, rather than in organizations that spring from the grass roots. Individuals are therefore accustomed to voting in free and fair elections and often participate in cooperatives or community associations formed by the state. This type of organization tends to foster personalistic and clientelistic forms of relationships.

Because of the role of the "benefactor state" in Costa Rica and the climate of relative social equality and respect for human rights, NGOs developed less rapidly in Costa Rica than in other Latin American countries where repression was a spur to this type of organization. During the 1970s, then, as many Latin American NGOs became aligned to the cause of social transformation, Costa Rican NGOs remained focused on the provision of charity and relief to fill in the gaps of state action. The reluctance of the Costa Rican Catholic Church in the postwar era to promote a social action philosophy undoubtedly contributed to this charity orientation.

Economic Crisis, Adjustment, and NGO Response in the 1980s

In general, the NGOs that existed prior to the debt crisis of the 1980s were charity-oriented, paternalistic, and apolitical. The effects of the crisis led to a dramatic increase in the number of NGOs, their access to foreign funding, and a radical reorientation in their operations. The US government's response to the Costa Rican crisis was not limited to stabilization funds and economic adjustment at the macroeconomic level. The Reagan administration's concern with Central America led to an influx of funds to Costa Rican NGOs and also instilled a new approach to the role of NGOs in civil society. The precipitous decline of living standards among the poor led to a concern for the stability of the Costa Rican liberal institutions. The director of USAID in Costa Rica believed that the unemployment and other social problems that would result from structural adjustment meant that a "shock absorber" was necessary to prevent violent social unrest. NGOs were explicitly promoted as a private-sector alternative to state paternalism.

In 1987, USAID created a separate organization called ACORDE (Asociación Costaricense de Organismos de Desarrollo) to take charge of USAID funding to the NGO sector. The board of directors was initially chosen entirely from the private sector by USAID. The criteria of eligibility for funding were also established by USAID. Control over US funds was given not to ACORDE but to PACT (Private Agencies Collaborating Together), a consortium of twenty-one US NGOs that is almost entirely funded by the USAID. PACT administered the grants in US dollars to US agencies operating in Costa Rica and appointed a technical adviser to ACORDE. Through support of NGOs in Costa Rica, the United States hoped to ease social tensions, diminish the reliance of lower-class groups on the state, and promote market-oriented production systems.

NGOs were seen as a means not only to supplement incomes for the poorest groups but also to promote the new entrepreneurial attitudes among the poor. ACORDE's eligibility criteria state that priority will be given to projects that contribute to socioeconomic development through "generation of employment, and the increase of productivity and the level of income of the beneficiaries." While projects may contain other (social or cultural) components, the productive aspect is paramount. ACORDE's approach thus clearly supports the economic strategy of structural adjustment promoted by USAID and other international donors, encouraging greater emphasis on short-term, market-oriented development and a greater role for the private sector as opposed to state-led development schemes.

In addition to the multiplication of Costa Rican agencies compatible with USAID objectives, the 1980s also saw the emergence of another form of local NGO associated with new Costa Rican social movements that appeared in the 1980s. The effects of the economic crisis on the popular sectors and the decay of the traditional organizations of the left led to the rise of new NGOs that sought to ally themselves with, and to spur the development of, independent popular organizations. Led by Costa Rican intellectuals, often linked to the universities or churches, or formerly to state agencies, these "organic NGOs" or "centers" were funded primarily by

European NGOs. These progressive NGOs engaged in a wide variety of activities, including popular education and conscientization, communications, research, organizational support to the popular sector, and promotion of appropriate technology, as well as productive projects. As elsewhere in Latin America, these progressive NGOs wished to distance themselves from the vanguardism of the traditional left.

How can the activities of the progressive and mainstream NGOs be distinguished in practice? A statement signed by members of the Concertación Centroamericana de Organismos de Desarrollo (CCOD), a grouping of like-minded Central American NGOs, states:

> What is the fundamental difference that distinguishes an NGO with a popular orientation from an NGO linked to the neoconservative strategy? Both implement small projects; they both link themselves with the most vulnerable social groups. Both even display participatory pedagogical techniques and approaches to promotion that seek to consolidate a capacity for economic self-management. In reality, what distinguishes a neoconservative wave of NGOs from an NGO movement committed to promoting the leadership of popular groups lies in how they view the problem of power. In the first case, the activity of the NGO is oriented at provoking changes in order to avoid modifications in the structure of power. In the second case, the NGOs try to promote changes in order to achieve transformations in the relation of social forces in a manner which favors the majority. (CCOD 1988, 24–25)

According to the CCOD, then, "participation" alone is not enough. Popular participation at the grassroots level must be linked with participation in social movements attempting to change the balance of power in the country. The question, however, is how this general orientation can be translated into action at the local level that genuinely empowers the beneficiaries, given the structural constraints with which all NGOs must contend.

Costa Rican Case Studies

During fieldwork in Costa Rica in 1988 and 1989, three NGO development projects were examined. Two of them are directed by US-based NGOs and funded by USAID, one (OEF International) directly from Washington, D.C., and the other (Catholic Relief Services) through an institution established by USAID to channel funds to NGOs in Costa Rica. The third project is directed by a Costa Rican NGO (CECADE — Centro de Capacitación y Desarrollo) that is part of the alliance of progressive NGOs (or "centers") and is funded by a West German NGO. All three of the projects work with peasants; the majority of the peasants live in remote, underdeveloped areas of the country and have received land under the agrarian reform process. The agencies examined all claimed to contribute to popular participation and democratization at the grassroots level. However, the conception of meaningful participation varied between the agencies, as did the strategies used to promote it.

CRS is the second largest US development agency, with many years of experience throughout the world. It is the foreign relief and development agency of the US Conference of Catholic Bishops, but it receives the majority of its funding from USAID. Like other established mainstream NGOs, CRS has evolved away from its initial charity and relief emphasis toward a more developmentalist approach. In addition to its secular development activities, CRS also provides institutional support to the Catholic Church in Latin America. Because of the disinterest of the Costa Rican hierarchy in social issues, however, CRS actions in Costa Rica are perhaps more heavily shaped by the philosophy and procedures of the head office and US staff than in other countries where the local church is stronger.

In 1989, CRS's work in Costa Rica was focused on rural and urban income generation. The rural projects were located in the three poorest areas of the country (the Nicoya Peninsula and the Atlantic and the southern regions). CRS established a new rural program in 1986 with a convention signed by CRS, ACORDE, and PACT (each agency provided part of the financing, ACORDE in colones and PACT in dollars, and CRS played the main operational role). The primary goal of the program was to provide organizational, technical, and financial support to small producers, primarily in the area of nontraditional agricultural products. The program was thus consistent with the Agricultura de Cambio program initiated by the Costa Rican government as part of its structural adjustment measures. This program was designed to encourage farmers to switch away from the production of basic grains and traditional

TABLE 6.1
"MAINSTREAM" NGO: CATHOLIC RELIEF SERVICES (CRS)

NGO analyzed	Catholic Relief Services
Type	"Mainstream"
Project studied	Support for cacao production by cooperative in Osa Peninsula
Main funder	USAID (through CRS, ACORDE, AND PACT)
Participation strategy	Instrumental participation of co-op members; no participation by women
Development strategy	Promotion of nontraditional exports
Role of international agency	Paternalistic
Link with local groups	COOPEALIANZA, a credit and service cooperative, is the implementing agency; cooperation with IDA, the state agrarian reform agency

exports toward nontraditional exports such as fruits, spices, and ornamental plants.

The project examined was based in the town of Uvita, on the coast of the OAS Peninsula, in the southern region of Costa Rica. The project was initially designed to provide financing, training, and technical assistance to local peasants for the production, processing, and marketing of cacao, one of the nontraditional crops being promoted by the government (see Table 6.1). Unfortunately, world cocoa prices had declined dramatically since the project was conceived, with very negative implications for the economic viability of the crop.

When the project began, the beneficiaries were organized into a "pre-cooperative." Since the beneficiaries were not legally incorporated and lacked experience with maintaining accounts, COOPE-ALIANZA, a credit and services cooperative located in the nearby town of San Isidro de El General, was designated as the implementing agency. This arrangement was planned to end once the community gained the legal and technical capacity to manage its own finances. The group gained formal cooperative status in mid-1988, but as of mid-1989, financial control remained in San Isidro.

Instrumental Participation

The CRS approach can be characterized as "institutional support" rather than concern for the quality of participation at the grassroots level or for participation in broader social and political processes. CRS did base its selection of the Uvita community on the level of organization and commitment of the group (as reported by the state agrarian reform agency). The level of community organization did appear to have advanced, at least in formal institutional terms. However, the design and implementation of the project were largely top-down in character and showed little popular input. This type of participation is quite compatible with the traditional patterns of Costa Rican society and does little to advance the interests of peasants at the national level in an era when the state is less disposed to meet the needs of the poor.

The Uvita group was initially brought to CRS's attention by the state agrarian reform agency, IDA. Peasants who had invaded lands in IDA's possession formed the settlement. Members of the community had formed a neighborhood committee after the invasion, and the committee had been working together in a more or less permanent form for six or seven years. Because the group displayed "much capacity and determination," IDA decided to seek financing for it.[10] Both CRS and IDA were very satisfied with the level of participation and organization in the cooperative. A June 1988 CRS report evaluated progress in group organization as good, based on two criteria: the formal inauguration of the cooperative and the provision of training and technical assistance in cacao-farming techniques by an IDA agronomist. According to the report, "[t]his assistance has also promoted an integration of the group and a positive collaborative attitude toward working as a collective."

However, a closer examination reveals many problems with the CRS approach to participation. Most important, the way in which the project was implemented and designed showed more attention to state and international donor priorities than to the needs identified by the group itself. The first two years of the initial three-year CRS-ACORDE-PACT project were spent on an academic study of economic, geographic, and social conditions in three regions of the country, with no popular input and little attention to political considerations or popular movements. The orientation of the project was decided in advance with the 1986 decision of the Costa Rican mission to promote nontraditional export production among campesinos. As a result of this orientation, groups could not expect CRS support unless they conformed to this strategy. The dominant attitude to participation was displayed in the response of the IDA promoter when asked how the decision was made to produce cacao:

> That was the idea of the members themselves. They had heard that CRS offered financing if they produced a product like that [a nontraditional export]. It seemed to them that they could grow cocoa, a permanent crop.

Peasants clearly recognized that they would not receive funding for other types of activities. Community control over the nature of the project was thus limited to the selection of the crop.

It also appears that the introduction of the project created some divisions within the community as a whole. Some residents opposed the project and were boycotting the group. One male member of the Vigilance Committee of the cooperative stated:

> There is a minority sector of the community which hasn't been in agreement with the cooperative. They are people with a low level of education. They believe the cooperative is bad because it's only for the leaders and not for the good of the community. Besides, there are people who don't want to leave basic grain production.

This community division created by the orientation of the project shows there was inadequate attention to the range of community needs and objectives prior to project design.

There was a well-consolidated leadership group in the cooperative but little sign of broader participation (apart from labor on the cacao crop and agricultural training). General meetings were held only twice a year, providing insufficient opportunity for community control over the project. Even basic knowledge of the project appeared limited outside of the leadership structure. One co-op member stated that he thought he would leave the cooperative soon because the co-op accounts were not explained to the members and because he did not understand how control was kept over project funds. He believed that he had been charged more than he had received. Even if this was not true, the belief shows a serious lack of confidence in and knowledge of the functioning of the organization.

At the evaluation session held in 1989 it was concluded that training had been successful with regard to productive requirements but that there had been no training in the administration of the cooperative.

Apart from the limitations on participation within the cooperative, the exclusive focus on cacao production also placed a serious limitation on community involvement. Farmers who did not wish to produce cacao, as well as landless peasants, were automatically excluded (although IDA obtained lands for a few men who expressed interest in joining the cooperative — unusual behavior on IDA's part, displaying the state agency's degree of commitment to this project). Women were also virtually excluded, since under IDA regulations only single or widowed women were eligible to receive entitlements for plots, and only landowners were eligible for co-op membership. According to the IDA officer, women "are indirect beneficiaries. Because it's a cooperative of producers and that's fundamentally men's work. There is only one woman in the cooperative." Many studies indicate, however, that projects need to be aimed directly at women's specific needs and to incorporate women directly if they are to benefit. Apart from links with state agencies, CRS, and other international donors, the group has few outside contacts. No ties were established with any peasant union, and there was no attempt to influence regional or national policy, apart from gaining land titles for members from IDA. This lack of broader political involvement, in fact, may be one reason why the group received special attention from both IDA and CRS.

OEF International (formerly known as the Overseas Education Fund) is a US-based NGO founded in 1947 by the League of Women Voters; it works primarily with women in developing countries (see Table 6.2 on the following page). Like CRS, OEF is very dependent on USAID funding: in 1987, almost 80 percent of its total budget came from USAID grants (OEF International 1988, 11). In the 1960s, OEF's primary activity was leadership training among upper- and middle-class women; in the early 1970s, though, the US New Directions legislation made this approach politically unsellable, and with some difficulty, the agency made the transition to working primarily with lower-class women.

In 1985, OEF launched two Costa Rican programs with very

TABLE 6.2
"CONTRADICTORY" NGO: OEF INTERNATIONAL —
PROGRAM FOR EDUCATION IN PARTICIPATION (PEP)

NGO analyzed	OEF International
Type	"Contradictory"
Project studied	Program for Education in Participation (PEP); organizational support to community banks created by FINCA (Fundación Integral Campesino), another US-based NGO
Main funder	USAID (through OEF in Washington)
Participation strategy	Local empowerment and increased participation by women
Development strategy	Mixed strategy: Basic needs + exports
Role of international agency	Donor-NGO conflict; substantial autonomy of Costa Rican office from main office in Washington, D.C.
Links with local groups	None

different goals and methodologies: Women in Business (WIB) and the Program for Education in Participation (PEP). I chose to focus on the latter program because of its emphasis on participation and community development. PEP was part of a broader OEF program titled "Women, Law, and Development," which had the stated goal of advancing "the understanding of women's subordinate and marginal status and provid[ing] them with forums through which they can build more responsive political and social structures" (OEF International 1986, 9). While the WIB program followed USAID's encouragement of micro and small enterprise in the Third World, the PEP program had a much more political orientation involving the promotion of social and political change. I therefore call OEF a "contradictory" NGO both because of these very different programs within the organization itself and because of the differences between USAID's general approach and the PEP program.

Among the results hoped for in the Central American program were that participants would "take concrete action to: (1) demand their share of public resources and services, and (2) participate in the municipal and national political processes" (Arnove n.d., 1). These are classic goals of liberal pluralism. However, the program also relied heavily on the use of participatory educational techniques, based on the philosophy of "conscientization" of Brazilian educator Paolo Freire, typical of an "empowerment" approach.

PEP was funded by a special USAID "Democracy Program" established on the recommendation of the Kissinger Commission and was primarily designed to promote electoral processes in Central America and candidates favorable to US foreign policy objectives. Because of this special status, funds were transferred from USAID to OEF International in Washington and then to San Jose rather than through the normal route of ACORDE. In the project I studied, OEF provided training and participatory education for peasants in the southern region of the country who were members of community banks established by FINCA (Fundación Integral Campesina) International, another US-based NGO. This collaboration with FINCA was one of the elements contributing to the project's contradictory profile, since FINCA has a much more mainstream orientation.

The groups with which PEP worked primarily consisted of peasant producers of basic grains and contained a high proportion of women. Participants received small loans from FINCA on an individual basis but repaid the loan to a rotating fund managed by a "solidarity group" of community members receiving FINCA support. The objectives of the PEP component of the project were to strengthen the "organizational capacity," "collective consciousness," and community orientation of the groups (OEF-PEP 1988).

When I visited OEF-PEP in Costa Rica in 1989, the initial three-year project had been completed. Another broader proposal had been made to USAID but had not been approved. When I visited the communities, therefore, the project had just ended.

Local Empowerment and Increased Women's Participation

As its title indicates, OEF's Program for Education in Participation had a deeper commitment to promoting grassroots participation than the CRS project, where participation appeared as a secondary objective. OEF literature defines "education for participation" as

> a global and integral process of education, in which men and women will analyze and critically interpret their world and their problems, and will

be able to acquire the skills necessary to respond to them in a cooperative and democratic way.

Thus, education for participation transcends a determined modality to become a general theoretical-methodological orientation. The aim is to "affirm the responsibility of members of community organizations to promote full, democratic, and cooperative participation in the decision-making process" (OEF 1988).

This statement displays a Freireian philosophy of education. The program is also influenced both by the liberal-feminist orientation of OEF's "Women, Law, and Development" program, which focuses on addressing legal obstacles to women's equality, and by the consciousness-raising methods of Western feminism in the 1970s. The result of these mixed origins was that PEP appeared very successful in increasing popular participation (especially by women) at the community level but had trouble developing a clear strategy for promoting broader forms of participation and a deeper insertion into Costa Rican popular struggles.

The PEP methodology involves extensive use of participatory techniques and popular education methods such as sociodrama, drawings, poetry, songs, folk sayings, and so on, to increase the level of participation by all group members. An evaluation of PEP commissioned by USAID states:

> The evaluations delivered by participants continually refer to what they have achieved in terms of self-esteem, and their ability to better express their problems and concerns, as well as what they have learned, in order to better organize meetings and plan activities. (Arnove n.d., 2)

This evaluation was confirmed by the interviews I carried out with the community banks in the southern zone. One woman from Las Parcelas stated:

> Ivania [the PEP promoter] has helped us a lot. At the beginning, people were more afraid to participate, but now we're more confident — especially the women. Women often didn't participate much before, but participating in the meetings gives you more confidence.

She also stated that she and other women got out of the house more through PEP activities (campesinas on dispersed parcels of land are often isolated from community activities because of household responsibilities and machista ethics that insist women should stay in the home) and that some of the men helped more with household tasks because of Ivania's involvement. Ivania attempted to address problems of machismo within the groups, so that women gained greater confidence to participate, and men allowed them to take on positions of leadership. Of course, not all men were amenable to this change in women's status, and undoubtedly many women were prevented from participation because of childcare and other responsibilities and because of their husbands' unwillingness to permit them to take on a more active role.[11] The PEP promoter also focused on creating more egalitarian forms of decision making within the groups. The groups met as a whole at least once a month, showing a higher level of regular participation by all members than in the CRS project.

PEP's encouragement of the groups to move beyond the narrow focus on financial aspects of the banks to greater community involvement also succeeded to some extent. The various groups took on such community projects as constructing a soccer field and a meeting house. A male member of the Las Parcelas group stated:

> We've changed a lot, through participation in the project. Before there was a community problem. We have now united a lot. Also, within the family, there's more unity. There's more agreement between spouses. The women have their own projects, a clearer idea of what they want, so women's work is valued more.

PEP was less successful in linking this project with broader regional and national issues, partly because of the constraints imposed by FINCA. PEP had hoped to encourage the groups to look beyond their communities and to create greater unity by supporting a "sectoral committee" with representatives of each of the 120 groups with which FINCA was working in Costa Rica. Through this organization, OEF hoped to strengthen the grassroots groups through feedback and support. Despite an initial agreement between OEF and FINCA that OEF would carry out educational work with the sectoral committee, FINCA subsequently decided that the committee would only deal with narrow economic issues. Thus, the groups with which OEF was working in the southern zone had no organized connection to other *comunidades*. It may also have been difficult for OEF to form open associations with peasant unions, which were viewed negatively by USAID. There was therefore the danger that these would

TABLE 6.3
"PROGRESSIVE" NATIONAL NGO: CECADE

NGO analyzed	CECADE (Centro de Capacitación y Desarrollo)
Type	"Progressive"
Project studied	Support for cacao production and small income-generating projects; organization of local producers' associations
Main funder	Agro-Action (West German NGO)
Participation strategy	Support for social movements; little participation by women
Development strategy	Basic needs + nontraditional exports
Role of international agency	Nonintervention
Links with local groups	Support for UPANACIONAL (Costa Rica's largest peasant union); member of the Concertation of Central American NGOs

become isolated experiments in participation at the local level. Increased individual capacity to participate would not be channeled into cooperation with other groups in similar positions in order to challenge the problems that confront them all. In addition, the fact that OEF's work in the *comunidades* ended with the cut-off in US-AID funding, while FINCA's activities in this area continued, meant that the more individualistic and capitalistic orientation may tend to predominate.

The third project examined was directed by a progressive Costa Rican center, CECADE, and funded by a West German NGO, Agro-Action (see Table 6.3). Like OEF-PEP, CECADE's approach heavily stressed the use of participatory techniques, but, like CRS, CECADE was supporting productive projects rather than focusing primarily on education. Because it was founded by intellectuals who had for many years been associated with the Costa Rican left, CECADE had a much stronger identification, however, with peasant organizations than either of the two US-based NGOs.

One of CECADE's productive projects was selected for study. This project was being implemented among small producers in the northern region of the country. The project was funded by Agro-Action, a West German NGO, which had little direct involvement in the project design or implementation. CECADE began working in this region in 1986 on the invitation of UPANACIONAL, the country's largest peasant union. The main focus of work was on San Jorge, a remote settlement 75 kilometers north of San Carlos; the settlement was formed by *precaristas* who occupied a large plantation there in 1976. In San Jorge, CECADE chose to support three separate activities: the production of cacao, the establishment of a concrete-block factory that would supply material for the construction needs of the community, and a model pig farm. The goal was to establish a rotating fund that would permit the projects to become (at least partially) self-sustaining. CECADE was politically opposed to the principle of structural adjustment but felt that given the cutbacks in subsidies to basic grain production, nontraditional exports represented the main alternative available to small farmers. However, like CRS, the CECADE project was negatively affected by the decline in cocoa prices.

Support for Social Movements

CECADE, less constrained by donors and with a clearer orientation toward political change, placed a greater emphasis on the participation of beneficiaries in national social movements. However, while local participation was also seen as a goal, it was not yet sufficiently developed. Because of the emphasis on productive strategies, and, specifically, on the launching of the cacao project, group learning and empowerment were to some extent sacrificed to productive efficiency. CECADE itself recognized the need to expand community participation. For example, a 1988 project report stated:

> The size of the nursery was very large and required a great deal of work which had to be done in very little time (one month) in order to take advantage of the rains. This meant that the process was carried out in a very directed manner, sacrificing more reflective and democratic styles of work.

There is, therefore, some evidence to support the view of critics of productive projects that such projects inevitably lead to emphasis on technocratic concerns and detract from more purely political and participatory work.

Part of the problem, as in the CRS project, was the initial heavy emphasis on a single export crop. A 1987 report by CECADE stated:

> The participation of the farmers has been neither constant nor massive, given that until the present the project has basically focused on the production of cacao, and not all of the farmers are interested in this crop. This has suggested the need to begin providing other alternatives which make possible a broader form of participation from the families involved. (CECADE 1987)

In San Jorge, there was relatively large participation in the initial phase of the cacao nursery by all social sectors (male farmers, women, and youth) because of the opportunity for paid labor, but some of those who participated were frustrated because labor was not immediately reimbursed. Participation in the project subsequently dropped off because job opportunities in the project were limited, and farmers struggling to survive found it difficult to leave their land to participate in the cement-block and pig projects.

The pig project offered employment to only three teenage girls, and about eight to ten day laborers worked in the cement-block factory. The projects were not offering opportunities for participation on a regular basis to small farmers or to women involved in childcare and household labor. The heavy emphasis on production meant that other opportunities for participation did not exist. It also limited the participation of women, whose household labor is generally not recognized as productive.

The fact, however, that the CECADE promoters were aware of these problems of participation at the local level and from the beginning were seeking strategies to overcome them shows that the organization takes the problem of participation very seriously. CECADE had initiated a radio project for the northern zone, financed by the Canadian Catholic Organization for Development and Peace. This communications project would permit dissemination of information about the problems of the peasantry in this region and allow peasants to participate in the mass media. A literacy project was also contemplated (a preliminary needs-identification study had been initiated) because of the low level of education in the community, which limited the ability of the association to take over full control of the project (particularly financial aspects).

The field staff also wished in the future to put more emphasis on projects that could be carried out on the participants' own parcels, in order to broaden the opportunities for participation. As one promoter stated:

> It has been difficult to break with the paternalistic mentality; the people expect us to arrange everything. They still don't feel like the project is theirs. Because they are projects which are carried out outside of their parcels, it is difficult for them to participate more actively.

Even though progressive NGOs may wish to develop a more collective orientation among Costa Rican peasants, they must learn to come to terms with peasant survival strategies related to the existing land tenure system, which makes collective work difficult on a regular basis.

CECADE's work also benefits from a close association with the peasant union UPANACIONAL (or UPA). The project was initiated partly on UPA's request, and all members of the Asociación de Agricultores established in the villages were also members of UPA. While UPA was not the most militant of the peasant organizations in Costa Rica, having been established by relatively well-off coffee farmers, the connection with UPA ensured that CECADE's work had a link with wider struggles of peasant producers. Further, CECADE's work to increase the organizational capacity of small producers may have acted to increase the political weight of more marginalized sectors within UPA.

CECADE also assisted the peasants in increasing their political power vis-à-vis the Costa Rican state. Unlike the *parceleros* in Uvita, the group in San Jorge had received little support or attention from IDA after the initial land invasion. When the project began, although the settlement had been in place for twelve years, only five of the original forty-four (male) *parceleros* had received official land titles. Along with the local Asociación de Desarrollo Comunal, the Asociación de Agricultores pressured IDA either to process the remaining land titles or to act as a guarantor with COOPESAN CARLOS for the residents to obtain loans from the co-op and allow them to participate in that group's cacao project. As a result, sixteen farmers received the guarantee, and IDA agreed to send a group of topographers to map out the dimensions of the parcels.

Unlike the Uvita project, the CECADE project did not accept the problems associated with cacao production passively, but promoted a political response. The CECADE promoters held workshops with farmers and technicians involved with cacao production in the northern zone in order to share information about problems of the crop and possible solutions. Some of the responses proposed to the government included increased financing, debt forgiveness, freezes on the price of inputs, establishment of support prices for cacao, and discouragement of cacao imports. The document produced by the CECADE promoters as a result of their encounters with cacao producers states that

> the implementation of these proposals, some of which clash with the government's economic policies, will depend on the strength and the power of negotiation developed by peasant organizations, and on the contradictions which exist within the government with respect to the economic adjustment plan, from which peasant groups may obtain some benefits. (Ramírez and Villalobos n.d., 8)

CECADE's strategic orientation thus created the political framework for transformative political action, turning the people from the objects to the subjects of their own development. However, participation at the grassroots level needed to become more authentic in order to sustain national social movements with the necessary strength to force changes on the plans of the state (and the international financial institutions).

Conclusion

These case studies from Costa Rica show that the view that presents NGOs as inherently participatory is naive and inadequate. As indicated above, NGOs display very different understandings of what participation means and how it is to be achieved. The problem of dominant models of development has not been that the concept of participation has been entirely lacking, but that it has been marginalized and depoliticized. Most NGOs have contributed to this process by accepting the apolitical vision of NGO work. As a result, participatory initiatives have all too often had only an instrumental value in ensuring the efficient promotion of the interests of dominant powers, rather than actually empowering the poor. In the present context, as the case of Costa Rica shows, the ideology of community self-reliance as a basis for NGO activity is perfectly compatible with the current drive toward privatization and the dismantling of Third World states.

This does not mean that the concept of participation must be rejected, but that it must be reclaimed and explicitly linked with national and international processes of democratization. If this link is not made, even the most participatory of NGO projects runs the risk of following the path of isolated nineteenth-century utopian communities in Britain and North America that were eventually extinguished by internal conflict and hostile external forces. However, even those NGOs that adopt broad-based democratization as a goal lack a systematic analysis of the relationship between participation and democratization. Some assume that increased organization at the local level will necessarily contribute to democratization. There are some reasons to support the idea that personal empowerment is a necessary element of democratization, but it is only a first step. Personal empowerment does not necessarily lead to the decision to participate in the political system as a whole, nor does it guarantee the conditions for greater participation. For example, the organization of cooperatives in Guatemala in the 1940s brought about increased state repression and the annihilation of local organizations and enforced popular passivity.

In contrast, some analysts of democratization in Latin America entirely discount the role of grassroots organizations. The influential 1986 study by Guillermo O'Donnell and Philippe Schmitter, *Transitions from Authoritarian Rule,* portrays the democratization that occurred in the Southern Cone in the 1980s as primarily a process of elite accommodation. Studies of and by NGOs could contribute to this debate by examining the relationship between participation at the community level, participation in social movements, and national processes of democratization. Under what conditions is this connection made?

Finally, supranational forces have to be confronted in order to make this connection possible. How can the internationalization of the state, which has occurred under structural adjustment, be confronted? NGOs must avoid co-optation by the World Bank, the IMF, and other international actors that see them as useful allies in antipopular projects. National and international NGOs can play an important role in representing popular interests on the global stage, but they must make constant attempts to make sure their efforts are rooted in popular experiences. NGOs themselves must be democratized in order to contribute to successful democratization of Third World (and First World) societies.

Notes

1. The term "aid regime" comes from Wood (1986). Wood does not include NGOs among the institutions of the aid regime. I would argue that NGOs should be considered part of the regime, although as actors less rigidly controlled by the dominant norms and rules.

2. Among other supposed qualities of NGOs (or "private voluntary organizations," as they are referred to in the United States) that have become articles of faith, according to Judith Tendler, are that, in contrast to aid institutions, they are more likely to be able to reach the poor; are more concerned with process than outcome; are more able to be flexible and experimental; and have a special ability to strengthen local organizations (Tendler 1982, 4–5).

3. See Carole Pateman's excellent review of the view of participation in classic liberal theorists (Pateman 1970).

4. An influential formulation was provided by Sherry Arnstein (1969) reflecting on her experiences with citizen participation in urban programs in the United States in the 1960s. She describes a "ladder of participation" in which each of the eight rungs of the ladder corresponds to a different extent of citizens' power in the political process. These range from "manipulation" and "therapy," which are, in fact, "non-participation," through "informing," "consultation," and "placation," up to the highest rungs, "partnership," "delegated power," and, at the highest level, "citizen control."

5. Robert Cox also views the rural development project aimed at self-sufficiency (of the type promoted by the World Bank but often implemented by NGOs) as the response of managers of the world economy to the recognition of the fact that the world capitalist system "would not absorb more than a fraction of the world's rural populations" (Cox 1987, 388).

6. In an influential typology, David Korten (1987, 145–59) describes the changes in NGOs as characterized by three "generations." According to Korten, an initial relief and welfare approach in the early postwar period was followed local development. Korten describes a third, more recent NGO strategy as involving commitment to sustainable systems development; that is, recognizing the limits of the impact of their emphasis on small-scale, self-reliant community development projects in the 1960s and 1970s, some NGOs have shifted their emphasis toward attempting to influence broader systemic factors, including government policy. Korten (1990, 11–32) has subsequently developed a conception of a fourth-generation strategy under which NGOs would "become facilitators of a global people's development movement." However, Korten's

description of this fourth generation is vague and not accompanied by specific examples of development agencies working in this area.

7. Stewart MacPherson notes that the term "community development" (which became a key feature of later NGO activities) was first coined by the British Colonial Office in 1948 (MacPherson 1982). Community development was defined as a movement designed to promote better living for the whole community with the active participation and if possible the initiative of the community; however, if this initiative was not forthcoming spontaneously, techniques for arousing and stimulating it were to be used in order to ensure the community's active and enthusiastic response to the movement (see MacPherson 1982).

8. Part of the hierarchy's response to these perceived threats was the establishment of Caritas, a social assistance organization composed mainly of Catholic laypeople in various countries of the region. See Williams (1989) for a description of the political motivations of the Central American bishops.

9. The Program of Action adopted by the 1976 World Employment Conference of the ILO states: "A basic-needs-oriented policy implies the participation of the people in making the decisions which affect them through organizations of their own choice" (cited in Cohen and Uphoff 1980, 213n). In a 1974 article ("ILO: Limited Monarchy"), Robert Cox offers a (former) insider's view of the internal politics of the ILO and its shifting position on basic needs (in Cox and Jacobson 1974, 102–38).

10. Interview with Alvaro Chanto, IDA "promoter," San Isidro, 1989.

11. In addition to the other contradictions between OEF's and FINCA's approaches, they also differ over their approaches to women's role in society. While FINCA does promote women's participation in community banks, it does not conceive of this participation as contributing to broader emancipation or challenge traditional family structures. In fact, small projects for women are seen as a response to the economic crisis that will maintain traditional structures. According to the FINCA president in Costa Rica, "We haven't tried to get women to do activities outside of the home — so as not to create conflict, because the men are machismo. We want to help so the men feel that the women can help economically, but still be round the house, to make lunch, take care of the kids, and so on. If the women go out to work in a factory, that could hurt the stability of the family."

SEVEN

Community Economic Development in El Salvador

Aquiles Montoya

The literature on Community Economic Development (CED) has been lacking a study that shows the actual state or level of development within most communities in a Central American country. This is as true for El Salvador as it is for other countries in the region. Such a study ideally would be both systematic and encompass a large number of communities, assessing their diversity with regard to origin, location, purpose, organization, and ideological outlook. This chapter reports on such a study conducted on a sample of one hundred communities selected from El Salvador's ten departments or provinces. The sample might not be statistically representative of the total community population in El Salvador, but we feel certain that we have studied the most important of the country's organized communities. We have also emphasized provinces where such communities are heavily represented. Representative data are given in absolute percentage form unless otherwise indicated.

Community Origins

The organized communities that we studied and that, as we see it, have undertaken to implement one form or another of CED were created during and after the political and military conflict of the 1980s and 1990s. That is, we are dealing with communities of fairly recent origin. When we speak of "communities," we do not refer to just any popular group, such as those that might be created by the government or some international or national NGOs (nongovernmental organizations). The communities in our study have their origin in three very precise phenomena associated with the civil war of the 1980s and 1990s, namely, repatriation, repopulation, and demobilization.

By "repatriation" we mean the formation of communities via the return of people from outside the country. Such communities, for example, would include Nueva Esperanza, formed by returnees from Nicaragua; Guarjila, formed by those repatriated from Mesa Grande in Honduras; and Ciudad Romero, formed by families coming from Panama. However, all these returnees are Salvadorans who were forced to emigrate because of the war and the scorched-earth strategy of the government's armed forces.

By "repopulation" we mean the constitution of communities by people who, although they did not leave the country, left the areas in which they had normally lived. In the repopulation process a community might be formed in some new location or reformed in that previously abandoned. Such communities would include, for example, Palo Grande and Milingo in Suchitoto.

By "demobilization" we mean the constitution of communities by those combatants associated with the Farabundo Martí por la Liberación Nacional (FMLN) who were demobilized as a result of the peace accords. But we also include in this category those peasants who were incorporated into the army by the government. Examples of such communities would be Marino II and Nuevo Amanecer in Usulután.

For the one hundred communities that comprise our study, the most important factor in explicating the origin and the formation of the communities was repopulation, or repopulation in combination with demobilization, which accounted for almost one-half of all communities. It was also a surprising result that one-fourth of the communities were constituted by demobilized persons. We expected that the demobilized would have joined already existing communities, and this was often the case; but they also formed their own communities in locations understandably determined by the availability of land under the terms of the Transfer of Land Program.

What we found is as follows. Only nine communities originated in the process of repatriation alone. But another nineteen had a partial origin in repatriation, combined with either repopulation, demobilization, or both, that is, with the three factors taken together. This is as expected. It would have been strange for the communities to keep themselves closed, given that, for the majority, they are quite small. A "closed" community can exist when the number of persons constituting the initial core is large, but such cases were exceptional.

Legal Status

According to the current municipal code, any community can become a legally incorporated society and thus create a community association, elect a directing council, create regulations, form a general assembly that would assist the mayor should there be one, and see that the acts of the constitution of the community association are faithfully kept. Thanks to this relatively simple procedure the majority of the communities are legally constituted. Of the one hundred communities studied, seventy-five had legal status; eighteen were in the process of legalizing their status; and only seven had no legal status and were not in the process of obtaining it. This indicates that 82 percent either have or are in the process of obtaining legal status. This is important because, with the conflict over, and in spite of the easy procedure for legalization, many mayors have refused to live up to their municipal obligations for either political reasons or because they still have not returned to their localities.

Having legal status is crucially important for the community's ability to obtain credit or to legalize property in the form of goods or shares (land, machinery, buildings, etc.) that have been donated to the community or have been acquired by it in the marketplace. We are not suggesting here that with legalized status the whole problem of property, or the question as to which form of property is most appropriate, is thereby resolved. We merely indicate that there does exist a collective legal entity with the capacity to confer the right of ownership or legal possession. That the property issue is not so easily resolved is shown by the fact that, in addition to legalizing their status, a number of communities have formed associations

TABLE 7.1
LEVEL OF AWARENESS ABOUT THE ADVANTAGES
OF LIVING IN A COMMUNITY

	Work	Social	Labor Organization
High	24	38	32
Medium	44	46	36
Low	28	12	28
No Response	4	4	4
Total	100	100	100

and cooperative societies in order to legalize the ownership of their assets.

Community Awareness and Intercommunity Relations

Community awareness may be shown in many ways, but we have only explored three dimensions: work, social interaction, and labor organization. Community life does not appear spontaneously but requires work, education, practice, will, and a lot of time. And so in those communities that enjoy a better life, the level of awareness (or *concientización*) should be greater, all other factors being equal (Table 7.1). But community awareness is also influenced by the origin of the community, with those communities formed by repatriation having a higher level of awareness. This may be explained by the fact that these communities are often formed by the repatriation of an entire community, which thus brings with it the community structure created during the years in exile.

In spite of the fact that communities originating from repatriation are in the minority and that those originating from repopulation and demobilization are only recent, the results given in the table under "high" are quite surprising in that the social dimension represents over a third, the labor organization almost a third, and the work dimension almost a quarter of all communities.

Given the composition of the communities regarding the cross tabulation for origin and age, the data corresponding to "medium" were what we had expected. Taken together with the data for "high," this presents a hopeful outlook for the future of the communities. One might even say that this future is assured if this were exclusively a function of the level of awareness of the advantages of living in a community situation.

Regarding this future, it was important to determine what the relations were among the communities themselves. We found that the most important of these relations were social, followed, in order, by political, economic, and mutual-aid. It appears to us that communities should seek to invert this rank order of priorities so that they could better articulate the economic relationships between themselves, such that these relationships not only would grow but the already-existent ones would be deepened. Research into local and rural development in other parts of Latin America has demonstrated the importance of this point. As argued by Marcelo Posado (1999, 326–46), the positive role of municipalities as a dynamic force in the development process generally depends on a high level of cooperation and articulation among them. For one thing, it allows for the constitution of larger spatial, economic, and social entities such as the "productive consortia" that have materialized in the peripheral regions of Buenos Aires province in Argentina.

Population and Families in the Communities

We left out of our study all communities in the three western provinces (Santa Ana, Sonsonate, and Ahuachapan) and in the most eastern province (La Unión). This decision was not capricious but rather was a result of the fact that since the civil conflict did not develop in the western part of the country, there was no repopulation or repatriation. It was much the same for La Union: even though this province did not entirely escape the conflict, we did not succeed in finding organized communities that might have been created in the 1980s and 1990s, and so we set this province aside.

The provinces with the most communities are those in which the armed conflict was most serious — Usulután, Cuscatlán, Chalatenango, San Miguel, San Vicente, and San Salvador. In the northeast of Chalatenango province a number of communities organized into

TABLE 7.2
POPULATION AND FAMILIES

Province	Number of Communities	Number of Families	Number of Persons
Cabañas	4	731	4908
Chalatenango	14	1983	11068
Cuscatlán	17	891	3293
La Libertad	3	227	1115
La Paz	2	145	740
Morazán	5	1579	8269
San Miguel	10	2337	9349
San Salvador	10	3741	3561
San Vicente	11	741	3561
Usulután	24	2305	11696
Total	100	14,680	57,560

important municipalities. They include Arcatao, San José Las Flores, and San Antonio Los Ranchos. The lack of correspondence between the number of communities and the population is due to our attempt to not leave out the more important communities, which in some provinces include relatively large ones such as Santa Marta in Cabañas (4,000 persons), Guarjila and Arcatao in Chalatenango (4,300 between them), Segundo Montes in Morazán (7,421), and Las Marias and Las Moritas in San Miguel (6,160 between the two). With their inclusion, a certain bias in the corresponding percentages may be introduced between the number of communities and the community population of the province. For example, Cabañas with 4 percent of the communities represents 8.7 percent of the total community population; Cuscatlán with 17 percent of the communities represents 6.9 percent of the population; Morazán with 5 percent of the communities represents 14.4 percent of the population; and San Miguel with 10 percent of the communities represents 16.2 percent of the population.

Even supposing there were no other communities, which is not the case, the total population making up this form of alternative development is very significant — fifty-six thousand persons, perhaps more. We know, for example, that the "Economic Social System," a group of fifteen communities situated to the south of Tecoluca in

San Vicente province, has a population of about four thousand, and yet our study only includes a few of these communities.

Communities and the Land

Land occupies an important place in rural communities because their livelihood, work, culture, and social and material existence are intimately associated with the soil, if not totally dependent upon it. It is important, therefore, to ascertain both their relationship to the land and its quality.

First, of all the communities we visited, fifty-five reported owning their own land; thirty-three reported that they either own their own land or are in the process of transferring ownership to themselves; and only twelve said that they do not own their own land. For these communities, land ownership has practically ceased to be a problem, a situation radically at odds with the national situation in which land remains the central problem for peasant producers. For example, the Alianza Democrática Campesina (ADC), an amalgam of some twenty peasant organizations, views land as the major object of its struggle (Veltmeyer 1999). The fact that land is no longer a major problem opens up many possibilities for improvement, conservation, and/or reclaiming of the land. It is only when agricultural workers are not owners of their land that difficulties arise regarding investment and conservation. Moreover, land ownership gives these communities a greater sense of permanence and raises the possibility that children and grandchildren will continue their efforts and be their beneficiaries, a situation not possible under conditions of insecure tenancy. The ownership of their own land can be seen as a triumph for the communities under study, a realized goal, a good amidst all the bad that the civil war has left them.

Second, we have the issue of land quality, which can be characterized generally as excellent, good, fair, and poor. Two percent of the communities consider the land they work as excellent; 24 percent consider their land good; 54 percent consider it fair; only 11 percent view it as poor; 9 percent of the communities either did not respond or reported a mixture of fair, good, and excellent. This too is important in that it shows that most communities can secure their existence and development on the basis of agricultural production, although not without effort.

But for a clearer understanding of the foregoing we should complete the analysis of land quality with a topography. For this category, 17 percent responded that they occupied flat land; 29 percent semiflat; 35 percent broken; and 19 percent variegated. The data show that for forty-six communities the land is either flat or semiflat, and they certainly do not mean deserts or swamps. Thus we may conclude that at least 46 percent of the communities can cultivate land that varies from excellent to fair in quality without major problems of erosion, since there is little important cultivation on hilly slopes.

We should add that the data presented regarding land quality and topography for each community reflect only the predominant features of the land. There are exceptional cases in which a community's land is both flat and of excellent quality, such as is the case with Las Canoas in the south of Usulután. On the other hand, it can be poor and broken, as is the case with the land in the Segundo Montes community in the north of Morazán.

Agricultural Techniques

It is important to understand the technical relationship between community producers and the land, and to do this we investigated two techniques: one arising out of the Green Revolution and the other organic agriculture. The first of these is characterized by the use of chemicals such as fertilizers, fungicides, insecticides, and herbicides, while the second, as its name indicates, uses only organic products.

Our data show that the communities have been influenced by the Green Revolution. Peasants are quite resistant to change, and when change has been brought about once, it is difficult to get them to change once again. Thus it is that the techniques of the Green Revolution must have been more or less imposed upon the peasantry through credit mechanisms and other aid. Moreover, the change may have been due to the loss of the soil's natural fertility that resulted in an urgent need for chemical fertilizers, especially when the importation of Peruvian guano was suspended.

In spite of the fact that the peasants use chemical inputs and improved seed, there is a certain presence within the communities of organic agriculture. Even though in eighty-six of the communities over 50 percent of peasant producers use chemical products, there are seven communities in which over one-half use organic fertilizers, the first step toward organic agriculture. Moreover, in twelve communities over half of all farmers combine the use of chemical and organic products. Further, there are six communities in which half of the farmers use organic fertilizers and eight that combine the use of chemical and organic products.

However, if we look at those communities in which fewer than half of all farmers use organic fertilizers or combine chemical and organic fertilizers, it is clear that the presence of organic agricultural techniques is significant, especially if we take into account the risks associated with passing from one technique to another.

It is also interesting to note that the majority of the farmers in the communities under study have attained a higher technological level in their cultivation of basic grains as a consequence of the Green Revolution. The percentage of those that use neither chemical inputs nor improved seed is very low, 2 and 5 percent, respectively. To use another technological indicator, that of soil analysis, we found that 76 percent of the communities use it, a useful practice if and when these farmers were to advance toward organic agriculture.

Environmental Problems and Solutions

Problems of deforestation, erosion, and water pollution are intimately connected with the land and agricultural techniques. And so before proceeding, we need to look at some of the environmental problems that communities are confronting, together with some possible solutions. These latter may take the form of programs and training that relate not just to economic activity but to the lives of communitarians in general.

Generally speaking, environmental problems of the communities are less serious than those that form the sad reality at the national level. The exception here is deforestation, which affects 87 percent of all the communities studied. Perhaps we should not expect anything different, because the whole country is seriously deforested. Yet this may change in the future because there is a very real concern within most communities with environmental problems in general and deforestation in particular.

Regarding the environmental concerns of the communities under study, deforestation is followed in importance by erosion, a serious problem for 62 percent of all communities. If there is deforestation, there is erosion. Fortunately, there are programs to cope with both problems, and even though such programs are not found in all the affected communities, they are in a large percentage of them — 52 percent (for deforestation) and 47 percent (for erosion), to be precise.

We found that in half of the communities some form of hillside cultivation was practiced, which creates the potential for erosion if we speak of annual crops and the use of no special techniques. Forty-seven percent of the communities report having swampy or marshy land, although for a high percentage of them drainage is possible, allowing such land to be incorporated into productive activities. Finally, the low reported level of water pollution is not due to a lack of familiarity with this problem, because the study of water quality is a general preoccupation of all these communities thanks to the work of a number of NGOs. The relatively low level of washouts is explained by the topography of the terrain that results in little hillside cultivation.

Aside from data about problems and the programs used to deal with them, we gathered data relating to the training of community agricultural producers. Eighty-three percent of the communities have set up courses on technical training, which surely would have to do with their agricultural practices. Only 54 percent of the communities provide some form of environmental education, which probably accounts for the low level of organic agriculture.

There are other activities in the communities apart from agriculture. Just because these communities are rural does not mean that they do not engage in nonagricultural activities. Eighty-six percent of the communities reported having cattle, which besides improving their daily diet constitutes an additional source of employment and income. Also, in the yards around their homes, as we shall see momentarily, they engage in activities such as raising fowl, pigs, and goats.

Nonagricultural Activities

Activities unrelated to farming, when developed, may form an important source of employment and income and thus warrant further technical and financial support. Our data show that in eighty-one communities there is a small store; in twenty-four of the communities there are individuals involved with transportation; and in twenty-three communities there are activities involving garment production. In a few communities we also found activities such as shoemaking (ten), carpentry (twenty), crafts (twelve), tinsmithing (eighteen), and the operation of small restaurants (seventeen). It seems clear that all these activities, with the exception of the small businesses, are not *typical* of the rural areas and are showing a metamorphosis associated with CED.

In some cases, these and other skills were obtained by the population while they were refugees within or outside the country. In other cases, their NGO supporters provided training in these activities through particular projects while also providing the requisite financial resources.

Employment Opportunities

Regarding employment, we found frequent recourse to a strategy of alternative development; that is, before asking for or demanding anything, community members have tended to propose the organization of economic activities aimed at employment and income generation. In this matter, either community leaders have tended to support the advice given by outside funding agencies and the NGOs or these agents have followed the direction of community leaders.

Yet the communities have not been able to count on permanent employment for all members of the community for the following reasons (among others): (1) even though they have the ability and the technical capacity, they may not be able to start new businesses for lack of financial resources; (2) recent training and attempts to abandon agricultural activities create a larger pool of unemployed labor; (3) the training of women has resulted in their demanding jobs; and (4) since the communities are relatively new, there is insufficient surplus for the reinvestment needed to create new jobs.

TABLE 7.3

PRINCIPAL ROLES ACROSS ALL COMMUNITIES, BY GENDER

Men		Women	
Farmers	100	Housewives	99
Bakers	29	Bakers	26
Shopkeepers	35	Shopkeepers	28
Service promoters	50	Service Promoters	46
Masons	65	Dressmakers	69
Shoemakers	26	Carpenters	55
Joiners	11	Nurses	17
Drivers	51	Midwives	57
Mechanics	15	Potters	13
Teachers	29	Teachers	37
Tailors	44	Weavers	8
Veterinarians	12		
Asst. Veterinarians	16		
Agronomists	7		
Asst. Agronomists	7		

Confronted with this situation, it is not surprising that employment opportunities in the communities are insufficient. We found that in only four of the communities was employment considered sufficient; in ninety-three it was insufficient; and three communities did not respond to this question. It is nonetheless highly satisfactory that in at least four communities employment opportunities are regarded as sufficient, for there are very few places on the national level that could say the same.

The second and third points indicated above are understandable when we ascertain what the principal roles are for men and women within the communities. This information is shown in Table 7.3.

As one would expect for the totality of communities, there are many persons dedicated to agriculture. Yet what is not obvious is the number of communities in which there are masons, carpenters, drivers, service promoters, teachers, bakers, and shoemakers. A most unexpected result is the presence of veterinarian assistants, mechanics, veterinarians, joiners, agronomists, and assistants to agronomists.

As to women, with the exception of obvious domestic roles, dressmaking, and shopkeeping, we find women working as midwives, service promoters, teachers, bakers, nurses, potters, and weavers.

Table 7.3 shows the enormous potential within the communities for all sorts of occupational undertakings — producing commodities, providing necessary and useful services — through which they can continue to organize and create the capacity for work. And all this has been done without having had recourse to technical specialists, who are reluctant to live in the communities and who have little knowledge of community life or little interest in it.

Family Income

Of all the data obtained, those dealing with family income are the most unreliable. First, people are reluctant to provide information about their income; second, when they do provide such information it is unlikely both monetary and nonmonetary incomes are considered. Incomes are certainly low and are insufficient to satisfy material necessities. Yet if we take into account that the communitarians do not pay for rent, water, or other services and that they have their own family gardens, we could say that living conditions in the communities are better than those of the average peasant in the country.

Because all community houses have a plot on which household economic activity, such as raising animals or growing vegetables, is carried out, and because this sort of activity contributes toward the meeting of their material necessities, we thought it best before proceeding to assess income sources. This is because it is common to think of income only in terms of money received for some sort of work.

The raising of chickens and garden produce are general activities found in most community households. In terms of importance these activities are followed by pig raising and the cultivation of fruit trees, and then goat raising. These activities, excluding garden produce and goats, are found in virtually all peasant households that have sufficient space to carry them out. Goat raising, while not typical, is common in certain northern areas of the country, as is garden produce in the more fertile and humid zones. Besides providing eggs for the daily diet, chicken raising makes possible the consumption of chickens or roosters that have passed their most productive stage. Moreover, raising these animals constitutes a sort of investment, since it is easy to sell them should money be required. Pigs and goats, for their part, form a type of medium-scale savings strategy over the period of about a year, after which time they may be sold for a respectable sum, at least for more than chickens. Pigs and goats also constitute a sort of reserve for emergencies, whatever these may turn out to be. Furthermore, goats provide milk, something greatly appreciated by peasants since it is high in nutrient content and they can also obtain income through daily sales of milk. Fruits and vegetables are both food and a complementary source of income, and even though peasant families do not include them in their itemization, they are really a form of monthly family income, a fact that leads us to suggest that family incomes are generally underestimated.

Sources of income for poor peasants cannot generally be reduced to those involving simply employment, for in El Salvador as in Mexico and elsewhere in the region remittances from migrants often are an important source of rural family incomes. In order to establish typical and atypical communities, from the point of view of including remittances, we surveyed income sources with the following results. First, remittances surprisingly do not play a significant role, there being fewer than ten communities in which some families count on remittances from abroad and nine on remittances from within the country. In sixty communities, families earn a living by working within the community; in only seventeen communities are there families that are compelled to take up work outside the community, a fact at variance with a pattern that is widespread in the rural economy.

In this regard, the traditional survival strategy for peasant producers in the country is subsistence production of basic grains on *minifundios* (minifarms) and the sale of labor on the coffee or sugarcane plantations in order to obtain sufficient income to live. That this practice is changing indicates that the peasant no longer has to sell his or her labor in order to acquire the necessities for living. This is a positive development in the sense that a new life strategy is in the making, and community economic development might be on the horizon.

Living Conditions within the Community

So far we have taken up the study of working conditions of families and their incomes. But now we are interested in how these incomes are related to or are translated into housing conditions, education, and health. These conditions, in one way or another, form the material goals of any family unit.

Housing and Basic Services

If we exclude housing that is in simply bad condition but include the various combinations of conditions from semi- to extremely bad, we find that at least 56 percent of the housing is in fair to excellent condition. Given the traditionally terrible conditions of housing in the country, this result is encouraging; and the figure does not appear to be exaggerated since there are a large number of communities in which houses are under construction or that have recently constructed houses.

In addition to the three basic factors — roof, walls, and floor — used to determine the condition of housing, we considered other features such as the availability of electricity and water in the homes. We feel that the condition of the foregoing three structural features tells us more than information about construction materials — whether a wall be of adobe, brick, cement block, or mud may well tell us nothing of its condition. Similarly, a roof could be made of tiles, asbestos, or shingles, and yet its condition could be indeterminate.

In terms of household services and amenities that affect living conditions, our findings are as follows. In forty-three communities there is electrical service, but in only seven communities does every household have it. But given that a solid infrastructure for electrical service is found in at least forty-three communities, sooner or later all the houses in these communities will have electricity. Regarding drinking water, the situation is somewhat better since forty-seven communities have some form of access to potable water, while in nineteen communities all households have water service. Regarding latrines, only two communities possess none whatsoever; in twenty-three some households have latrines; in forty-seven communities all have them; and in twenty-eight communities most households have latrines, a fact of the greatest importance in that they help prevent the spread of infectious and contagious diseases from which the rural population has chronically suffered. In this regard, it would seem that the families in these communities enjoy better living conditions than those of the general rural population.

Finally, we investigated the use of wood in the communities, and it is clear that all of them do make some use or other of wood. There are twenty-one communities in which some houses do not use wood for cooking, a significant advance over the situation found in rural communities in general.

Infrastructure and Social Services

In addition to housing, it is important to ascertain the conditions of education, health, and spiritual needs. Searching out these parameters, we collected information on infrastructure and social services. The interesting fact regarding education in the communities is that only twenty-three communities had no school. Moreover, there is the novel feature that of the seventy-seven schools in as many communities, sixty-three belong to the communities themselves. That is, the members of the communities, with the help of outside agencies, have constructed the schools in which their children are educated. Thirteen of these sixty-three communities even pay their own teachers. It is these novel aspects of the communities under study that have engendered so much enthusiasm in outside observers. Besides educational infrastructure, thirty-nine communities have a clinic and eighty-three have a health worker. Although some communities receive only periodic visits from medical personnel, in others doctors have committed themselves on a full-time basis.

As to spiritual needs, eighty-two communities have a place that serves as a commons or cultural center. Further, fifty-two communities have a church or some space to carry out religious activities.

Development Assistance

When we speak of assistance we are technically speaking of economic assistance. But there is also technical and scientific assistance that could place a community on the path to development. On this point we might clarify that when we speak of "development" or "economic development" we have in mind conditions in which people are able to satisfy both their material and spiritual needs. We concur here with Manfred Max-Neef's notion of "human-scale development" — that human needs are relatively stable while the ways of satisfying them are many.

It is not surprising that paid technical help for the communities is low, given that we are speaking of poor communities in the search for ways to develop; there are, in fact, only sixteen communities that are in a position to attract technical assistance. This does not mean that the communities receive no technical support whatever, since NGOs also provide technical assistance and they are present in eighty-seven communities. The support of NGOs is quite variable, and they play a very important role in community development. Without NGOs we could not even think about development. At least this appears to be the case for the initial phase of the development process encountered in the majority of our communities.

Nonetheless, we do not think that NGOs should be a permanent factor in community development. On the contrary, a good NGO accompanies a community in development without replacing the community's own role in this process, one that recognizes that the members of the community and not the NGO field workers are the real development actors. From the very first, an NGO should be planning its exit. It is of the utmost importance to realize that communities must eventually and preferably sooner go it alone.

NGO assistance takes the form of financial assistance for a variety of programs. These programs may be for credit, marketing, structuring of and training for a cooperative, environmental assistance, local development, agriculture, textiles, water, electricity, health, education, housing, and so on. The "menu" of NGO programs is as varied as the needs of the communities. Yet the support they receive is still insufficient and appears to us to be unequally distributed, with some communities receiving a good deal of support while others receive nothing, even though the needs across the communities are the same.

Moreover, the presence of NGOs is dependent on the number of communities in a province, with the more privileged communities being closer to the national capital. And although the majority of NGO workers are people who work in solidarity with the poor and the marginalized, there are also those who are more motivated to serve themselves than to serve others. On this point the analysis on the role of NGOs in the development process by Velt-meyer (1999) and Veltmeyer and Petras (1997, 2000) is apropos. We have, for example, DIGNAS, which is dedicated solely to women; or FUNPROCOP (Fundación para la Promoción de Cooperativismo), which is dedicated to cooperatives; and others, whose work is mainly to support development through economic and social activities. Other NGOs emphasize economic development. There are also NGOs concerned with human rights, with demobilization of the FMLN, and with labor organization. Support received by the government, although neither magnanimous nor widespread, is associated with education, health, water, electricity, agriculture, and local development.

Although fifty-nine communities report receiving support from the government, it is unfortunate that such support is not present in all communities as much as it should be, at least insofar as education and health are concerned. Moreover, such support continues to be in the form of aid and not in a form conducive to community development. For a long time now we have understood that rather than receiving fish, people must be taught how to learn to fish. But the government now is not enthusiastically engaged in, so to speak, teaching people how to fish; it seems primarily interested only in handing out aid.

Real and Potential Economic Resources and Problems

We have referred to the problematic relating to incomes and employment, and a critical part of this problematic is financing — especially relating to the generation and disposal of any surplus. On this issue we wanted to find out what resources in addition to land the communities have available. But most importantly our concern was to establish the potential for surplus generation, investment, and population growth. In each community the tendency is to grow both by including new members and through normal population growth.

According to our data, sixty-nine communities have grown; nineteen have stabilized; and only eight have diminished in size (there was no response from four). A decrease in population is frequently due to a relocation of the population into other organized communities, including the splitting off that results in the founding of a new community. This is a more important factor than people retiring from the community and its way of life.

Community Financing

Seventeen communities operate with their own resources. The remainder are associated with some type of credit in the form of loans (48 percent), combined loans and personal resources (27 percent), and combined loans and grants-in-aid (4 percent). There was no response from four communities. This situation suggests that it would be worthwhile to pause for a look at the perception of the costs of credit. We found that forty-five communities found interest rates high; eight found them low; twenty-four found them acceptable; and twenty-three did not respond to the question. Since a large majority of these communities operate without a commercial bank, but often with NGOs, the three perception categories make a lot of sense. That is, they do not reflect subjective opinion so much as distinct sources of financing. Even so, for the great majority the rates are high, and this may have to do with the low returns on agriculture or perhaps with the form in which credit was obtained or the moment in which it was obtained. Regarding the manner of obtaining credit, we found that forty-nine communities obtained it individually; eleven got it collectively; and nineteen used a combination of these. There was no response from twenty-one communities.

It is clear that when entering markets, even money markets, it is possible to get better prices collectively than individually. It surprised us that the majority of the credit in the communities was obtained on an individual basis — 49 percent as opposed to 11 percent collectively. The reason for this has to do with repayment, which seems to be more assured when the obligation is an individual one. The high number of "no response" is due to those who do not use loans at all.

Lastly, on the matter of opportuneness for obtaining credit, the specific data are these: 36 percent obtained credit opportunely; 23 percent obtained it late; and 10 percent got it ahead of time. There was no response in 31 percent of the sample.

Profitability

Although we believe that community profitability should be understood primarily in social terms and only secondarily in economic terms, our data nonetheless refer primarily to the latter conception. The data collected on profitability show that for twenty-one communities the past year had been profitable; for thirty-one it had been a loss; and for forty-six it was neither profitable nor a loss. There was no response from two communities.

By social profitability we refer to the following features: first, when there is an equality between income and expenses, and income and employment have been created for community workers, which they otherwise would not have obtained; second, when, thanks to community life, a number of needs are satisfied that could not be satisfied in some other manner; and, third, when, thanks to the community, people have access to nonmaterial satisfactions such as security, liberty, self-esteem, and participation. Almost half the communities are in a situation of socioeconomic profitability, while a third reported losses. The latter is a very serious situation since there is little likelihood of even simple reproduction; to operate with losses is to be on the downward slide to extinction. The fact that a third of the communities find themselves in this predicament necessitates further inquiry. However, we find that a fifth of all communities operate at a profit and have a surplus. And so we can confirm that around 70 percent of all communities are socially or economically profitable. We can thus conclude that community economic development, as an alternative development strategy, should be considered a serious development option.

We conclude this section by looking at where the surplus is going. Given the lack of employment, the surplus should be used primarily for job-creation, since this would increase economic activity and thus create yet more employment. We found that in seventy-one communities, the surplus was reinvested; in five it was distributed; in another five it was used for debt repayment; and in nineteen communities it was used for all of these.

Available Material Resources

In order to explore the possibilities these communities have for development, we need to know the factors of production that exist within them. We have seen that they have land and labor in abundance and that the latter is fairly skilled. We have also looked at agricultural techniques and the financial resources that are used. Now we want to determine what the other factors of production, such as cattle, machinery and agricultural equipment, irrigation capacity, and infrastructure, are; and we also want to see if there is any arable land that is underutilized.

We pointed out above that as a savings strategy, the yards surrounding community homes contain chickens, pigs, and goats. But besides these smaller animals, they also keep cattle, from which the people obtain milk and meat. Cattle raising is one of the most important economic activities in farming, and so it is gratifying to see that eighty-six communities engage in this activity.

The machinery and equipment used to increase farm labor productivity require a certain amount of capital investment that is not always available to these communities, which explains why only thirty-five communities had these sorts of implements.

Another element that factors into annual labor productivity is irrigation. We sought to determine whether there was a capacity to irrigate and then if there was an infrastructure to do so, since without it, water, even if present, cannot be utilized. Results show that eighteen communities have an irrigation infrastructure, while thirty-two have an unused capacity for irrigation. We can conclude, then, that half of the communities could make use of irrigation for farming, cattle raising, and fish ponds.

Potential Economic Resources

Seeking a deeper look at these matters, we had to explore potential economic resources, ones that could be used to take advantage of present water resources. Knowledge of such resources is the key to any strategy for medium- and long-term development.

Water capacity was explored using the three indicators: agriculture, cattle raising, and aquaculture. Our data show that by using irrigation, twenty-six of the communities could cultivate grain and thirty could grow vegetables. This would increase work opportunities during the dry season, which is precisely the season in which there are fewer opportunities for work. But it would not only increase employment and family incomes; it would also increase the amount of goods produced within the community, whether these are for consumption or sale.

Nineteen of the communities would be able to grow hay under irrigation, a development that would allow them to increase their herds and diminish the costs of production. This would make possible an increase in the economic surplus as well as the other factors of production we have already pointed out. There is also sufficient water to enter into aquaculture, with the raising of shrimp and fish in fifteen and thirteen communities, respectively. This not only would improve and vary the diet but would also generate new jobs and incomes.

What is interesting about all this is that we are not speaking here of theoretical possibilities, for the communities have already undertaken studies and projects in order to further these and other activities. This is the case for at least one-fifth of the communities, while another two-fifths already have projects underway.

Since the future of the communities depends upon their ability to succeed in developing economic activities, and given their high level of initiative regarding proposals and seeking out opportunities, we can say, first, that the future for the majority of the communities is promising. Second, if we take in to account how much they have achieved in so short a time — the oldest community is barely ten years old — we have no doubt that they are on their way to better work and living conditions.

Since it is well known that the development of farming presupposes diversification, we sought to determine what possibilities there were for the communities to develop new activities besides those associated with irrigation. Since we did not wish to include data regarding the development of something purely for novelty's sake, we asked that only those new projects be indicated for which they had sufficient land, water, and/or the experience to bring the activity to fruition. The results are shown in Table 7.4 on the following page.

The diversity of activities here is surprising, some being quite novel. They cover a wide spectrum, from the traditional agricultural exports such as coffee and sugarcane to things that have only recently begun to be exported to the United States, such as iguanas. Traditional farming activities are mentioned, such as raising fowl, bees, and pigs, and there is even rabbit breeding, which in this country is

TABLE 7.4

PROJECTS THAT THE COMMUNITIES COULD UNDERTAKE

Project	Number of Communities
Various fruits	58
Cattle	44
Citrus fruits	42
Firewood lots	32
Turkeys	24
Nurseries	29
Lumber lots	36
Rabbits	14
Coffee	23
Vegetables	50
Iguanas	16
Hot peppers	24
Peanuts	15
Goats	13
Lorocos	38
Chickens	55
Bees	24
Green produce	44
Sugarcane	19
Pigs	29

Total Activities=20

only at its beginning stages. Vegetables and green produce are here alongside the newer cultivation of lorocos (the leaves of a vine, used in preparation of the national dish, *pupusas*), as are those already introduced, such as hot peppers and peanuts. Were these communities able to succeed in bringing into reality all these farming projects, in conjunction with other nonagricultural undertakings for which they have a recently skilled workforce, the possibilities for endogenous development would be great.

It appeared to us that the communities had a high degree of organization and participation at the level of consultation and resolution, and continue to have a high level of awareness about the advantages of living in a community. Given the importance of participation not just for the individual but for the sake of the whole community, we tried to ascertain the members' participation in the community assemblies. Recall that all these communities are organized, and it is this organization that is the very first requirement for a community to be considered as an agent of, and a fit subject for, community economic development. We found that for the most common form of participation, attendance at the community assembly, 41 percent always attended, 38 almost always, 18 percent sometimes, 1 percent never, and 2 percent did not respond. Participation in assemblies is not the only form of participation, nor even the most gratifying, but it does show us the level of interest people have in the matters pertaining to their community.

These results for participation are quite high, with the level of constant or regular participation at almost 80 percent. Any labor organization would cry out for such levels of participation, and we are not speaking here of mere attendance at meetings, but rather an active participation in which enthusiastic voices can be heard, something we discovered in more than a few of our visits to the communities.

Women in the Communities

In daily rural life, especially in the exceptional circumstances created by civil war, women have a much more central role than usual. These conditions are also part of the new alternative development, and so women continue to be guiding hands with significant responsibility and important bastions of support. This reality is evident when visiting any community, but it is surprisingly evident in communities such as Nuevo Gualcho in which the majority of the members are women.

Among the communities studied, the majority have households headed by women. Along with this datum come all the associated implications — such as women having responsibility for material and spiritual/moral well-being in the functioning and development of the home. It is encouraging, therefore, that in forty-one communities there is some form of organization for women. The latter makes possible not only individual but also collective development; and it creates a dynamic awareness of gender theory and raises the self-esteem of women, something that all too frequently is low even among female professionals and intellectuals. Such organizations not only make possible the spiritual and psychological development of women, but also open many possibilities for bettering their eco-

TABLE 7.5
THE GENDER PROBLEMATIC

	Yes	No	No Response
Are there homes in which women are heads of the household?	89	9	2
Do women have an organization?	41	58	1
Are there workshops on gender?	29	71	0
Are there economic projects for women?	37	57	6

nomic conditions and therefore creating the possibility for a better and more dignified life for women and their families. As we see in Table 7.5, twenty-nine communities have started seminars on gender, and in thirty-seven there are economic projects that directly promote the financial conditions of women.

This is a cause for satisfaction. In contrast to the traditional peasant community in which women are the victims of the machismo of their husbands and other men in the community in general, these communities — in seeking a real alternative development of their lives, their families, their social interaction, and themselves — are undergoing positive changes with regard to matters of gender.

Natural Disasters

It is of the utmost importance to include within a socioeconomic study of farming communities what their experience of natural disasters has been, for a flood or a drought can cause marked differences in annual economic activity. These may result in the success or failure of one or more projects and so are very important in determining the efficacy of an alternative economic development.

The most serious natural disasters are floods, and it is precisely from these that the majority of the communities in the coastal zone suffer. In a flood, the communities lose not only harvests and animals but also housing and domestic utensils, not to mention human life. It is lamentable that almost one-fifth of the communities have experienced floods, for the latter have most assuredly affected their living conditions and work. But the communities have also had to endure hurricane-force winds that work mayhem on crops, and such destruction was visited upon almost a quarter of the communities. Similar in their effects are late-season rains that, coming as they do at the end of the rainy season, level coffee and sesame crops and cause great economic losses. Finally, there are droughts that affect the production of basic grains, a commodity that the communities depend on for their daily food. The material living conditions of these communities would have been better had they not experienced natural disasters. Such disasters not only destroy existing material resources but also require new resource inputs that could have otherwise been put to better use to increase the reproductive potential of the community.

Conclusions

After more than three years of regretting that general information on the communities within El Salvador was unavailable, we have finally (in 1997) generated some systematic data on one hundred communities made up of repatriated, demobilized, and relocated persons. These persons are the subjects of a new strategy of development, a strategy that in some circles is known as community economic development (CED). These subjects — the members of these communities — create day in and day out a new reality with their lives and activities that we have called the New Popular Economy. We call it "new" because a simple popular economy is not new, but the form it now takes is indeed novel. It seeks to attain collective well-being in an organized manner through a practice of new values of solidarity, community, cooperation, and mutual aid. This is all very new. Thus in order to differentiate it from past practices — those of the traditional peasantry — it is necessary to call it something else, and yet continue to point out its popular character. It is this novel undertaking — whereby people through their own efforts seek to obtain a material and spiritual well-being that cannot be reduced to simple economics — that we call community economic development.

"Development" does not have solely an economic dimension. By focusing on the economics of development we are merely drawing attention to a characteristic feature of popular strategies, namely, that they seek to develop, on their own terms and in an organized collective manner, economic activities conducive to their development. This goes a long way toward satisfying their material and spiritual needs. We do subscribe to the idea that development presupposes economic growth. But it is obvious that economic growth alone does not necessarily lead to economic development. In order to avoid an often somewhat scholastic discussion about such terms as "development," "economic development," and "socioeconomic development," we use the expression "community economic development" to capture the aforementioned ideas. There is a definite understanding within communities about how best to bring about development, namely, to have jobs and incomes that will allow them to satisfy their material and spiritual needs. However, since in recent times others are creating neither adequate jobs nor the associated incomes for them, they have had to create these for themselves, and this has meant engaging in various sorts of economic activities. Yet it is proven that to do so in an individual and isolated manner is fruitless, and hence they enter into these activities in a collective and organized manner.

The results have not been as satisfactory as they might have been. But if one thing is clear from our study it is that there is still much undeveloped potential, and this has led us to indicate elsewhere that the real importance of the communities' efforts is not in what they have attained but in what they could attain given their potential, their resources and constraints, the barriers to development, and the facilitating conditions. In order to avoid any possible anticollectivist prejudice, we should note that "collective" is not applied in any sort of mechanical way to land ownership, means of production, productive labor, the management of finances, or the marketing of products. Rather, collectivity is present in certain activities only because it is functionally relevant. For example, if production requires collective work, then it will be done collectively; if it is better to do marketing collectively rather than individually, then it will be done collectively.

Nonetheless, perhaps the most important feature is that no superior authority imposes the requirement of being collective or individual; it is the people themselves who decide on the most relevant form for their activities. This applies to property ownership and work, as it does to everything else. All this leads us to insist that beyond being agents or actors, these persons are subjects, subjects of their own lives and work, of their own destiny grouped into some sort of community or federation. The most important thing is that the basic unit is the community, and thus any discussion of spatial extension or size is irrelevant. All the discussion about local development or regional development — at least from the perspective of CED — is also of little relevance. CED may be conceived of as taking place on a local level, a regional level, or a national level, within a small community or within an enormous group of organized communities. The basic unit continues to be the community.

It is obvious that social, political, and economic relations between communities are desirable and necessary. Yet it is erroneous to think that the lack of a regional strategy makes CED impossible; regional development is not in and of itself a determining factor in CED. Our idea of CED is that it includes the small and the large, the simple and the complex, and the local, district, regional, and national levels. Development must be conceived as a process, and such a process demands, further, some conception of itself that not only will unfold its own dynamic but will also allow for the inclusion of other perspectives. Thus, in our case, the conceptions of local or regional development could be included perfectly within the perspective of CED.

These observations suggest a number of conclusions:

1. On the national scale a new and unprecedented reality exists, namely, a community sector with a large population that is seeking to resolve its problems of poverty and marginalization in an organized manner. What is more, they are succeeding in carrying out this CED.

2. There is a high level of awareness among the communities about legalizing their status, and as a consequence a large majority of them are legally constituted entities.

3. A large majority of the communities either own their own land or are in the process of acquiring ownership, a situation from which they may then derive great advantages.

4. Even though there are indeed environmental problems, there is both an awareness that these must be confronted and efforts already underway to do so.

5. If we look at the principal trades of the members of the communities we studied, it is gratifying to see that there is quite an ample diversification of economic activity; this suggests a high level of potential development for these communities.

6. Employment opportunities are insufficient in most communities, and so this problem must be confronted decisively and immediately.

7. There is a problem with incomes, which for the majority are low even when we make our parameters more precise in order to obtain more objective data on incomes, and so we conclude that as long as employment opportunities are insufficient, incomes will be low for the majority of families.

8. In spite of what we have just said, these communities do not promote economic strategies based solely on agricultural exports, for the majority of community members acquire their income by working in the community itself.

9. Community families use the raising of chickens, pigs, and goats as a savings strategy, and this also contributes, to a greater or lesser extent, to their daily diet.

10. CED appears to us to be a successful strategy if we consider the living conditions of community families, which, for the most part, are significantly better than those in the country in general; further, the quality of these living conditions is due to improvements in the material conditions of housing and/or the presence of public services such as water, electricity, education, and health.

11. A large part of the success that communities have enjoyed has been associated with the human, material, and technical support and collaboration of the various NGOs that have worked with them.

12. These communities are not closed or in some sense stuck in a rut but are open and growing communities experiencing serious pressures on their economic resources and social services and hence must put in place planning and projects for the medium and long term.

13. The communities are in fact generally profitable, with only a third of them reporting financial losses, something that we should seriously seek to remedy.

14. In the majority of cases, whenever the communities have an economic surplus, they reinvest it, thus making possible future growth.

15. The communities have economic resources that are not being utilized; these include land that can be irrigated and recently accumulated skills, such as those coming from projects and initiatives that have sought financial backing to convert project ideas into reality.

16. Current conditions in the communities are very favorable for making development possible, especially the focus on gender and on human development with a heavy environmental emphasis; this should not be confused with the "sustainable human development" focus, which has little to do with the experience of these communities.

17. In general, the experience of the communities studied has been a successful instance of CED, and therefore they merit continued support. Although the results have been excellent, the situation must be consolidated in order to realize its potential and be reproduced on a larger scale.

In conclusion, we want to underscore the necessity of national and international NGO support for the communities since they cannot yet get along completely on their own. Recall that many were started after the peace accords in 1992 and so are still very young. Moreover, it is of the greatest importance that they develop and give depth to the structure of economic, social, and political relations among themselves, as this may be the only sure way of facing the influence of capitalist market forces. In this context, it is absolutely necessary to carry out research on this community sector on a continuing basis, making information available about the life and aspirations of the communities. This not only would be of assistance to the development of this sector but also would assist other researchers, other NGOs, and anyone else interested in the problems of development as these presently inform the reality of El Salvador.

EIGHT

Neoliberalism and Sustainable Popular Development

David Barkin

Neoliberalism is exacerbating the polarization of society in all of its dimensions. Structural adjustments, with their program for international economic integration and public-sector austerity on the domestic front, have radically reduced the possibilities for equitable growth and the satisfaction of social needs. For most Latin Americans, this neoliberal opening is a nightmare. Falling real income, increasing unemployment, and the accelerated withdrawal of social safety nets leave us with few alternatives. A significant number of people, however, have chosen to attempt to construct their own independent paths to survival. At present many of these strategies are no more than precarious arrangements to assure the income needed to hold body and soul together. They involve a combination of traditional forms of production for increasing local self-sufficiency, financed by other activities in the same region or elsewhere; at present, people are forced to migrate, often accepting jobs in the most unfortunate of circumstances, with a consequent deterioration of their own lives and contributing to the unraveling of culture and society.

This unexpected response by millions who are unwilling to accept the inevitability of their absorption into the neoliberal quagmire offers a point of departure for alternative strategies. These alternatives are now being explored by myriad communities and scholars throughout the hemisphere; the contradictions of neoliberal development are so profound that even the international development community now recognizes their importance as a way of responding to the present crisis and searching for a progressive transitional route toward a better world. They are so important that a new literature is focusing on grassroots approaches, including the exploration of problems related to participation and gender, while new organizations have emerged to take advantage of the political space that this opening is creating and to use the resources that are becoming available.

Many of these alternatives are emerging from concern about the need to search for a new approach to sustainability. This chapter focuses on the problems of developing a strategy for sustainable development. Sustainability has become an important part of the discussion of development. It is increasingly clear to practitioners and academics alike that our thinking about development strategies must change; unless different approaches are allowed to thrive, the prevailing strategy of international economic integration with open borders will destroy our capacity to undertake these tasks. These new approaches require more than the defense of our natural environment. The conservation of a region's ecosystems depends on more than a political recognition of the importance of the problem. It also requires the strengthening and reconstruction of the social and economic capacity of people with the knowledge and ability to engage in the productive activities required for protecting and enriching the natural systems in which these resources exist. This chapter turns to the task of exploring a strategy of sustainable development; it builds upon the principles of a diversified productive base, creative use of the local resource base, and local participation in planning and implementation.

The Heritage of Development

Today's dual economy is an anachronism. While internationalization promises higher profits for capital than ever before, the contradictions bred by impoverishment are provoking a worldwide rebellion. The international expansion of capital integrates resources and people into a polar system of great wealth accompanied by poverty and despoliation. This expansion has created vast extensions of land that have been denuded of their primary cover and so can no longer be profitably cultivated; in the process, large numbers of people are forced into precarious conditions in rural areas or urban slums; this waste of natural and human resources imposes a huge burden on society, in terms not only of opportunities forgone but also of the costs of managing the social control and welfare tasks.

Official development theory seeks the solutions to poverty in market-led structural changes. International development experts and environmentalists alike join in an effort to wrench these groups from their regions, blending the arguments of economic efficiency with those of natural destruction to justify their removal. But these strategies raise two important questions: (1) Is a new era of growth in its current mode either possible or desirable given environmental limitations? and (2) Given the historical record, is there demonstrated evidence that new levels of growth will provide for greater economic (and therefore political and social) equity among diverse groups of nations, regions, communities, and people?

The answers to both these questions are a resounding no. A market-driven strategy will not bridge the chasm between rich and poor, with all its negative implications, characteristic of today's dualisms. Instead, an approach that recognizes the limits of natural resource exploitation and capital expansion is proposed, one that addresses the issues of poverty and sustainability by offering a program of rural development for those presently excluded, a program that eventually would also ameliorate conditions in the rest of society. Both the increasing number of poor people and the accumulating environmental problems require solutions that are less market-dependent, solutions that take into account the redundancy of large portions of the population to the current framework for production and economic growth, and, therefore, provide for these people by creating a system in which communities can survive without complete integration into the global marketplace.

Investigations show that when given the chance and access to resources, the poor are more likely than other groups to engage in direct actions to protect and improve the environment. From this perspective, then, an alternative development model requires new ways to encourage the direct participation of peasant and indigenous communities in a program of job creation in rural areas to increase incomes and improve living standards. By proposing policies that encourage and safeguard rural producers in their efforts to become once again a vibrant and viable social and productive force, this chapter proposes to contribute to an awareness of the deliberate steps needed to promote sustainability.

The chapter identifies many opportunities to reflect on the importance of sustainability and the possibilities of implementing approaches that take us in a new direction. But it also suggests that there are significant obstacles to such progress. Overcoming these obstacles requires more than well-intentioned policies; it requires a new correlation of social forces, a move toward broad-based democratic participation in all aspects of life, within each country and in the concert of nations. Strategies to face these challenges must respond to the dual challenges of insulating these communities from further encroachment and assuring their viability.

In this alternative view, the world-system is one of increasing duality, polarized between the rich and poor nations, regions, communities, and individuals. A small number of nations dominate the global power structure, guiding production and determining welfare levels. The other nations compete among themselves to offer lucrative conditions that will entice the corporate and financial powers to locate within their boundaries. Similarly, regions and communities within nations engage in self-destructive forms of bargaining — compromising the welfare of their workers and the building of their own infrastructure — in an attempt to outbid each other for the fruits of global growth. This dynamic is not conducive to promoting sustainable development. The regions unable to attract investment suffer the ignoble fate of losers in a permanent economic Olympics, condemned to oblivion on the world stage. In their struggle for survival within the global marketplace, many of the world's rural populations are doomed to marginality and permanent poverty.

Among the many questions raised by this discussion, some of the more important ones might be grouped into the following areas:

- What is the relationship between poverty and environmental degradation?

- Can the obstacles to sustainability be overcome by raising national per capita income levels?

- Can policies directed toward poverty eradication also contribute to reducing pressures on the environment?

- Are wealthier people around the world confronting the problems of sustainability responsibly? What is their level of responsibility to support environmental protection and conservation in areas inhabited by the poor?

Sustainability is not possible in rural Latin America as long as the expansion of capital enlarges the ranks of the poor and impedes their access to the resources needed for mere survival. Capitalism no longer needs growing armies of unemployed to ensure low wages, nor need it control vast areas to secure regular access to the raw materials and primary products for its productive machine; these inputs are now assured by new institutional arrangements that modified social and productive structures to fit the needs of capital. At present, however, great excesses are generated, excesses that impoverish people and ravage their regions. Profound changes are required to facilitate a strategy of sustainable development. In the last section we explore such an approach, suggesting that it may be possible and necessary to promote a new form of development: a structure of local autonomy that allows people to rebuild their rural societies and produce goods and services in a sustainable fashion while expanding the environmental stewardship services they have always provided.

Sustainability

Sustainable development has become a powerful and controversial theme, creating seemingly impossible goals for policy makers and development practitioners. Virtually everyone now couches his or her proposals for change in terms of its contribution to sustainability. There is a widespread acknowledgment that present levels of per capita resource consumption in the richer countries cannot possibly be generalized to people living in the rest of the world; many argue that present levels of consumption cannot be maintained even for those groups who now enjoy high levels of material consumption.[1] In this new discourse, resources encompass not just inherited natural capital, including raw materials (such as soil, subsoil products, good quality air and water, forests, oceans, and wetlands), but also the earth's capacity to absorb the wastes produced by our productive systems; of course, the analysis of resources also includes considerations about the quality of the built environments in which we live and work.

The concern for sustainability has become global, reflecting the widespread fear of the deterioration in the quality of life. Existing productive systems and consumption patterns threaten the continuity of the existing social organization. The inequitable and undemocratic nature of current patterns of development raises the specter of the unraveling of present systems — social, political, productive, and even those of personal wealth. A different structure, more attuned to the earth's possibilities for supporting and reproducing life, must replace them.

To address questions of sustainability, then, is to confront the fundamental dilemmas facing the development community today. While the trickle-down approaches to economic progress enrich a few and stimulate growth in "modern" economies and sectors within traditional societies, they do not address most people's needs; moreover, they contribute to depleting the world's store of natural wealth and to a deterioration in the quality of our natural environment.

In the final analysis, we rediscover that in present conditions the very accumulation of wealth creates poverty. While the poor often survive in scandalous conditions and are forced to contribute to further degradation, they do so because they know no alternatives. Even in the poorest of countries, social chasms not only prevent resources from being used to ameliorate their situation but actually compound the damage by forcing people from their communities and denying them the opportunities to devise their own solutions. For this reason, the search for sustainability involves a dual strategy. On the one hand, it must involve an unleashing of the bonds that restrain people from strengthening their own organizations, or creating new ones, in order to use their relatively meager resources to search for an alternative and autonomous resolution to their problems. On the other hand, a sustainable-development strategy must contribute to the forging of a new social pact, cemented in the recognition that the eradication of poverty and the democratic incorporation of the disenfranchised into a more diverse productive structure are essential.

Sustainability is not "simply" a matter of the environment, economic justice, and development. It is about people and our survival as individuals and cultures. Most significantly, it is a question of whether and the way in which diverse groups of people will continue to survive. In fact, the burgeoning literature about the move toward sustainability celebrates the many groups who have successfully adapted their cultural heritages, their unique forms of social and productive organization, and their specific ways of relating to their natural environments. Sustainability, then, is about the struggle for diversity in all its dimensions. International campaigns to conserve germplasm, to protect endangered species, and to create reserves of the biosphere are multiplying in reaction to the mounting offensive, while communities and their hard-pressed members struggle against powerful external forces to defend their individuality, their rights, and their ability to survive while trying to provide for their brethren. The concern for biodiversity, in its broadest sense, encompasses not only threatened flora and fauna but also the survivability of these human communities, as stewards of the natural environment and as producers.

Globalization has stymied this movement toward diversity. The powerful economic groups that shape the world economy (transnational corporations, transnational financial institutions, and influential local powers, among others) are striving to break down these individual or regional traits, molding us into more homogenous and tractable social groups. They would position us to support the existing structure of inequality and to engage in productive employment — and, for those lucky enough to enjoy high enough incomes, to become customers.

The Literature on Sustainable Development

In contrast to the generalized theories about the development process and sophisticated models of economic growth, the literature on sustainable development offers a mixture of high ethical principles, manuals for practical organization and implementation, and very concrete case studies of successes and failures. In this section we offer a rapid overview of some of the general approaches and solutions characteristic of this literature that might be suitable for various regions and problems. Rather than attempt to be comprehensive, this discussion is meant to convey the flavor of the discussion and the directions for future work. More than anything else, it is meant to reinforce the growing conviction that sustainable development may be an idea whose time has come; its implementation requires challenging not only the self-interest of the wealthy minority but also the consumption package that is defining our quality of life. This is the real challenge we face today.

Sustainability is a process rather than a set of well-specified goals. It involves modifying processes in nature, the economy, and society. It has become more fashionable as people have discovered that increasing production or even national wealth does not guarantee improving living standards and a higher quality of life; but the challenges of environmental protection are perhaps the most immediate force making the discussion so important. There are fundamental ethical questions about the sustainability of a global structure that perpetuates high degrees of international inequality. These overall questions go far beyond the scope of this chapter, which addresses strategies to promote a greater degree of sustainability in rural development. But for an effort to be successful it will also contribute to modifications in national development programs conducive to greater popular participation in their design and implementation.

A strategy to promote sustainability must focus on the importance of local participation and control over the way in which people live and work. The question of local or regional autonomy and autarchy is an important part of any discussion of national and international integration. The issues of autonomy versus cooperation and coordination are very much related to others having to do with self-sufficiency versus international specialization. The analysis of the previous sections places strategies for sustainability at the opposite end of the spectrum from the prescriptions of the neoliberal reforms. Yet the advocates of sustainability recognize that the choices are not this simple: industrial products and technologies will not be rejected simply because they involve hierarchical control and maddeningly alienated work. The response must be more reflective and confront the realities of an urbanized global society in crisis, with some nations incapable of providing for the most elemental needs of their citizens, while at the same time permitting others to enrich themselves while ransacking the storehouse of natural resources. In what follows we will briefly review some of the strategies proposed to promote sustainable development in different contexts.

Self-Sufficiency and the Relationship between Production and Consumption

The first issue that must be dealt with squarely is that of self-sufficiency versus integration into the global trading system with a tendency toward specialization based on monocropping systems. Sustainability need not be tantamount to autarchy, although it is conducive to a much lower degree of specialization in all areas of production and social organization. Food self-sufficiency emerged as a necessity in many societies because of the precariousness of international trading systems; specific culinary traditions developed on the basis of highly localized knowledge of fruits and vegetables, herbs and spices. Although the introduction of Green Revolution technologies raised the productive potential of food producers tremendously, we soon found out how hard it was to reach this potential and the high social and environmental costs that such a program might entail.

Food self-sufficiency is a controversial objective that cogently raises the question of autonomy. Development practitioners are virtually unanimous in rejecting calls for an extreme position, although Third World representatives broadly applauded Mexico's declaration in favor of such a program in 1980 to the World Food Council. Today the discussion is more complex, for there is general agreement on two contradictory factors in the debate. On the one hand, local production of basic commodities that can be produced equally well but more efficiently elsewhere is a luxury few societies can afford, if and only if the resources not dedicated to the production of these traded goods can find productive employment elsewhere.[2] On the other hand, there are probably few exceptions to the observation that greater local production of such commodities contributes to higher nutritional standards and better health indexes. In the context of today's societies, in which inequality is the rule and the forces discriminating against the rural poor legion, a greater degree of autonomy in the provision of the material basis for an adequate standard of living is likely to be an important part of any program of regional sustainability. It will contribute to creating more productive jobs and an interest in better stewardship over natural resources.

There are many parts of the world in which such a strategy would constitute a wasteful luxury. It would involve the diversion of resources from other uses that could be more productive in contributing to the availability of goods for trading. But even in circumstances in which wholesale importation of basic commodities is advisable, people concerned with sustainable development raise questions about modifying local diets so that they are more attuned to the productive possibilities of their regions; in the current scene, the tendency to substitute imported products for traditional foods is particularly troublesome, with terrible consequences for human welfare in many societies.[3]

Food self-sufficiency, however, is only part of a broader strategy of productive diversification whose tenets are very much a part of the sustainability movement. The principles of greater self-reliance are fundamental for the whole range of products and services that a society would like to assure itself. Historically, rural denizens never have been "just" farmers, or anything else, for that matter. Rather, rural communities were characterized by the diversity of the productive activities in which they engaged to assure their subsistence. It was only the aberration of transferring models of large-scale commercial agriculture to development thinking in the Third World that misled many into ignoring the multifaceted nature of traditional rural productive systems. Sustainable development strategies directly face this problem, attempting to reintroduce this diversity, as they grapple with problems of appropriate scales of operation and product mix.

Productive diversification related to a pattern of local needs and resources is another important expression of this line of thought. To the extent that people are not involved in the design and implementation of programs to assure their own consumption needs, they are also going to have less appreciation of the impact of their demands on the rest of society and the natural environment. Thus, the approach discussed in the literature being reviewed here places a great deal of importance of some direct relationship among the people involved in the planning of production and those examining the question of what levels of consumption are possible.

Popular Participation, Social Justice, and Autonomy

Sustainability is about direct participation. If there is one constant in the diverse literature in the area, it is the recognition that the movement has emerged from the grassroots to participate in and support intermediate-level NGOs that claim to speak for the extraordinary proliferation of community groups and civic organizations that are beginning to demand an increasing role in the national policy debate.

These demands and the responses from official agencies on the multilateral and national levels are quite instructive. There is a generalized agreement among practitioners that sustainable development policies cannot be designed or implemented from above.[4] To be successful they require the direct participation of the intended beneficiaries and others who might be impacted. But there is also general agreement that this participation must involve more than a mere consultative role. For such an approach to work, it requires that the powerful become aware of the need to integrate people into real power structures in order to confront the major problems of our day; this entails a redistribution of both political and economic power, a fundamental prerequisite for any program for sustainability, as most of the technical analyses point out that existing patterns of creating and perpetuating these inequalities lead to environmental degradation (Boyce 1994; Goodland and Daly 1993).

In this formulation, sustainability is not simply about environmental preservation. It is about the active participation of people in the understanding of the dynamics of natural systems and the redesign of productive systems that will allow them to be productive while conserving the planet's ability to host uncounted future generations. It is an approach to the problem of "empowerment," another word that has also become popular. Perhaps the most telling aspects of the literature on sustainability is the cumulus of examples of the way in which people can and do "act in solidarity with each other when the state isn't watching" to solve common problems and initiate creative experiments for social innovation (Friedmann 1992, 168–71; also see Ostrom 1993). Of course, the life work of Albert Hirschman offers countless examples of the ways in which the NGOs and other

grassroots groups have been successful in exerting pressure to modify development projects as part of their own (local) perception of
development priorities.[5] Interestingly enough, however, under special circumstances, the state itself may (be forced to) play a creative
role in encouraging or "liberating" creative participatory energies to
promote programs of local development and social justice that also
contribute to moving the society in the direction of sustainability
(Alves Amorim 1994; Tendler 1993).

Lest we become too sanguine, much of the literature shows how
and why the state does not operate to "empower" the downtrodden.
The difficult juncture of the late 1980s forced the Mexican government to finance grassroots development schemes through local
mobilization in communities dispersed throughout the country; the
Solidarity Program was highly regarded by the international press
and development community as an effective welfare (and vote) program, but did little to create permanent productive opportunities for
the participants, who were rarely able to continue once the official
programs were terminated;[6] Colombia's later copy of the program
promises to offer no more opportunities for the poor. In his path-
breaking examination of problems of soil erosion, P. Blaikie goes
further to explain that market signals generally push government
into programs that benefit the rich and that much of the productivity-
enhancing research is misguided, but his most general criticism is
one that neatly encapsulates much of the criticism of development
experience of the past half-century: "the emphasis is upon particular commodities isolated from social, economic and environmental
context" (Blaikie 1985, chap. 2).

In the final analysis, a program focusing on sustainability must
also deal with poverty. There is a widespread recognition that poverty and environmental destruction go hand in hand, although less
thought has been directed toward the enormous environmental problems occasioned by the present consumption standards of the affluent
throughout the world. In the coming period, economic progress itself
will depend on involving the grassroots groups to help the affluent
find ways to control their consumption and on the organization of
development programs that offer material progress for the poor and
better stewardship of the planet's resources.

A Strategy of Democratic Participation for
Rural Diversification and Productive Improvement

Sustainable development is an approach to productive reorganization that encompasses the combined experiences of local groups throughout the world. The techniques for implementation vary greatly among regions and ecosystems. A single common denominator pervades this work: the need for effective democratic participation in the design and implementation of projects; its centrality is evident in the titles of some the excellent writing on the subject: Abdallah and Engelhard (1993); Calderón, Chiriboga, and Piñeiro (1992); Machado, Castillo, and Suárez (1993); Nuñez (1993). Another lesson from recent experience is the importance of creating networks to support and defend this work; without the mutual reinforcement that the international grouping of NGOs provides, the individual units would not be as effective in obtaining funds for their projects, technical assistance for their implementation, and political support against intransigent or incredulous local and national politicians and institutions (Arruda 1993; Friedmann and Rangan 1993).

The successes, however, are due not just to the tenacity and sacrifice of committed organizational workers and local participants, but also to the forging of a support structure, nationally and internationally, of workers, peasants, scholars, and activists who are willing to mobilize to support the spontaneous or well-organized efforts of individual groups throughout the world who are promoting projects of democratic participation for sustainable development. Organizations are forming; alliances are being recast; experiences are being reevaluated. In Latin America one of the most promising examples of this is RIAD (Red Interamericana de Agriculturas y Democracia), with headquarters in Chile.

Sustainable development is not an approach that will be accepted simply because "its time has come." The opening of the multilateral development community to the NGOs and other grassroots groups — including the long-term commitment of organizations like the Inter-American Foundation in the United States and numerous foundations from western Europe to support such efforts — is not just a token gesture by powerful agencies to the powerless; rather, it reflects the recognition that these base-level groups have been effectively mobilizing people and resources to achieve measurable improvements in living standards while contributing noticeably to protect the environment. Such victories signal the beginning, not the end, of a process.

Furthermore, recognition does not mean acceptance of the goals or even the principles of the sustainable development community. As we have repeatedly stressed in the preceding pages, the prevailing model of industrial development has created structures of concentrated wealth and power that systematically generate social and environmental problems on a global scale. In the process, small but powerful elites have consolidated their control in many societies, and countless others benefit from the spoils of a consumption model that the system has engendered; this is an unsustainable pattern of production and consumption, a model that can be made to be more efficient, less contaminating, but which in the end will continue to be nonviable. Vested interests actively deny access to resources, to employment opportunities, and to even the minimum standards of amenities to enormous segments of humanity, while wasting exorbitant amounts on ostentatious expressions of consumption for a privileged few.

Sustainable development, in the final analysis, involves a political struggle for control over the productive apparatus. It requires a redefinition not only of what and how we produce but also of who will be allowed produce and for what ends. For organizations involved in projects of sustainable development in rural areas, the conflict will center on control of mechanisms of local political and economic power, and the use of resources. The struggle to assure a greater voice in the process for peasants, indigenous populations, women, and other underprivileged minorities will not assure that their decisions will lead to sustainable development. But such broad-based democratic participation will create the basis for a more equitable distribution of wealth, one of the first prerequisites for forging a strategy of sustainable development.

Varieties of Sustainable Development

The Regions That Get Left Behind

International economic integration will not affect all peoples equally. In the case of NAFTA, for example, large segments in all three countries will remain in the backwaters of international progress. To some degree, these people are in regions that have the unique opportunity to take advantage of their status as marginal. Many of these regions are peopled with groups of indigenous origin who still treasure much of the experience that has been passed down through the generation; recent research in the Third World on ethnobotany, ethnobiology, agrobiology, and agroforestry is attempting to capture some of this wisdom. This work is showing that the productive potential of traditional agriculture is many times what is currently obtained, that there are cultural factors that prevent the full application of this knowledge (including, of course, the prevalent disdain for indigenous culture, except as a consumption good for tourists and eccentric intellectuals), and that some of our discoveries about these systems are transferable among cultures, as well as useful in improving cultivation systems used by "modern" farmers. Finally, as we conduct more research on these native cultural practices, we are learning that the native practitioners have begun to integrate more recent technological advances to improve productivity and reduce the amount of labor required in production.

In these regions the redevelopment of the "peasant economy" is both desirable and urgent. It is not simply a matter of rescuing ancient cultures, but rather of taking advantage of an important cultural and productive heritage to provide solutions to the problems of today and tomorrow. It is not a question of "reinventing" the peasant economy, but rather of joining with their own organizations to carve out political spaces that will allow them to exercise their autonomy, to define ways in which their organizations will guide production for themselves and for commerce with the rest of the society.[7] Once again, the technocratic identification of productive mechanisms and the cataloging of systems of indigenous knowledge (which, for example, are now the order of the day among transnational corporations looking for new sources of germplasm for their biotechnological advances) are not going to reverse the structure of discrimination, unless accompanied by effective political participation (Nuñez 1993).

These regions that get left behind will have many opportunities to explore ways in which to use their resource endowments creatively. Among the most important are projects administered by local community groups that begin to diversify their productive base, using sources of renewable energy and evaluating the natural environment to develop new products or find new ways of adding value to traditional technologies and goods; projects mentioned in the literature include the harnessing of solar, geothermal, and aeolic energy for food processing, improving the quality and developing systems to increase the output of artisan crafts (or marketing them so that they command better prices), and developing facilities for recreation and institutional arrangements to permit outsiders to gain an appreciation of indigenous cultures. The opportunities to seek out new ways of organizing the natural resources base are great, and the initiatives to implement such programs are gradually finding respondents interested in exploring this and other alternatives (Barkin 1994).

Centers of Biodiversity

The world's scientific and environmental community has mobilized to identify and protect an increasing number of particularly valued areas. These "biosphere reserves" in the wilds and urban "heritage" centers are guardians of part of the ecosystem's natural and produced treasures. But they are also controversial battlefields where science and community are struggling for an operational definition of environmental protection and sustainability. The lines are drawn most clearly in the efforts to create nuclear areas in the designated biosphere reserves where people are not permitted to intrude; in some cases, the designation — or some similar status, such as national park — actually involves the removal of local inhabitants from the area in the name of the environment. On a more general level, the growing concern for protecting endangered species has led to conflicts with local populations that have traditionally coexisted with these species, exploiting them in sustainable ways, until the powerful forces of the market led to increased kill rates that threatened their very survival.

While there is no one generalized solution to the conflicting needs and goals of the groups involved in these regions, it does seem that the philosophical approach of "sustainability" does offer some insights. One promising proposal suggests creating "peasant reserves of the biosphere" or "neighborhood restoration clubs" in which local communities are encouraged to continue living within a region, husbanding the resources. In exchange, the "outside world" would accept the obligation to ensure that the community was able to enjoy a socially acceptable quality of life with economic opportunities similar to those of other groups and full political participation at all levels. One particularly interesting example of this approach is the attempt to create such a model in the Chimalapas region of southwestern Oaxaca in Mexico, an attempt that has overcome many political obstacles but still has not been completely successful. Other examples that embody this approach involve organizing the local communities that formerly were engaged in predatory activities to participate in (or actually help design) protective activities as part of a strategy of productive diversification for community development, which would include ecotourism but could not be limited to this type of activity, because research has shown them to be too sporadic and insecure to offer economic security for most communities.

Autonomous Development:
A Strategy for Sustainability

Sustainable development is not consistent with the expansion of "modern" commercial agriculture. Specialized production based on the use of machinery and/or agrochemicals that emerged from the Green Revolution approach to technological development has produced vast volumes of food and other primary products; the social and environmental costs, however, are proving to be incalculable. Commercialized rural development has brought in its wake the progressive marginality of peasant and indigenous populations.

Global integration is creating opportunities for some, nightmares for many. Domestic production is adjusting to the signals of the international market, responding to the demands from abroad and importing those goods that can be acquired more inexpensively elsewhere. Urban-industrial expansion has created poles of attraction for people and their activities that cannot be absorbed productively or healthfully. Urban slums and deteriorating neighborhoods house people seeking marginal jobs while local governments are overwhelmed by the impossible tasks of administering these burgeoning areas with inadequate budgets. At the same time, peasant communities are being dismembered, their residents forced to emigrate and abandon traditional production systems. They also cease to be stewards of the ecosystems of which they are a part.

In this juxtaposition of winners and losers, a new strategy for rural development must be considered: a strategy that revalues the contribution of traditional production strategies. In the present world economy, the vast majority of rural producers in the Third World cannot compete on world markets with basic food stuffs and many other primary products: the technology and financial might of farmers in the richer nations combine with the political necessity to export their surpluses to drive down international prices, often below the real costs of production in the Third World, especially if these farmers were to receive a competitive wage. Unless insulated in some way, their traditional products only have ready markets within the narrow confines of communities that are suffering a similar fate.

Marginal rural producers offer an important promise: if encouraged to continue producing, they can support themselves and make important contributions to the rest of society. In contrast, if prevailing rural policies in Third World countries define efficiency by the criteria of the international market, based on the political and technological structure of the industrialized nations, peasants will be driven from their traditional planting programs, and food imports will begin to compete for scare foreign exchange with capital goods and other national priorities, as has happened in many countries (Barkin, Batt, and DeWalt 1990). The approach suggested by the search for sustainability and popular participation is to create mechanisms whereby peasants and indigenous communities find support to continue cultivating in their own regions. Even by the strictest criteria of neoclassical economics, this approach should not be dismissed as inefficient protectionism, since most of the resources involved in this process would have little or no opportunity cost for society as a whole.[8]

In effect, we are proposing the formalization of an autonomous production system. By recognizing the permanence of a sharply stratified society, a country will be in a better position to design policies that recognize and take advantage of these differences to improve the welfare of groups in both sectors. A strategy that offers succor to rural communities, a means to make productive diversification possible, will make the management of growth easier in those areas developing links with the international economy. But more important, such a strategy will offer an opportunity for the society to actively confront the challenges of environmental management and conservation in a meaningful way, with a group of people uniquely qualified for such activities.[9]

Local autonomy is not new. Unlike the present version of the dual economy that permeates all our societies, confronting rich and poor, the proposal calls for creating new structures to permit those communities that choose to live in rural areas to receive support from the rest of the nation to implement an alternative regional development program. The new variant starts from the inherited base of rural production, improving productivity by using the techniques of agroecology. It also involves incorporating new activities that build on the cultural and resource base of the community and the region for further development. It requires very site specific responses to a general problem and therefore depends heavily on local involvement in design and implementation. While the broad outlines are widely discussed, the specifics require specific investment programs from direct producers and their partners. Our work with local communities in the over-wintering area of the Monarch Butterfly in west central Mexico is one example of this approach to development.[10]

What is new here is the introduction of an explicit strategy to strengthen the social and economic base for an autonomous production system. By recognizing and encouraging the marginal groups to create an alternative that would offer them better prospects for their own development, the approach suggested here might be mistaken to be the simple formalization of the "war on poverty" or "solidarity" approach to the alleviation of the worst effects of marginality. This would be an erroneous understanding, because the key to the proposal is not a simple transfer of resources to compensate groups for their poverty, but rather an integrated set of productive projects that offer rural communities the opportunity to generate goods and services that will contribute to raising their living standards while also improving the environment in which they live.

Notes

1. In this sense, we reject the notion that what is being sustained is growth itself, rather than a process that aims to contribute to improved welfare of people in an environment whose integrity is being protected.

2. A historical study of twenty-four nations shows that many of the resources released as a result of the import of basic food grains are left idle and the peasant societies that produced them suffer from serious unemployment (Barkin, Batt, and DeWalt 1990).

3. The complexity of the task of ending hunger is widely recognized. But recent literature has stressed the social rather than the technical (or supply-based) origins of famine and hunger; Amartya Sen (1992) is a particularly effective exponent of this point, while others have gone into greater detail about the "social origins" of food strategies and crises (Barraclough 1991).

4. This is the theme of Matthias Stiefel and Marshall Wolfe's book (1994), which summarizes a broad range of experience about popular participation. They point to the "declining state capacity to provide services and reduce income inequalities," accompanied by an equal reduction in "public confidence in the legitimacy of its efforts." When joined with the processes of political democratization, it is not surprising that the international community is "looking to 'participation' as a means of making their development projects function better, helping people cope . . . [and] as an indispensable dimension of the environmental policies . . . that can no longer be evaded or postponed" (19).

5. In their review of Albert Hirschman's contributions to development theory and practice, Lloyd Rodwin and Donald Schön (1994) emphasize his insistence on placing people at the center of the process, becoming actors in the larger processes of which they are a part.

6. Some of the cadre of the Zapatista Army of National Liberation were participants in official programs that were abruptly canceled.

7. Eric Wolfe (1982) offers a rich catalog of experiences among the "peoples without history" who successfully adapted to the European expansion, as well as a litany of tragic cases of those who did not.

8. This is crucial. Many analysts dismiss peasant producers as working on too small a scale and with too few resources to be efficient. While it is possible and even necessary to promote increased productivity, consistent with a strategy of sustainable production, as defined by agroecologists, the proposal to encourage them to remain as productive members of their communities should be implemented under existing conditions. In much of Latin America, if peasants cease to produce basic crops, the lands and inputs are not often simply transferable to other farmers for commercial output. The low opportunity costs of primary production in peasant and indigenous regions derive from the lack of alternative productive employment for the people and the lands in this sector. Although the people would generally have to seek income in the "informal sector," their contribution to national output would be meager. The difference between the social criteria for evaluating the cost of this style of production and the market valuation is based on the determination of the sacrifices society would make in undertaking one or the other option. The theoretical basis

for this approach finds its latest expression in the call for a "neostructuralist" approach to development for Latin America (Sunkel 1993).

9. Much of the literature on popular participation emphasizes the multi-faceted contribution that the productive incorporation of marginal groups can make to society (Friedmann 1992; Friedmann and Rangan 1993; Stiefel and Wolfe 1994). While very little has been done on specific strategies for sustainability in poor rural communities, it is clear that much of the experience recounted by practitioners with grassroots groups (e.g., Glade and Reilly 1993) is consistent with the principles enunciated by theorists and analysts like Miguel Altieri (1987).

10. For the more general discussion, see Barkin 1998. Boyce (1995) offers a specific program for the reconversion of El Salvador based on the principles discussed in this chapter. The proposals of groups like RIAD offer specific examples of ongoing grassroots efforts to implement initiatives like those discussed in the text. The Centro de Ecología y Desarrollo (Barkin 1998) continues to advocate a program to protect the Monarch Butterfly by intensifying local participation in regional development.

NINE

The Prospects for Community-Based Development

Anthony O'Malley

Postmodernism and Community Development

The concept of community has had a long role in the history of social analysis. As an idea, the feeling-tone of "community" is positive, encouraging, and reinforcing, emphasizing as it does what Émile Durkheim called *solidarité sociale,* what Ferdinand Tönnies called *Gemeinschaft,* and what grassroots postmodernists like Gustavo Esteva and M. S. Prakash regard as "complicity in the political and subjective struggle to pioneer postmodern paths out of the morass of modern life." This positive emphasis on "community" is offered as an anodyne for the very real conflicts, not only personal and political but also objective and structural, that beset social groups by virtue of their involvement in the macro-/microdynamics of modern social structures. This inherently positive feeling about "community" is reinforced by its connotations of local and everyday life experiences. "Community" in this context means not only sharing (economically, politically, culturally, and psychologically) but doing so on a human scale.

The notion of community has played an important role in the development of classical social thought, but for our purposes we can sort the variety of views about "community" into one of two understandings that dominate the theoretical landscape:

1. That "community" is at best a fanciful indulgence in wishful utopian thinking and at worst an ideological conception

of specious solidarity, used to obscure fundamental structural inequalities or the objective conditions of social class. This understanding of "community" is often supported by the ancillary understanding that economic relations are primary and that simply sharing a language or a culture or some identity or common activity does not suffice ipso facto in the constitution of a community. We might call this the *conflict* understanding of "community."

2. That in the concept of community we have lost sight of the fundamental character of human sociability and have laid ourselves open to the existential malaise produced by industrial capitalist society and its scientific technocratic culture. From this perspective, a brighter human future is only possible by retrieving the basic unit of social, political, economic, and cultural interaction — the community — with its human properties. This we might call the *romantic* understanding of "community." Despite its implicit idealism, such an understanding has a practical dimension in that it provides a clear center of reference for a politics of resistance and opposition to the dominant model of capitalist development and an alternative development path. For many proponents of development, realists as well as romantics, the most appropriate response to the global sway of world free-market capitalism and technocracy is the formation and/or strengthening of communities. Within the nongovernmental sector of development practitioners there is a virtual consensus on this point.

This consensus among development practitioners in the popular sector is based on various new currents of thought that have emerged in the wake of the theoretical impasse of the 1980s. One of these currents relates to the notion of grassroots postmodernism propagated by Esteva and Prakash (1998), among others. This notion in turn derives from the postmodern view that development in both theory and practice is a misbegotten enterprise that is disrespectful of the principle of cultural diversity as well as the capacity of people at the grassroots level to construct their own solutions — to weave the fabric of their own lives on the basis of their own resources and relations of solidarity.[1]

The postmodernist emphasis on individuals as the human subject, relations of difference, and the politics of social identity allows only a very limited scope for analyzing social entities larger than or beyond the "community." Admittedly there is more scope for treatment of "multivocal" concepts such as "gender" and "ethnicity" and the subjective experiences and the identity politics that they define. But these notions do not provide the sense of empirical localization that "community" does.

Thus, the natural object of postmodern theory as applied to social analysis is the community. In this connection, a postmodern discourse on development is rife with notions of community action, community strengthening, community development, community awareness, community responses, and so on. All these variations on the concept community — and the different policies and practices they imply — are conceived of as alternatives to received notions of progress in the human condition. However, nowhere in this postmodernist discourse is there any analysis of the real conditions that inhibit or facilitate the development process. That is, it is grounded in a *romantic* rather than a *realist* view of community, and it is predicated on a post- or nonstructural analysis of these conditions.

On this point, with reference to ideas advanced by the various contributors to this book, I would argue that a structural class or *conflict* perspective on community provides a more reasonable approach to an analysis of the development process, namely, the programs, plans, policies, and actions that issue from analysis. It is suggested that the romantic cum postmodernist approach has critical weaknesses that render it not only unsatisfactory at the level of understanding but also seriously deficient at the level of practical strategies when it comes to dealing with large-scale, independent, and very well organized socioeconomic forces such as transnational capitalism.

As for the source of this deficiency, I have already indicated that the currently fashionable use of "community" is the outcome of a convergence between two modalities of development thought — romanticism and postmodernism. But we need a more precise understanding of this convergence. This will help us understand how the vices of community development discourse arise out of its virtues.

By itself, community discourse has the virtue of drawing our attention to human social activities organized around cooperation, mutual aid (as Kropotkin famously called it), and various forms of dynamic reciprocity. This emphasis is especially welcome in an epoch in which the competitive social and economic relations of market capitalism have become fundamental and unquestioned even by former socialists. By themselves, postmodern forms of social understandings, especially in development, have the virtue of pressing us into a recognition of the absolute value and fundamentally necessary existence of diversity in all its forms, particularly cultural. This is the case, for example, with Esteva and Prakash's *Grassroots Postmodernism,* in which the romantic idea of community is combined with a postmodernist emphasis on relations of difference and conditions of cultural diversity. However, in this and other instances of postmodernist discourse the real world of community-based development does not materialize in a form that leads either to understanding of the forces and dynamics involved or to practical action. The discourse is so ethereal and convoluted as to induce a sort of theoretical levity or perhaps a levitation, in that postmodern musings on community tend to rise "light as feathers" (as the Czech writer Milan Kundera might say — unbearably light) into a rarefied and progressively unbreatheable atmosphere of "the countertextual imaginary," to speak in postmodernist terms. In this context, postmodern discourse on community development can be likened to a hot-air balloon anchored to the real world. The real world of class conflict, divided communities, and power structures does not materialize. This is a fatal flaw in postmodern versions of community development, including that of Esteva and Prakash.

Community-Based Development as a Means or an End

In assessing the role of the community in development, one might well ask if community-*based* development (CBD) refers to a development process that starts at the community level and ensures thereby a subsequent regional or national development or whether it means that development is best formulated in community terms and at the community level.

Another question that can be raised is whether community-based development refers to a *means* or an *end*. This question is complicated by the lack of agreement among development thinkers about just what constitutes a community or even what constitutes development. These difficulties are not indicative of theoretical anarchism or disarray in development thought so much as they are evidence of important transitions in the contemporary world that have caused fundamental changes over the past quarter-century and, concomitantly, altered thought and policy responding to this change. This new objective context — the more or less complete dominance of free-enterprise market capitalism — is in many respects, particularly because of its unchallenged hegemony, more complex than the old world order of the early postwar years (1948–73).

It is not that the impetus toward development has changed. There are still hundreds of millions of human beings in the world living in conditions of the most hideous and appalling degradation and billions living in conditions of permanent insecurity with regards to an adequate or even minimal livelihood. Development involves efforts to change this ghastly situation, not only out of empathy with our fellow human beings but also to secure our own humanity in the process. For no one can be fully human in a world in which such suffering is, to a large extent, the effect of human social organization. It is to this situation that development thinking and activism are directed.

But it is a new situation, one in which capitalism operates on a global scale without any effective opposition, that forces us to view this inhumanity as the outcome of the system in place, a new world order in which the fruits of development are appropriated by the few, an acquisitive elite that owns the means of social production, and a few crumbs are allowed to trickle down to the many, the "wretched of the earth."

CBD is a response to this new situation. The chapters in this volume have sought to assess this response both in its objective context and in terms of its self-proclaimed program. What conclusions can be drawn from this assessment? There are quite a number, but some emerge from a comparison between CBD as "a means" and CBD as "an end in itself" in terms of the objective context and development program for each.

CBD as a Means: The Objective Context

From one point of view, CBD is the most fruitful *means* for generating socioeconomic betterment on the regional, the national, and, ultimately, the global level by fostering development at the root level of human socioeconomic activity — the community. By itself, this understanding is politically and culturally neutral; that is, it is used by both moderate community theoreticians and NGO activists who wish to throw off what they see as the predations of transnational capital and yet keep some sense of national development. But it is also used by multilateral development agencies that seek to see some form of capitalist development succeed through instigating the socioeconomic participation of those (the majority) who find that the "trickle" vanishes before reaching their upturned hands. Giving communities the appearance of having a stake in the socioeconomic enterprise, even suggesting that they are an important, perhaps the most important, part of the "engine of growth," goes a long way toward ensuring the requisite political stability for consolidating economic power and postponing yet longer the redemption of free-market IOUs. In the early 1980s, an era of prosperity for those countries that turned toward free-market capitalism was seen to be just around the corner. Over the years, the pain of the process was extended from the immediate short term to an unanticipated longer term — now some twenty years — while the projected and anticipated gains have been pushed further and further into the foreseeable (and unforeseeable) future. Kari Levitt (1992) encapsulates this process in her characterization of the neoliberal Structural Adjustment Program as "short-term gain for long-term pain."

The objective context of CBD as a means for development is the global structure of a now-hegemonic neoliberalism. According to this dominant ideology, the opening up of national economies all over the world, the liberalization of trade and capital flows, the deregulation of the environments in which capitalist enterprises must operate, the redemocratization of decision making through popular participation in these decisions, as well as targeted "aid," will all create conditions for reactivating a development process that, when compared to still-outstanding, old, mainstream-development IOUs, has failed miserably. In practice, however, these changes and strategies, pursued by the World Bank Group, the International Monetary Fund (IMF), the Organization for Economic Cooperation and Development (OECD), their associated institutions, multilateral agencies, and national governments all over the world, have in fact undermined the development efforts of community-based organizations.

On the receiving end of "decentralization," and thus left to their own devices and with few resources, communities all over the world have been increasingly forced to adjust their local economies to the forces and requirements of a world economy in terms of whose dynamic structure they are relative nonentities. Very few communities have been able to make this adjustment successfully. For one thing, the transitional social costs are extremely high and are borne by and large by local direct producers in developing countries together with an increasing number of impoverished "working poor," as Eduardo Aquevedo puts it in his contribution to this volume. The structural obstacles that these communities must overcome to realize any form of socioeconomic betterment are enormous because they find themselves, for all the talk of participatory democracy, simply passengers in an economic Leviathan whose ineluctable course they have not plotted and whose momentum they apparently cannot stem. Under such conditions, the mental grasp of a plan for local betterment, if seen as principally a *means* to a greater development, can become seriously dependent on the logic and dynamic of an economic global enormity whose daily effects are all too real: a felt power that alternately entices and repels but whose earnest, curiously vacant pronouncements on growth, equitable treatment, and level playing fields constantly seek to meddle with and adjust the reality of perceptions at the local level. In this objective context, the necessary conditions for community-based or local development as a *means* are difficult to achieve and in extreme cases may not be available at all no matter what the leadership, the resources, or the energy expended in the process.

CBD as a Means: The Program

Community-based development sees communities as the agents of development. Moderate CBD sees communities as the principal agents of development, while multilateral agencies conceive of them as lesser but nonetheless important participants in a market-driven development led by international capital. Neither of these is committed to the long-term existence of the community, however it may be defined, as an end in itself. Neoliberals perceive that many people in developing countries like to talk about communities and like to see themselves as belonging to a community in which the locality provides a means of securing their livelihood and acquires the significances that inform their lives and justify their actions. But necessary as this may be for development *realpolitik,* it has no ulterior meaning beyond expediency for those advocating local, participatory development from the desks of multilateral agencies. The principal actors remain as autonomous, individual economic agents doing what they do best in a market-governed socioeconomy. In a manner generic to market understandings, participation by communities continues to mean only guaranteed participation in the polity (redemocratization). Regarding participation in the economy, the most that can be hoped for in the long run is an opportunity to have a chance at the possibility of participating. *Guaranteed* popular participation in economic outcomes is neither warranted nor desirable and would ruin the entire *force vital* of the system. But it is just this participation in economic outcomes to which communities aspire, and from this thwarted desire issues the necessary doublespeak of neoliberal *realpolitik* at the local level.

CBD moderates, often connected to NGOs, who see communities as a means to a greater, perhaps national, form of development are constantly toying with this *realpolitik*. As nationalists they tend to see through the expediency of agency or "Washington consensus" claims but are themselves caught up in a form of expediency in their conception of the community as a useful politico-economic tool for furthering regional or local development, and thus national development. In this project they are often funded by international or governmental mainstream agencies, and some have to protest too loudly to force us to distinguish their program from that of the multilateral agencies. It is not difficult to see why in conditions of immiseration or relative poverty communities come to cast off the dependence on extracommunity wealth generation and reject the utilitarian advances of neoliberals and CBD moderates alike — and come to see CBD as an end in itself.

CBD as an End: The Objective Context

We have already provided some of the features of the objective conditions and structural context within which community development takes place. In cases where CBD is considered by members of a community to be an end in itself — as in, for example, the community of Segundo Montes in El Salvador — the same conditions apply, but their effects are different.

In the deliberate rejection of a dependence on outside sources of wealth generation and other socioeconomic inputs that put the community in a subservient and petitioner position with regard to more economically powerful forces, this type of CBD strives for a self-sufficiency, an endogenous growth, and forms of accumulating surplus over which it has, ideally, complete control. In this way it comes to control both the generation and the distribution of wealth. This control includes community decisions about property ownership and ownership of the means of production, which, as Montoya suggests in his chapter, may or may not be as a collective, but the decisions regarding the nature of such ownership are made on a collective basis. This essentially removes the community from the tremendous pressures brought to bear by extracommunity structures, especially the national class structure, on local socioeconomic dynamics.

If this delinking is successful, and the community is fortunate in both its talent and its environmental circumstances, it may enjoy a considerable advance in the well-being of its members, a development that serves to further justify the original strategy of pursuing CBD as an end in itself. If such a community lacks talent or is unfortunate in its circumstances, then the demise is fairly rapid. This is because the same delinking that promotes success in the first case now ensures rapid failure in the second, as there are no reciprocal links with either government agencies or even other communities that may be exploited to furnish a buffer for the hard times. In this event, the community usually disperses. This may be contrasted with the normally different fate of the "CBD as a means" sort of community in whose continued existence both mainstream agencies, governments, and moderate NGOs have a political and ideological stake and who will intervene in times of stress, not luxuriously but sufficiently to maintain the viability of the community and prevent its dispersion.

It is an interesting question. Can "CBD as an end" communities continue to exist in a steadily shrinking world in which transnational capital is continuously making exploratory incursions into the re-motest parts of the planet in search of profitable opportunities? One condition for such a continued existence would most certainly be the outright ownership of sufficient land to provide food for its mem-bers, but a dependency on outside sources for an input so crucial to survival would vitiate the entire point of constructing a commu-nity. This is often problematic, particularly in the current climate of land consolidation under mainstream development policies promot-ing capitalist industrialized agriculture and the neoliberal emphasis on cash-crop exports. Such ownership can sometimes come about as a land settlement between national governments and an indige-nous community, but this too is not often smooth if the land in question is particularly rich in agricultural, mineral, or petroleum resources. There is no point trying to escape to the forest as sooner or later such valuable woods as there may be — as with the tropi-cal hardwoods of the Lacondian jungle — will attract the attention of transnational forestry companies, and the usual game will begin of maneuvers between indigenous owners (if indeed they have title to the land), national governments, corrupt local governments, and transnational companies to leverage an extraction of the resource in a manner profitable to capital and, especially in developing countries, rarely of long-term benefit to the indigenous community.

This situation is not helped in the long run by the fact that among middle-class intellectuals, agencies, or government officials there is currently something of a radical chic in promoting the well-being of indigenous communities, an opportunity these communities and their leaders have wisely grasped with the knowledge that such at-tention is often evanescent and fickle and that they and their people cannot fall back on the prebends of a system of positional property. They must, then, make as much of this situation as they can during the time they find themselves in the international spotlight. But the effect of what one might call an "anthropological conscience," and which accounts, at least in part, for the present center-stage position of indigenous communities, does not fall on the hundreds of millions of immiserated persons who do not belong to such communities and whose only real claim to anthropological fame is the fullness of their galling poverty. For these anthropologically uninteresting communi-ties and under these objective conditions, going it alone or CBD as an end in itself may be risky, but it may be the only option they can create in what appears to them to be a world without options.

CBD as an End: The Program

One of the advantages of the "CBD as an end" approach is the high level of morale its sense of purpose, exclusiveness, and mission confers upon community undertakings. This morale can act as a support through hard times in a way that is uncommon for "CBD as a means" communities. Moreover, the socioeconomic self-sufficiency that generally forms a major goal of such communities forces into the public arena a discussion of what exactly constitutes the good life for human social groups. The point is that such self-sufficiency is really a form of isolation, and this isolation means nonparticipation, in theory if not in fact, in features of the dominant socioeconomic system that are based on extreme interdependency such as telecommunications, infrastructure, large and dependable quantities of energy, and specific forms of access to the production and exchange of expensive durables and machines. The acquisition of such inputs becomes problematic and has a direct bearing on the creation of an economic surplus within the community; it also has the salutary effect of bringing to the fore a reassessment of what the community really *needs* as opposed to what its members might *want*. And it would likely provoke a general discussion of what sort of material level the community would find satisfactory.

Then, too, this striving for independence, which begins necessarily with an immediate focus on socioeconomic programs and plans, is based on the political and cultural awareness that in the "outside," society produces not a creative interdependency, as the regulative ideal of its ideology would have it, but simply provides greater opportunities for the more powerful, usually capitalist, employers to leverage profit and concessions from the weaker, mostly workers or employees, through the manipulation of these crucial dependencies. It is the exploitation and oppression emerging from this control that exclusionary communities seek to deflect through nonparticipation.

However, the virtues of delinking and nonparticipation are entangled with their vices. The self-absorption of communities that see CBD as an end in itself is a difficult attitude to pass on to the next generation. Young people, whose horizons reach to the "outside" world with a natural curiosity, often have not shared the experiences that produced the community, and they are also attracted in a typically youthful way to what their elders reject and place beyond their reach. The leaching of the young from such communities poses a serious problem for community reproduction and cannot be stemmed by the provision of what the community believes to be an adequate and rewarding existence. Nor can it be stemmed by drumming into youthful heads the "community story"; the world is larger than the community, a fact that even the most isolated youth eventually ferret out, and the vaguer world is a greater receptacle for dreams and ambitions than the concrete community, with its predictable routines, could ever be. New members who are consciously seeking to join such a community sometimes replace such generational losses, but even this new recruitment poses its own problems for the continuity of the original community vision or program.

Moreover, such youthful desertion points to what is perhaps the Achilles heel of closed and even partially closed communities, namely, the simple fact that no community can any longer be truly isolated from the world. Such communities are now artifacts even when draped with the trappings of indigenous or crypto-indigenous culture. Self-proclaimed or voluntary exclusion entails being left alone; yet it is quite clear that one of the realities of "globalization" is that no one, be it sooner or later, will ever again really be left alone. In a world of such relentless proximity, a community as a world unto itself will require so much energy and so much mystification and denial as to collapse under the weight of its own self-delusion.

In the end, the only concrete meaning that can be given to CBD is, perhaps, the *fostering* of local initiatives undertaken by local people for local, socially created self-improvement. This means learning how to seize the *responsibility* for creating collective well-being, however big or small this collectivity may be and under whatever terms it may characterize itself within the ambit of daily existence. One of the great lessons emerging from this conscious attempt at collective empowerment is how little control persons and their collectivities normally have over the most important dimensions of their daily lives. The subsequent attempt to seize control of these dimensions through collective local creation of the ways and means for their satisfaction, that is, empowerment, in reality is only symptomatic relief for a particular community in search of the means of its survival or sustainable development. However, local efforts and improvements, while ameliorative, cannot confront the *source* of loss of control at the local level effectively because the source is not local. Nor can the source of loss of local control be addressed by the simple integration of a number of collective efforts.

In our time, in our society, the source of such control is systemic and structural and can only be confronted and dealt with through a broadly based *movement,* a coalition of social forces that among other things have led to difficult and frustrating lessons learned in efforts to promote diverse forms of CBD. In this case, the greatest contribution will *not* be in the generation of a new and alternative form of development. Rather, it is a type of school whose curriculum of resistance, social consciousness, and collective responsibility encourages its graduates to move out and beyond it and to confront as well as change the larger reality that surrounds and exploits them. This is no small achievement, and it is one that should be promoted by all development thinkers and practitioners.

Class and Community

One of the major points made in this volume, particularly in chapter 2, is that community-based forms of local development cannot escape or move beyond their inherent limits and weaknesses, the wall against development put up by the power structure of the dominant system. As argued above in diverse contexts, particularly Bolivia and Chile (chapters 4 and 5), communities are generally surrounded and penetrated by macroeconomic policies and institutionalized practices that create conditions that they cannot control but that need to be taken into account — and resisted collectively. In order to bring about development at the level of the community, and to broaden it into a nation- and regionwide process, what is required is a radical change in the institutionalized structure of the dominant system and its neoliberal model of macroeconomic policies. Grassroots community-based organizations, even with the supportive network of national and international NGOs, cannot easily constitute such an agency. This is a conclusion that can and should be drawn from the various studies reviewed in this volume. The chapter by Macdonald on NGOs in Costa Rica is revealing in this regard. An appropriate and effective agency for change and development requires an antisystemic social movement capable of mobilizing diverse popular forces in a confrontation with the existing power structure of the dominant capitalist class.

Although this is a complex topic that reaches well beyond the scope of this book, neither grassroots social organizations nor NGOs are capable of this mobilization. Nevertheless, elements of such an antisystemic movement are very much in evidence in Latin America's rural society. An important social base of this social movement is formed by the peasantry, one of the most oppressed, exploited, and marginalized social or class groupings in the region. This applies, for example, to the Landless Rural Workers' Movement (MST) in Brazil; the Revolutionary Armed Forces (FARC) of Colombia; the Confederation of Indigenous Nationalities (CONAIE) in Ecuador; and the Zapatista Army of National Liberation (EZLN) of Chiapas in Mexico. On this issue see Veltmeyer and Petras (2000).

The peasantry in Latin America and elsewhere has been subject to the most diverse and conflicting interpretations. On the one hand, peasants are often viewed as a premodern social force, a drag on the development process, but one reduced to numerical irrelevancy and fated to disappear into the dustbin of history (see, for example, Eric Hobsbawn). On the other hand, in recent years they have been socially constructed as a postmodern social category, clear evidence of a new postmodern world in which structural forces are no longer operative (see, for example, Mallon 1994, 1995). Although this issue needs much closer study, the new wave of peasant-based social movements sweeping across Latin America by some accounts has the potential to bring about the changes needed for a broad process of economic and social development. It is bringing in its wake a number of practical solutions and strategic responses that under certain conditions could constitute an effective form of community- and class-based alternative development. But whether these conditions are pregiven or can be generated is by no means clear. What is required is careful documentation of the diverse struggles involved and an analysis of the social forces being mobilized in the process. It is hoped that the studies collected and edited in this volume provide a useful starting point in this regard.

Notes

1. This notion of grassroots postmodernism is part of a broad spectrum of ideas associated with what could be seen as a school of thought. Based on principles of poststructuralism and a postmodernist sensibility, this school encompasses scholars as diverse as Wolfgang Sachs, discourse theorists like the Colombian sociologist Arturo Escobar (1997) and the Argentinean sociologist Ernesto Laclau (Laclau and Mouffe 1985), writers in an emerging tradition of postdevelopment, Florencia Mallon (1994, 1995) and other members of the Subaltern (Historical) Group, various theorists of the emergence of "new social movements," and proponents of a feminist ecological perspective (Mies and Shiva 1993) and a postmodern approach toward gender and development (see Marchand and Parpart 1995). For a critique of these modalities of what we might term "counterdevelopment," see, among others, Veltmeyer (1997b).

Acronyms

ACORDE	Asociación Costaricense de Organismos de Desarrollo
ADN	Alianza Democrática Nacionalista
ASDI	Asociación Salvadoreña del Desarrollo Integral
BINGO	Business-Interest NGO
CASEN	Caracterización Socioeconomica Nacional
CBD	community-based development
CBO	community-based organizations
CCOD	Concertación Centroamericana de Organismos de Desarrollo
CECADE	Centro de Capacitación y Desarrollo
CED	Community Economic Development
CEDLA	Centro de Estudios para el Desarrollo Laboral y Agrario
CEDOIN	Centro de Documentación e Información Nacional
CEPAL	Spanish acronym for ECLAC
CID-COTESU	Centro de Información y Desarrollo — Cooperación Técnico Suiza
COB	Central Obrera Boliviana
COLACOT	Confederación Latinamericana de Cooperación y Mutuales de Trabajadores
COMIBOL	Corporación Minera de Bolivia
CONAIE	Confederación de Nacionalidades Indígenas de Ecuador
CONAPSO	Corporación Nacional de Planificación Social
COOPEALIANZA	Cooperativa Alianza
COOPESAN CARLOS	Cooperativa San Carlos
CRS	Catholic Relief Services
DFID	Department for International Development (UK)
DRU	Dirección Revolucionaria Unitaria
EBS	Estrategia Boliviana Social

220

ECLAC	Economic Commission for Latin America and the Caribbean (UN)
EZLN	Ejército Zapatista de Liberación Nacional
FAO-FFHC	Food and Agriculture Organization (of the UN)
FARC	Fuerzas Armadas Revolucionarias de Colombia
FINCA	Fundación Integral y Campesina
FIS	Fondo de Inversion Social
FLACSO	Facultad Latinoamericano de Ciencias Sociales
FMLN	Farabundo Martí por la Liberación Nacional
FOSIS	Fondo de Solidaridad e Inversion Social
FSB	Falange Socialista Boliviana
FSE	Fondo Social de Emergencia
FSTMB	Federación Sindical de Trabajadores Mineros de Bolivia
FUNPROCOP	Fundación para la Promoción de Cooperativismo
GONGO	Government-Owned NGO
IDA	Institución de Desarrollo Agricola
IDB	Inter-American Development Bank
IDRC	International Development Research Centre (Canada)
IFDA	International Foundation for Development Alternatives
ILD	Instituto para la Libertad y Desarrollo
ILDIS	Instituto Latinoamericano de Desarrollo y Investigación Social
ILO	International Labour Office
IMF	International Monetary Fund
INEGI	Instituto Nacional de Estadística, Geografía e Informática
IRD	Integrated Rural Development
LPP	Ley de Participación Popular
MBL	Movimiento Bolivia Libre
MIDEPLAN	Ministerio de Planificación y Cooperación
MIR	Movimiento de la Izquierda Revolucionaria
MNR	Movimiento Nacional Revolucionario
MNRI	Movimiento Nationalista Revolucionario de Izquierda
MRTKL	Movimiento Revolucionario Túpac Katari de Liberación
NAFTA	North American Free Trade Agreement
NEM	New Economic Model

NEP	New Economic Policy
NGO	Nongovernmental Organization
NSI	National Statistics Institute
NSP	New Social Policy
OECD	Organization for Economic Cooperation and Development
OEF	Overseas Education Fund
OTB	organizaciones teritoriales de base
PCD	People-Centered Development
PEP	Program for Education in Participation
PINGO	Public-Interest NGO
PPL	Popular Participation Law
PREALC	Programa Regional del Empleo para América Latina y el Caribe
PRONASOL	Programa Nacional de Solidaridad
RIAD	Red Interamericana de Agricultura y Democracia
RIDAA	*Revista Iberoamericana de Autogestión y Acción Comunal*
SAP	Structural Adjustment Program
SEWA	Self-Employed Women's Association
SIF	Social Investment Fund
SLA	Sustainable Livelihoods Approach
SMSB	Small and Medium-Sized Business
UCS	Unión Cívica de Solidaridad
UDP	Unidad Democrática Popular
UNCED	United Nations Commission on the Environment and Development
UNDP	United Nations Development Programme
UNEP	United Nations Environmental Programme
UNRISD	United Nations Research Institute for Social Development
UPA	abbreviated form of UPANACIONAL
UPANACIONAL	Union de Pequeños Agricultores Nacionales
USAID	United States Agency for International Development
WIB	Women in Business
WID	Women in Development

Bibliography

Abdallah Taoufik, Ben, and Phillippe Engelhard. 1993. *The Urgency of Fighting Poverty for Democracy and the Environment.* Occasional Paper no. 5. Geneva: UN Non-governmental Liaison Service.

Acosta-Belén, Edna, and Christine Bose, eds. 1993. *Researching Women in Latin America and the Caribbean.* Boulder, Colo.: Westview.

Aglietta, M. 1979. *Theory of Capitalist Regulation.* London: New Left Books.

———. 1982. "World Capitalism in the 1980s." *New Left Review* 136.

Aguirre, Alvaro, et al. 1990. *La nueva política economía: Recesión económica.* La Paz: CEDLA.

Alamos, Rodrigo. 1987. "La modernización laboral." *Estudios Públicos* (Santiago) 26 (autumn).

Alburquerque, F., et al. 1990. *Revolución tecnológica y reestructuración productiva: Impactos y desafíos territoriales.* Buenos Aires: Editorial Grupo Latinoamericano.

Alimir, Oscar. 1994. "Distribución del ingreso e incidencia de la pobreza a lo largo del ajuste." *Revista de CEPAL* 52 (April): 7–32.

Altieri, Miguel. 1987. *Agroecology: The Scientific Basis of Alternative Agriculture.* Boulder, Colo.: Westview.

Alves Amorim, Monica. 1994. "Lessons on Demand." *Technology Review* (January): 30–36.

Amalric, E., and T. Banuri, eds. 1995. *People, the Environment, and Responsibility. Case Studies from Rural Pakistan.* London: Parthenon.

Amsden, Alice. 1995. "La revolución industrial asiática." *Economía Política, Trayectorias y Perspectivas* (March-April).

Andrae, Gunilla, and Bjorn Beckman. 1985. *The Wheat Trap.* London: Zed.

Antinao, Fernando. 1997. "Indicadores económicos, sociales y demográficos en la región del BioBío, 1960–1996." Mimeo. Centro Eula, Universidad de Concepción.

Aporto, Henry. 1994. *Más democracia, más gobierno: Un buen gobierno para el desarrollo humano.* La Paz: Vice-Presidencia de la República de Bolivia.

Aquevedo, Eduardo, and Jorge Rojas. 1996. *Morfología social de la pobreza en la región del BioBío.* Concepción, Chile: Editorial Vicaría Pastoral.

Arnove, Robert F. N.d. "Resúmen de la evaluación hecha al Programa de Educación Para la Participación." Unpublished document.

Arnstein, Sherry. 1969. "A Ladder of Citizen Participation." *Journal of the American Institute of Planners* 35, no. 4 (July).

223

Arocena, José. 1995. *El desarrollo local: Un desafío contemporáneo.* Caracas: Editorial Nueva Sociedad.

Arrieta, Mario. 1991. "Mecanismos para incorporar a la política económica a nuevos actores sociales." In *Ajuste estructural y política social,* ed. Carlos Toranzo Roca. La Paz: ILDIS.

Arrighi, Giovanni. 1990. "Marxist Century — American Century: The Making and Remaking of the World Labour Movement." In Samir Amin et al., *Transforming the Revolution.* New York: Monthly Review.

Arrizabalo, Xavier. 1995. *Milagro o quimera: La economía Chilena durante la dictadura.* Madrid: Editorial Los Libros de Catarata.

Arruda, Marcos. 1993. "NGOs and the World Bank: Possibilities and Limits of Collaboration." Mimeo. Geneva: NGO Working Group.

Baker, Dean, and Lawrence Mishel. 1995. "Profits Up, Wages Down: Worker Losses Yield Big Gains for Business." Washington: Economic Policy Institute (http://epn.org/epi/eppuwd.html).

Banuri, T., et al. 1994. *Sustainable Human Development: From Concept to Operation: A Guide for the Practitioner.* New York: UNDP, Bureau for Policy and Programme Support.

Barkin, David. 1990. *Distorted Development: Mexico in the World Economy.* Boulder, Colo.: Westview.

———. 1992. *Morelia hacia finales del milennio: Las ciudades medias.* Mexico City: Red Nacional de Investigación Urbana.

———. 1994. "Las organizaciones no-gubernamentales ambientalistas en el foro internacional." In *La diplomacia ambiental: México y la conferencia de las naciones unidas sobre medio ambiente y desarrollo,* ed. A. Glender and V. Lichtinger. Mexico City: Secretaría de Relaciones Exteriores/Fondo de Cultura Económica.

———. 1998. *Wealth, Poverty, and Sustainable Development.* Mexico City: Centro de Ecologia y Desarrollo.

———. 2000. "Winning Strategies for Rural Development: Traditional Societies and Environmental Protection with Global Support." Paper prepared for the Tenth World Congress of Rural Sociology, Rio de Janeiro, July 31.

Barkin, David, R. Batt, and B. DeWalt. 1990. *Food Crops vs. Feed Crops: The Global Substitution of Grains in Production.* Boulder, Colo.: Lynne Rienner.

Barraclough, Solon. 1991. *An End to Hunger? The Social Origins of Food Strategies.* London: Zed.

Beneria, Lourdes, and Shelley Feldman, eds. 1992. *Unequal Burden: Economic Crises, Persistent Poverty, and Women's Work.* Boulder, Colo.: Westview.

Benjamin, Thomas. 1989. *A Rich Land, a Poor People: Politics and Society in Modern Chiapas.* Albuquerque: University of New Mexico Press.

Benko, G., and A. Lipietz. 1992. *Les régions qui gagnent: Districts et réseaux: Les nouveaux paradigmes de la géographie économique.* Paris: Ed. PUF.

Besave Kunhardt, Jorgé. 1996. *Los grupos de capital financiero en México, 1974–1995.* Mexico City: IIE, UNAM/Ediciones El Caballito.

Bielschowsky, R., and G. Stomper. 1996. "Empresas transnacionales manufactureras en cuatro estílos de reestructuración en América Latina, Argentina,

Brasil, Chile y México despues de sustitución de importaciones." In *Estabilización macroeconómica, reforma estructural y comportamiento industrial,* ed. J. Katz. Santiago de Chile: CEPAL.

Bienefeld, Manfred. 1995. "Assessing Current Development Trends: Reflections on Keith Griffin's 'Global Prospects for Development and Human Security.' " *Canadian Journal of Development Studies* 16, no. 3.

Blaikie, P. 1985. "Why Do Policies Usually Fail?" In *The Political Economy of Soil Erosion in Developing Countries*. London: Longman.

Blauert, Jutta, and Simon Zadek, eds. 1998. *Mediating Sustainability: Growing Policy from the Grassroots*. West Hartford, Conn.: Kumarian Press.

Boisier, Sergio, and V. Silva. 1990. "Propiedad del capital y desarrollo regional endógeno en el marco de las transformaciones del capitalismo actual (Reflexiones acerca de la región del BioBío, Chile)." In Alburquerque et al. 1990.

Boisier, Sergio, et al. 1992. *La descentralización: El eslabón perdido de la cadena Transformación Productiva con Equidad y Sustentabilidad*. Santiago de Chile: CEPAL.

Bolivia, Ministerio de Desarrollo Sustenible y Medio Ambiente. 1994. *Plan general de desarrollo economico y social: El cambio para todos*. La Paz: Ed. Ministerio de Desarrollo Sustenible y Medio Ambiente.

Bolivia, Ministerio de Planeamiento. 1992. "Desarrollo social, democracia y crecimiento económico." International conference of the government of Bolivia and BID-CEPAL.

Bolivia, Ministerio de Planeamiento y Cooperación. 1970. *Estrategia socioeconómica del desarrollo nacional 1971–1991*. La Paz: MPC.

———. 1991. *Estrategia social de desarrollo*. La Paz: MPC.

Boom, Gerard, and Alfonso Mercado, eds. 1990. *Automatización flexible en la industria*. Mexico City: Ed. Limusa Noriega.

Borja, J., et al. 1989. *The Decentralization of the State, Social Movements, and Local Management*. Santiago: FLACSO.

Bose, Christine, and Edna Acosta-Belén, eds. 1995. *Women in the Latin American Development Process*. Philadelphia: Temple University Press.

Boserup, Ester. 1970. *Woman's Role in Economic Development*. London: Allen and Unwin.

Botz, Dan la. 1994. *Chiapas and Beyond: Mexico's Crisis and the Fight for Democracy*. Boulder, Colo.: Westview.

Boyce, James. 1994. "Inequality as a Cause of Environmental Degradation." *Ecological Economics* 11.

Boyer, Robert. 1989. *La teoría de la regulación: Un analísis critico*. Buenos Aires: Ed. Humanitas.

Bray, David. 1991. "The Struggle for the Forest: Conservation and Development in the Sierra Juarez." *Grassroots Development* 15, no. 3.

Brodsky, Melvin. 1994. "Labor Market Flexibility: A Changing International Perspective." *Monthly Labor Review* (November).

Bromley, Daniel. 1994. "Economic Dimensions of Community-Based Conservation." In *Natural Connections: Perspectives in Community-Based*

Conservation, ed. David Western and Michael Wright. Washington, D.C.: Island Press.

Brown, Flor, and Lilia Domínguez. 1989. "Nuevas tecnologías en la industria maquiladora de exportación." *Comercio Exterior* (Mexico) 39, no. 3 (March).

Bulmer-Thomas, Victor. 1996. *The New Economic Model in Latin America and Its Impact on Income Distribution and Poverty.* New York: St. Martin's Press.

Cabrero Mendozo, Enrique. 1995. *La nueva gestión municipal en Mexico: Análisis de experiencias innovadores en gobiernos locales.* Mexico City: Porrúa/CIDE.

Calderón, Fernando, Manuel Chiriboga, and Diego Piñeiro. 1992. *Modernización democrática e incluyente de la agricultura en América Latina y el Caribe.* Serie Documentos de Programas No. 28. San José, Costa Rica: IICA.

Calderón, Fernando, and Roberto Laserna. 1983. *El oder de las regiones.* Cochabamba: Ed. CERES.

――――. 1990. "Estado, nación y movimientos socieles regionales (1971–1983)." In *Los movimientos en América Latina,* ed. D. Camacho and R. Menjivar. Mexico City: Siglo XXI.

Campbell, Alastair, et al. 1977. *Worker-Owners: The Mondragón Achievement.* London: Anglo-German Foundation for the Study of Industrial Society.

Campfem, Hubert, ed. 1997. *Community Development around the World: Practice, Theory, Research, and Training.* Toronto: University of Toronto Press.

Carley, Michael, and Ian Christie. 1993. *Managing Sustainable Development.* Minneapolis: University of Minnesota Press.

Carrion, Fernando. 1996. "La descentralización: Un proceso de confianza nacional." *Nueva Sociedad* 142 (April–May).

Castedo-Franco, Eliana, and H. C. E. Mansilla. 1993. *Economía informal y desarrollo socio-político en Bolivia.* La Paz: CEBEM.

CCOD (Concertación Centroamericana de Organismos de Desarrollo). 1988. "Memoria: Reunión de organismos no-gubernamentales para la Constitución de la Concertación Centroamericana de Organismos de Desarrollo." San Jose, Costa Rica (November).

CECADE. 1987. "Proyecto — diversificación y capacitación para el desarrollo de pequenos agricultores — informe de labores, II semeestre." San Jose, Costa Rica.

CEDIB. 1995. *La capitalizacíon en proceso (1993–1995).* Cochabamba: CEDIB.

CEPAL. 1985. *La pobreza en América Latina: Dimensiones y políticas.* Santiago de Chile: CEPAL.

――――. 1989. *Transformación ocupacional y crisis en América Latina.* Santiago de Chile: CEPAL.

――――. 1991a. "Internacionalización y regionalización de la economía mundial: Sus consequencias para Latina América." *LC/L* 640 (3 September).

――――. 1991b. *Magnitud de la pobreza en América Latina.* Santiago de Chile: CEPAL.

————. 1993. *La transformación de la producción en Chile: Cuatro ensayos de interpretación.* Santiago de Chile: CEPAL.

————. 1995. *Focalización y pobreza.* Colección Cuadernos de la CEPAL 71.

————. 1995/1996. *Panorama social de América Latina y el Caribe.* Santiago de Chile: CEPAL.

————. 1996a. *Situación de la pobreza en Chile.* Encuesta CASEN 1994. Mimeo.

————. 1996b. *Balance preliminar de la economía de América Latina y el Caribe.* Santiago de Chile: CEPAL.

Cernea, Michael. 1987. In *Research in Rural Sociology and Development: Third World Contexts,* ed. Harry Schwarzweller. International Rural Sociology Association.

Chambers, Robert. 1997. *Whose Reality Counts?* London: IT Publications.

Chapela, Gonzalo, and David Barkin. 1995. *Monarcas y campesinos: Una estrategia de desarrollo sustentable.* Mexico City: Centro de Ecología y Desarrollo.

Chatan, Jacobo. 1996. "Crecimiento económico, equidad y pobreza en Chile: Una visión diferente." In Lavanderos 1996.

Chile, Departamento de Programas Sociales. 1992. *Solidarity and Social Investment Fund (FOSIS): Investment with the People.* Santiago de Chile: DPS.

————. 1993. *Promoting Local Development.* Santiago de Chile: DPS.

CID-COTESU. 1993. *Politicas sociales y ajuste estructural: Bolivia 1985–93.* La Paz: CID-COTESU.

Cohen, John, and Norman Uphoff. 1980. "Participation's Place in Rural Development: Seeking Clarity through Specificity." *World Development* 8.

Collins, Joseph, and Jon Lear. 1995. *Chile's Free Market Miracles: A Second Look.* Oakland, Calif.

Colomer Viadel, Antonio, ed. *Sociedad solidaria y desarrollo alternativa.* Mexico City: FCE.

CONAPSO. 1991. *Estrategia social.* La Paz.

Cox, Robert. 1987. *Production, Power, and World Order: Social Forces in the Making of History.* New York: Columbia University Press.

Cox, Robert, and Harold Jacobson. 1974. *The Anatomy of Influence: Decision-Making in International Organizations.* New Haven, Conn.: Yale University Press.

Crouch, C., and A. Pizzorno. 1978. *Resurgence of Class Conflict in Western Europe since 1968.* London: Holmes and Meier.

Davis, Mike. 1984. "The Political Economy of Late-Imperial America." *New Left Review* 143 (January-February).

Denham, Mark. 1992. "The World Bank and NGOs." Paper prepared for presentation at the annual meeting of the International Studies Association, Atlanta, April.

De Paula Leite, Marcia. 1993. "Innovación tecnológica, organización del trabajo y relaciones industriales en el Brasil." *Nueva Sociedad* 124 (March-April).

De Soto, Hernán. 1987. *El otro sendero.* Mexico City: Editorial Diana.

De Soto, Hernán, and S. Schmiedheiny. 1991. *Las nuevas reglas del juego: Hacia un desarrollo sustenible en América Latina*. Bogotá: Ed. Oveja Negra. *Development* 41, no. 2 (1998).

Díaz, Alvaro. 1989. "Chile: Reestructuración y modernización industrial autoritoria: Desafíos para el sindicalismo y la oposición." In *Industria, Estado y sociedad*. Caracas: Editorial Nueva Sociedad.

———. 1994. "Dinámicas del cambio tecnológico en la industria Chilena: Desafíos para la década de los noventa." *Proposiciones* (Santiago) 23.

Dohse, Knuth, et al. 1984. "From 'Fordism' to 'Toyotism'?" In *The Social Organization of the Labour Process in the Japanese Automobile Industry*. Berlin: International Institute for Comparative Social Research.

Duhart, S., and J. Weinstein. 1998. *Pesca industrial: Sector estratégico y de alto riesgo*. Vols. 1 and 2. Santiago de Chile: PET.

Durand, Jean-Pierre, ed. 1993. *Vers un nouveau modèle productif?* Paris: Ed. Syros.

Dutrénit, Gabriela, and Mario Capdevielle. 1993. "El perfil tecnológico de la industria mexicana y su dinámica innovadora en la década de los ochenta." *El Trimestre Económico* (Mexico City) 60, no. 239 (July-September).

Eberts, Paul, and Frank Young. 1971. "Sociological Variables of Development: Their Range and Characteristics." In George Beal et al., *Sociological Perspectives of Domestic Development*. Ames: Iowa State University Press.

ECA (Estudios Centroamericanos) 551 (1994); 564 (1995).

ECLAC. 1990. *Productive Transformation with Equity*. Santiago de Chile: ECLAC.

———. 1992. *Social Equity and Changing Production Patterns: An Integrated Approach*. Santiago de Chile: ECLAC.

———. 1996. *Statistical Yearbook for Latin America and the Caribbean*. Santiago de Chile: ECLAC.

Economic Policy Institute. 1998a. "Median Annual Earnings, for Men and Women Full-Time/Full-Year Workers, 1960–1996." http//www.epinet.org/datazone/datapages (January 19).

———. 1998b. "Share of Aggregate Income Received by Each Fifth and Top Five Percent of Families, 1947–1996." http//www.epinet.org/datazone/datapages (January 19).

Escobar, Arturo. 1997. "The Making and the Unmaking of the Third World." In *The Post-development Reader*, ed. M. Rahnema and V. Bawtree. London: Zed Books.

Escobar, B., and A. Repetto. 1993. "Efectos de la estrategia de desarrollo Chilena en las regiones: Una estimación de la rentabilidad del sector transable regional." *CIEPLAN* (Santiago de Chile) 37.

Espinosa, Juan, and Andrew Zimbalist. 1978. *Economic Democracy: Workers' Participation in Chilean Industry, 1970-1973*. New York: Academic Press.

Esteva, Gustavo, and Madhu Suri Prakash. 1996. "Grassroots Postmodernism." *Interculture* 29/2, no. 13 (summer-fall).

———. 1998. *Grassroots Post-modernism*. London: Zed Books.

Faber, Daniel. 1993. *Environment under Fire: Imperialism and the Ecological Crisis in Central America*. New York: Monthly Review Press.

Fajnzylber, Fernando. 1983. *La industrialización trunca de América Latina.* Mexico City: Ed. Nueva Imagen.

Fals Borda, Orlando, ed. *The Challenge of Social Change.* Beverly Hills, Calif.: Sage Publications.

FAO-FFHC. 1987. "NGOs in Latin America: Their Contribution to Participatory Democracy." *Development: Seeds of Change* 4.

Finot, Ivan. 1996. "Institucionalización política y económica de participación popular." In ILDIS 1996.

FIS. 1992. Presentation of Consultant Group. October.

Foster, John Bellamy. 1994. *The Vulnerable Planet: A Short Economic History of the Environment.* New York: Monthly Review Press.

Foxley, Alejandro. 1982. *Experimentos neoliberales en América Latina.* Santiago de Chile: Ed. CIEPLAN.

Friedmann, John. 1992. *Empowerment: The Politics of Alternative Development.* New York: Basil Blackwell.

Friedmann, John, and Haripriya Rangan. 1993. *In Defense of Livelihood: Comparative Studies on Environmental Action.* West Hartford, Conn.: Kumarian Press.

Fundación Nacional para el Desarrollo (FUNDE). 1994. *Bases para la construcción de un nuevo proyecto económico nacional para El Salvador.* Mimeo. San Salvador.

FUSADES (Fundación Salvadoreña para el Desarrollo Economico y Social). 1996. *Boletin Economico y Social* (San Salvador) 128 (July).

Garofoli, Gioachino. 1992. "Les systèmes de petites entreprises: Un cas paradigmatique de développement endogène." In Benko and Lipietz 1992.

Garretón, Manuel, ed. 1975. *Economía política en la unidad popular.* Barcelona: Fontanella.

Gazier, Bernard. 1996. *Implicites et incompletes: Les théories économiques de l'exclusion.* In Paugam 1996.

Glade, William, and Charles Reilly, eds. 1993. *Inquiry at the Grassroots: An Inter-American Foundation Reader.* Arlington, Va.: Inter-American Foundation.

Gledhill, J. 1988. "Agrarian Social Movements and Forms of Consciousness." *Bulletin of Latin American Research* 7, no. 2.

Gleich, Albrecht von. 1999. "Poverty Reduction Strategies: The Experience of Bolivia." In *Waging the Global War on Poverty: Strategies and Case Studies,* ed. Raundi Halvorson-Quevedo and Hartmut Schneider. Paris: Development Centre— OECD.

Godinez, Armando. 1995. "Fondo Social de Emergencia de la Presidencia de la République (FSE) y Fondo de Inversión Social (FIS): Dos experiencias de focalización en Bolivia." In *Focalización y Pobreza.* Santiago de Chile: CEPAL.

Gómez Solórzano, Marco. 1992. "Las transformaciones del proceso de trabajo en gran escala internacional." In *La reestructuración industrial en México,* ed. Josefina Morales. Mexico City: IIE, UNAM, Editorial Nuestro Tiempo.

González, Pablo. 1996. "Normativa y política laboral en Chile." *Colección Estudios CIEPLAN* 43.

Goodland, Robert, and Herman Daly. 1993. "Why Northern Income Growth Is Not the Solution to Southern Poverty." *Ecological Economics* 8.

Goulet, Denis. 1989. "Participation in Development: New Avenues." *World Development* 17, no. 2.

Green, Duncan. 1995. *Silent Revolution: The Rise of Market Economics in Latin America.* London: Cassell.

Griesgraber, Jo Marie, and Bernhard Gunter, eds. 1996. *Development: New Paradigms and Principles for the 21st Century.* London: Pluto Press.

Griffin, Keith. 1995. "Global Prospects for Development and Human Security." *Canadian Journal of Development Studies* 16, no. 3.

Griffin, Keith, and Rahman Khan. 1992. *Globalization and the Developing World.* Geneva: UNRISD.

Guerra Rodríguez, Carlos. 1994. "Democracia y cuidadana: En busca de la equidad o de nuevos recursos?" *Revista Mexicana de Sociología* 3 (July–September).

Guillén, Abraham. 1988. *Economía libertaria.* Bilbao: CNT-AIT.

———. 1990. *Economía autogestionaria.* Madrid: Fundación de Estudios Libertarios Anselmo Lorenzo.

———. 1993. "La autogestión como alternativa en un mundo en crisis." In *Sociedad solidaria y desarrollo alternativa,* ed. Antonio Colomer Viadel. Mexico City: FCE.

Guimarães, Roberto. 1989. *Desarrollo con equidad: ¿Un nuevo cuento de hadas para los años de noventa?* LC/R 755. Santiago de Chile: CEPAL.

Harrison, Bennett, and Barry Bluestone. 1988. *The Great U-Turn: Corporate Restructuring and the Polarization of America.* New York: Basic Books.

Head, Simon. 1996. "Das Ende der Mittleklasse." *Die Zeit* (April 26).

Hirst, Paul. 1994. *Associative Democracy: New Forms of Economic and Social Democracy.* London: Polity Press.

Hobsbawn, Eric. 1994. *The Age of Extremes: The Short 20th Century, 1914-1991.* London: Michael Joseph.

Honadle, George, and Jerry Van Sant. 1985. *Implementation for Sustainability: Lessons from Integrated Rural Development.* West Hartford, Conn.: Kumarian Press.

Hopenhayn, M. 1989. *The Postmodern Debate and the Cultural Dimension in Development.* Santiago de Chile: ILPES.

Ikenberry, John. 1996. "The Myth of Post–Cold War Chaos." *Foreign Affairs* 75, no. 3 (May–June).

ILDIS. 1996. *Democracia y participación popular.* La Paz: ILDIS.

ILDIS-CEDLA. 1995. *Informe social Bolivia 2: Diez años de ajuste estructural.* La Paz: ILDIS-CEDLA.

ILDIS-Grupo UDAPE. 1992. *La estrategia social y su implementatación.* La Paz: ILDIS-Grupo UDAPE.

International Bank for Reconstruction and Development. 1989. "Meeting of the World Bank–NGO Committee and Recent Progress in Bank-NGO Cooperation." Internal memorandum. Washington D.C., 13 February.

International Labour Office. 1996. *World Employment 1996.* Geneva: ILO.

International Monetary Fund. 1992. *Finance and Development.* December.

Iriarte, Gregorio. 1996. *Analisis crítico de la realidad*. 6th ed. Cochabamba: Colorgraf Rodríguez.
Jazaïry, Idriss, Mohiuddin Alamgir, and Theresa Panuccio. 1992. *The State of World Rural Poverty*. London: Intermediate Technology Publications (for the International Fund for Agricultural Development).
Kay, Cristóbal. 1989. *Latin American Theories of Development and Underdevelopment*. London: Routledge.
Kennedy, Paul. 1996. "Forecast: Global Gales Ahead." *New Statesman and Society* (31 May).
Korten, David. 1987. "Third Generation NGO Strategies: A Key to People-Centered Development." *World Development* 15 (autumn supplement).
———. 1990. *Getting to the 21st Century: Voluntary Action and the Global Agenda*. West Hartford, Conn.: Kumarian Press.
Kothari, Rajni. 1984. "Party and State in Our Times: The Rise of Non-party Political Formations." *Alternatives* 9 (spring).
———. 1986. "NGOs, the State, and World Capitalism." *Economic and Political Weekly* 21, no. 50 (December 13).
Laclau, Ernesto, and Chantal Mouffe. 1985. *Hegemony and Socialist Strategy*. London: Verso.
Landim, Leilah. 1988. "ONGs y estado en América Latina." Unpublished document, February.
Larrazabal, A. Erick, and Victor Hugo de la Barra. 1997. *Capitalización y pensiones: Análisis y reflexiones sobre modelos de reforma*. La Paz: Sociedad de Análisis de Políticas Públicas.
Laserna, Roberto. 1995a. "La democracia en Bolivia: Problemas y perspectivas." In *La democracia en América Latina*, ed. Pablo Gonzáles and Marcos Roitman Rosenmann. Mexico City: Jornada Ediciones.
———. 1995b. "Reforma del estado y politicas sociales en Bolivia: Los desafíos del desarrollo humano sostenible." In *Estado y politicas sociales despues del ajuste,* ed. Carlos Vilas. Caracas: Nueva Sociedad.
Laserna, Roberto, ed. 1985. *Crisis, democracia y conflicto social*. Cochabamba: CERES.
Laurell, Ana Cristina. 1994. "Pronasol o la pobreza de los programas contra la pobreza." *Nueva Sociedad* 135.
Lavanderos, Jorgé. 1996. *El dilema de Chile: ¿Crecimiento sin equidad?* Santiago de Chile: LOM.
Lazarte, Jorgé. 1988. *Movimiento obrero y procesos políticos en Bolivia (Historia de la COB 1952–1987)*. La Paz: ILDIS.
Leborgne, Daniel, and Alain Lipietz. 1992. "Flexibilité offensive, flexibilité défensive: Deux stratégies dans la production des nouveaux espaces économiques." In Benko and Lipietz 1992.
Lechner, Norberto. 1990. "In Search of the Lost Community." In *Working Document*. Santiago: FLACSO.
Leiva, Fernando, and James Petras, with Henry Veltmeyer. 1994. *Poverty and Democracy in Chile*. Boulder, Colo.: Westview Press.
Leiva, Fernando, and R. Agacino. 1995. *Mercado de trabajo flexible, pobreza y desintegración social en Chile: 1990–1994*. Santiago: Arcis.

Levitt, Kari. 1992. "IMF Structural Adjustment: Short-Term Gain for Long-Term Pain? *Economic and Political Weekly* (January 18).

Lewis, Arthur. 1963. "Economic Development with Unlimited Supplies of Labour." In *Economics of Underdevelopment*, ed. A. N. Agarwala and S. P. Singh. New York: Oxford University Press.

Liamzon, Tina, et al., eds. 1996. *Toward Sustainable Livelihoods*. Rome: Society for International Development.

Lipietz, Alain. 1982. "Toward Global Fordism." *New Left Review* 13 (March–April).

———. 1987. *Mirages and Miracles: The Crisis of Global Fordism.* London: Verso.

———. 1989. "The Debt Problem: European Integration and the New Phase of the World Crisis." *New Left Review* 78 (November–December).

Lisk, Franklyn. 1985. Introduction to *Popular Participation in Planning for Basic Needs,* ed. Franklyn Lisk. Aldershot, England: Gower House.

Lissner, Jorgen. 1977. *The Politics of Altruism: A Study of the Political Behavior of Voluntary Development Agencies.* Geneva: ILO.

Lummis, D. 1994. *Radical Democracy.* Ithaca, N.Y.: Cornell University Press.

Lustig, Nora, ed. 1995. *Coping with Austerity: Poverty and Inequality in Latin America.* Washington, D.C.: Brookings Institution.

Machado, A., L. C. Castillo, and I. Suárez. 1993. *Democracia con campesinos, ó campesinos sin democracia.* Bogotá: Ministerio de Agriculture, Fondo DRI, IICA, and Universidad del Valle.

MacPherson, Stewart. 1982. *Social Policy in the Third World: The Social Dilemmas of Underdevelopment.* Brighton: Wheatsheaf Books.

Maddison, Angus. 1997. *La economía mundial 1820–1992: Análisis y estadísticas.* Paris: OECD.

Magdoff, Harry. 1992. *Globalisation: To What End?* New York: Monthly Review Press.

Mallon, Florencia. 1994. "The Promise and Dilemma of Subaltern Studies: Perspectives from Latin American History." *American Historical Review* 99, no. 5 (fall).

———. 1995. *Peasant and Nation: The Making of Postcolonial Mexico and Peru.* Berkeley: University of California Press.

Malloy, James, and Eduardo Gamarra. 1988. *The Transition to Democracy in Bolivia.* Pittsburgh: University of Pittsburgh Press.

Marchand, Marianne, and Jane Parpart, eds. 1995. *Feminism/Postmodernism/Development.* New York: Routledge.

Marcio Camargo, José, et al. 1995. *Stability, Growth, Modernization, and Pervasive Flexibility: A Feasible Combination?* Santiago de Chile: ILO.

Marcos, Jaime. 1994. "Disolución de comunidades campesinos y dinámica municipio-comunidad." *Debate Agrario* (CEDES, Lima) 19.

———. 1996. "Las comunidades campesinas en el proceso de regionalización del Perú." *Nueva Sociedad* 142 (April-May).

Marglin, Stephen, and Juliet Schor. 1990. *The Golden Age of Capitalism: Reinterpreting the Postwar Experience.* Oxford: Clarendon Press.

Marini, Ruy Mauro. 1981. *Dialéctica de la dependencia.* Mexico City: Era.

Martin, Hans-Peter, and Harald Schumann. 1997. *The Global Trap*. London: Zed Press.

Martínez Alier, Juan. 1991. "Ecology and the Poor: A Neglected Dimension of Latin American History." *Journal of Latin American Studies* 23, no. 3 (October).

Max-Neef, Manfred. 1986. *La economía descalza*. Montevideo: Nordan Comunidad.

———. 1989. "Human Scale Development: An Option for the Future." *Development Dialogue* 1.

Max-Neef, Manfred, Antonio Elizalde, and Martin Hopenhayn. 1965. "Desarrollo a escala humana: Una opción para el futuro." *Development Dialogue* (special issue).

Mayorga, Fernando. 1993. *Discurso y política en Bolivia*. La Paz: CERES/ILDIS.

———. 1997. *Ejemonias? Democracia representativa y liderazgos locales*. La Paz: PIEB-Sinergia.

McKnight, J. 1997. *The Careless Society: Community and Its Counterfeits*. New York: Basic Books.

Medina, Javier. 1995. *La participación popular como fruto de las luchas sociales en Bolivia*. La Paz: Ministerio de Desarrollo Humano.

Melgar Rojas, Jorgé. 1995. *Ley de Participación Popular, detras del texto*. La Paz: Ministerio de Desarrollo Humano.

MIDEPLAN. 1994. *Areas y localidades de extrema pobreza: Región del BioBío*. Santiago de Chile: MIDEPLAN.

———. 1996. *Realidad económico-social de los hogares en Chile: Algunos indicadores relevantes encuesta CASEN 1992–1994*. Santiago de Chile: MIDEPLAN.

MIDEPLAN-SERPLAC. 1991. *Estrategia para el desarrollo regional: La región el Bío-Bío al encuentro del Siglo XXI*. Concepción, Chile.

Mies, Maria, and Vandana Shiva. 1993. *Ecofeminism*. London: Zed Books.

Molina, M. Fernando. 1997. *Historia de la participación popular*. La Paz: Ministerio de Desarrollo Humano.

Montesinos, Mario, and Roberto Góchez. 1995. "Salarios y productividad." *ECA* 564 (October).

Montmollin, Pastre. 1984. *Le taylorisme*. Paris: Editions La Decouverte.

Morales, Josefina. 1992. "La reestructuración industrial. . . . " In *La reestructuración industrial en México*, ed. Josefina Morales. Mexico City: IIE, UNAM, Editorial Nuestro Tiempo.

Morales, Juan Antonio. 1990. "Democracia y política económica en Bolivia." In *El difícil camino: Hacia la democracia*. La Paz: ILDIS.

———. 1994. *Governance, Capacity, and Adjustment in Bolivia*. La Paz: ILDIS.

Morley, Samuel. 1995. "Structural Adjustment and Determinants of Poverty in Latin America." In *Coping with Austerity: Poverty and Inequality in Latin America*, ed. Nora Lustig. Washington, D.C.: Brookings Institution.

Muñoz, Oscar. 1989. "Crisis y reorganización industrial en Chile." In Oscar Muñoz et al., *Industria, estado y sociedad: La reestructuración industrial en América Latina y Europa*. Caracas: Editorial Nueva Sociedad.

Neaera Abers, Rebecca. 2000. *Inventing Local Democracy: Grassroots Politics in Brazil.* Boulder, Colo.: Lynne Rienner.

Nozick, Marcia. 1993. "Five Principles of Sustainable Community Development." In *Community Economic Development: In Search of Empowerment,* ed. Eric Shragge. Montreal: Black Rose Books.

Nuñez, Oscar. 1993. *Desarrollo sostenible y economía campesina.* Mimeo. Managua: Centro Para la Promoción, la Investigación y el Desarrollo Rural y Social (CIPRES).

O'Connor, James. 1973. *The Fiscal Crisis of the State.* New York: St. Martin's Press.

O'Donnell, Guillermo, and Philippe Schmitter. 1986. *Transitions from Authoritarian Rule: Tentative Conclusions about Uncertain Democracies.* Baltimore: Johns Hopkins University Press.

OECD. 1988. *Voluntary Aid for Development: The Role of Non-governmental Organisations.* Paris: OECD.

———. 1991. *Economic Studies* 16 (spring).

———. 1994. *The OECD Jobs Study: Facts, Analysis, Strategies.* Paris: OECD.

———. 1996a. *International Direct Investment Statistics Yearbook.* Paris: OECD.

———. 1996b. *OECD Economic Outlook.* No. 60 (December). Paris: OECD.

OEF International. 1988. *Documento del Programa Educación para Participación (PEP) para Centroamérica.* San Jose, Costa Rica.

OEF-PEP. 1988. "Informe de actividades del 88, sub-proyecto bancos comunales—FINCA." OEF (22 December).

Olave, Patricia. 1994. "Reestructuración productiva bajo el nuevo patrón exportador." In *América Latina en los ochenta: Reestructuración y perspectivas,* ed. Juan Arancibia Córdova. Mexico City: IIEC-UNAM.

Omae, Kenichi. 1990. *The Borderless World: Power and Strategy in the Interlinked World Economy.* New York: Harper Business.

Oman, Charles. 1996. "The Political Challenges of Globalisation and Regionalisation." *OECD Development Centre Policy Brief* (Paris: OECD) 11.

Ominami, Carlos, ed. 1986. *La tercera revolución industrial, impactos internacionales el actual viraje tecnológico.* Mexico City: RIAL-Anuario-Grupo Ed. Latinoamericano.

Organization of American States (OAS). 1994. *Statistical Bulletin of the OAS.* Washington, D.C.: OAS.

Ostrom, Elinor. 1993. *Institutional Incentives and Sustainable Development: Infra-structure policies in Perspective: Theoretical Lenses on Public Policy.* Boulder, Colo.: Westview Press.

Otero, María, and Elisabeth Rhyne. 1994. *The New World of Microenterprise Finance.* West Hartford, Conn.: Kumarian Press.

Patel, Surendra. 1994. "East Asia's Spectacular Development: Its Lessons for Others." *Asia-Pacific Development Journal* (UN Commission for Asia and the Pacific) 1, no. 1 (June).

———. 1995. *Technological Transformation.* Vol. 5 of *The Historic Process.* Aldershot, England: Averbury.

Pateman, Carole. 1970. *Participation and Democratic Theory.* Cambridge: Cambridge University Press.

Paugam, Serge, ed. 1996. *L'exclusion: L'etat des savoirs.* Paris: La Découverte.

Peredo Leigue, Antonio. 1995. *La COB: El poder obrero en Bolivia.* La Paz: CEDOIN.

Perrot, Anne. 1995. *Les nouvelles théories du marché de travail.* Paris: La Découverte.

Petras, James, and Henry Veltmeyer. 1995. "La recuperación económica en América Latina: El mito y la realidad." *Nueva Sociedad* 137 (May–June).

Piori, M., and C. Sabel. 1984. *The Second Industrial Divide: Possibilities for Prosperity.* New York: Basic Books.

Posada, Marcelo. 1999. "Desarrollo rural y desarrollo local: Un estudio de caso en la Argentina." *Espacio Abierto* 8, no. 3 (September–December).

Poulton, Robin. 1988. "On Theories and Strategies." In *Putting People First: Voluntary Organisations and Third World Organisations,* ed. Robin Poulton and Michael Harris. London: Macmillan.

PREALC. 1991. *Retrospectiva del sector informal urbano en América Latina.* Geneva: ILO.

———. 1993. *PREALC informe.* Santiago de Chile: ILO-PREALC.

Quiroz Martin, Teresa, and Diego Palma Rodrígues. 1997. "Chile." In Campfem 1997.

Raczynski, Dagmar. 1995. *Social Policies in Chile: Origins, Transformations, and Perspectives.* Democracy and Social Policy Series no. 4. Notre Dame, Ind.: Kellogg Institute.

Rahman, Anisur. 1991. "Toward an Alternative Development Paradigm." *IFDA Dossier* 81.

Rahman, Khan. 1993. *People's Self-Development: Perspectives on Participatory Action Research.* London: Zed Books.

Rahnema, Majid. 1990. "Participatory Action Research: The 'Last Temptation of Saint' Development." *Alternatives* 15.

Ramírez, José, and Angel Villalobos. N.d. "Los riesgos economicos y sociales de los productores de cacao de la zona norte." CECADE, unpublished document.

Ramos, Pablo. 1979. *Siete años de economía Boliviana.* La Paz: Universitaria.

Rao, Aruno, Rieky Stuart, and David Kelleher. 1999. *Gender at Work: Organizational Change for Equality.* West Hartford, Conn.: Kumarian Press.

Razeto, Luis. 1985. *Economía de solidaridad y mercado democrático.* Santiago de Chile: PET.

———. 1987. "Sobre la inserción y el aporte de la economía de la solidaridad en un proyecto de transformación social." In *Estrategias de vida en el sector popular urbano,* ed. J. Diaz Albertini and Roelfien Haak. Lima: DESCO.

———. 1988. *Economía de solidaridad y mercado democrático.* Vol. 3. Santiago de Chile: PET, Academia de Humanismo Cristiano.

———. 1993. *De la economía popular a la economía de solidaridad en un proyecto de desarrollo alternativo.* Santiago de Chile: Programa de Economía del Trabajo (PET).

Red Interamericana de Agriculturas y Democracia (RIAD). 1993. *Qué es la agricultura sustentable?* Mexico City: Grupo de Estudios Ambientales y RIAD.

Reich, Robert. 1993. *The Work of Nations: Toward the Capitalism of the Twenty-First Century.* Madrid: Javier Vergara.

Robinson, William. 1996. "Globalization: Nine Theses on Our Epoch." *Montelibre Monthly* (March–April).

Rodríguez, A., and F. Velásquez. 1994. *Municipios y servicios públicos: Gobiernos locales en ciudades intermedias de América Latina.* Santiago de Chile: SUR.

Rodwin, Lloyd, and Donald Schön, eds. 1994. *Rethinking the Development Experience: Essays Provoked by the Work of Albert O. Hirschman.* Washington, D.C.: Brookings Institute.

Rojas, Claudio. 1995. "Génesis y desarrollo de la conformación socioproductiva de Concepción — Talcahuano (Crónica de un desarrollo trunco)." *Estudios Regionales* 1.

Sachs, Ignacy. 1981. *Initiation a l'écodéveloppement.* Paris: Ed. Private.

Sachs, Jeffrey, and Juan Antonio Morales. 1988. *Bolivia 1952–1986.* San Francisco: International Center for Economic Growth.

Saenz, J., and R. Menjivar. 1991. *Urban Informality in Central America: Between Accumulation and Subsistence.* Caracas: Editorial Nueva Sociedad.

Saldías, Rodrigo. 1997. "Inversión extranjera directa en la Octava Región." *Informe Económico Regional* (Departamento de Economía, Universidad de Concepción) 28.

Salop, Joanne. 1992. "Reducing Poverty: Spreading the Word." *Finance and Development* 29, no. 4.

Sanfuentes, Alejandro. 1987. "Effects of the Adjustment Policies on the Agriculture and Forestry Sector." *CEPAL Review* 3 (December).

Sau, Ranji. 1996. "On the Making of the Next Century." *Economic and Political Weekly* 31, 14 (6 April).

Schroyer, Trent, ed. 1997. *A World That Works: Building Blocks for a Just and Sustainable Society.* New York: Bootstrap Press.

Schuurman, Franz. 1993. *Beyond the Impasse: New Directions in Development Theory.* London: Zed Books.

Sen, Amartya. 1981. *Poverty and Famines.* New York: Oxford University Press.

———. 1992. *Inequality Reexamined.* Cambridge, Mass.: Harvard University Press.

Sen, G., and C. Grown. 1987. *Development Crises and Alternative Visions.* New York: Monthly Review Press.

SERPLAC/BIOBIO. 1995. *Estrategia regional de desarrollo: Región del BioBío.* Ed. Gobierno Regional/Serplac.

Smith, Gavin. 1989. *Livelihood and Resistance: Peasants and the Politics of Land in Peru.* Berkeley: University of California Press.

Sotelo Valencia, Adria. 1995. "La reestructuración del trabajo y el capital en América latina." In *La teoría social Latinoamericana: Cuestiones contemporáneas,* ed. Ruy Mauro Marini and Márgara Millán. Vol. 4. Mexico City: Ediciones El Caballito/UNAM.

Stepan, Alfred. 1988. "Caminos hacia la redemocratización: Consideraciones teóricas y analísis comparativos." In *Transiciones desde un gobierno autoritario*. Vol. 3. Buenos Aires: Paidós.

Stiefel, Matthias, and Marshall Wolfe. 1994. *A Voice for the Excluded: Popular Participation in Development: Utopia or Necessity?* London: Zed Books.

Sunkel, Osvaldo. 1991. *Desarrollo desde dentro*. Mexico City: Fondo de Cultura Económica.

———. 1993. *Development from Within: Toward a Neostructuralist Approach for Latin America*. Boulder, Colo.: Lynne Rienner.

Tendler, Judith. 1982. *Turning PVOs into Development Agencies: Questions for Evaluation*. Program Evaluation Discussion Paper no. 12. Washington, D.C.: United States Agency for International Development.

———. 1993. "Tales of Dissemination in Small-Farm Agriculture: Lessons for Institution Builders." *World Development* 21, no. 10 (October).

Tetelboin, Carlos. 1992. "Chile: Políticas neoliberales y salud." In *Estado y políticas sociales en el neoliberalismo*, ed. A. C. Laurrell. Mexico City: Fundación Fredrich Ebert.

Therborn, Goran. 1995. *European Modernity and Beyond: The Trajectory of European Societies 1995–2000*. London: Sage.

Tönnies, Ferdinand. 1963. *Community and Society*. New York: Harper.

Toranzo Roca, Carlos. 1980. "Bolivia: Un nuevo modelo de acumulación?" *Estudios Preliminares IESE* (Cochabamba: Universidad Mayor de San Simon).

Toranzo Roca, Carlos, and Mario Arrieta. 1989. *Nueva derecha y desproletarización en Bolivia*. La Paz and Cochabamba: CERES.

Toye, John. 1987. *Dilemmas of Development: Reflections on the Counterrevolution in Development Theory and Policy*. Oxford: Basil Blackwell.

UNCTAD. 1990. *Analytical Report*. New York: UNCTAD Conference Secretariat.

———. 1994/1995. *World Investment Report*. New York: UNCTAD.

UNDP. 1993. *Cooperation for Development: Bolivia Report*. La Paz: UNDP.

———. 1996. *Desarrollo humano en Chile*. Ed. PNUD [UNDP].

UNIDO (UN Industrial Development Organization). 1991/1992. *Industry and Development Global Report*. Vienna: UNIDO.

United Nations. 1996. *Estudio económico y social mundial 1996: Tendencias y políticas en la economía mundial*. New York: UN.

Vanek, Jaroslav. 1974. *La economía de participación*. Buenos Aires: Amorrortu Editores.

Velasco, Ramiro. 1985. *La democracia subversiva*. Buenos Aires: CLACSO.

Veltmeyer, Henry. 1983. "Surplus Labour and Class Formation on the Latin American Periphery." In *Theories of Development*, ed. Ron Chilcote and Dale Johnson. Beverly Hills, Calif.: SAGE.

———. 1997a. "Latin America in the New World Order." *Canadian Journal of Sociology* 22, no. 2 (June).

———. 1997b. "New Social Movements in Latin America: The Dynamics of Class and Identity." *Journal of Peasant Studies* 25, no. 1 (October).

————. 1999. *The Labyrinth of Latin American Development.* New Delhi: APH Publications.

————. 2000. *América Latina: Capital global y la perspectiva del desarrollo alternativo.* Zacatecas, Mexico: UAZ; UNESCO.

Veltmeyer, Henry, and James Petras. 1997. *Neoliberalism and Class Conflict in Latin America.* London: Macmillan.

————. 2000. *The Dynamics of Social Change in Latin America.* London: Macmillan.

Vieira, Pedro Antonio. 1994. "Luchas obreras, control de la fuerza de trabajo y automatización de los medios de trabajo." Ph.D. diss., Economics Faculty, UNAM, Mexico City.

Vuskovic, Pedro. 1975. "Distribución del ingreso y opciones de desarrollo." In Garretón 1975.

————. 1993. *Pobreza y desigualdad en América Latina.* Mexico City: Centro de Investigaciones Interdisciplinarias en Humanidades, UNAM.

Waldon, John, and David Seddon. 1994. *Free Markets and Food Riots: The Politics of Global Adjustment.* Oxford: Blackwell.

Weaver, James, Michael Rock, and Kenneth Kusterer. 1996. *Achieving Broad-Based Sustainable Development.* West Hartford, Conn.: Kumarian Press.

Western, David, and Michael Wright, eds. 1994. *Perspectives in Community-Based Conservation.* Washington, D.C.: Island Press.

Williams, Philip J. 1989. *The Catholic Church and Politics in Nicaragua and Costa Rica.* London: Macmillan.

Wilson, Edward. 1992. *The Diversity of Life.* Cambridge, Mass.: Harvard University Press.

Wolfe, Eric. 1982. *Europe and the People without History.* Berkeley: University of California Press.

Wood, Robert. 1986. *From Marshall Plan to Debt Crisis: Foreign Aid and Development Choices in the World Economy.* Berkeley: University of California Press.

World Bank. 1990. *Bolivia: Poverty Report.* Washington, D.C.: World Bank.

————. 1995a. *Policy Research Bulletin* 6, no. 4 (August–October).

————. 1995b. *World Development Report: Workers in an Integrating World.* Oxford: Oxford University Press.

————. 1996. *World Development Report: From Plan to Market.* Oxford: Oxford University Press.

World Conference on Environment and Development (Bruntland Commission). 1987. *Our Common Future.* Oxford: Oxford University Press.

Zamosc, Leon. 1986. *The Agrarian Question and the Peasant Movement in Colombia.* Cambridge: Cambridge University Press.

Zavaleta, René. 1974. *El poder dual.* Mexico City: Siglo XXI.

Contributors

EDUARDO AQUEVEDO SOTO. Professor of Sociology, Universidad de Concepción de Chile. President of the Asociación Latinoamericana de Sociología (ALAS). Author of numerous studies on development in Chile and Latin America, including "Neoliberalismo, mercado de trabajo y pobreza en Chile," *Revista Mexicana Estudios Latinoamericanos* 10 (July–December 1998); "Neoliberalismo, mercado de trabajo y pobreza en Chile: El caso de la región del BioBio," *Revista de Ciencias Sociales* 14 (Uruguay) (1998); and "Neoliberalismo y pobreza en Chile," in *Democracia sin exclusiones ni excluídos* (Nueva Sociedad/ALAS/CLACSO/UNESCO, 1998).

DAVID BARKIN. Professor of Economics at the Universidad Autónoma Metropolitana, Xochimilco, Mexico City. Well-known author of numerous studies on the political economy of development in Mexico and elsewhere in Latin America, including *Distorted Development: Mexico in the World Economy* (Westview, 1990), and *Wealth, Poverty, and Sustainable Development* (Ed. Ruz, Mexico, 1998).

LAURA MACDONALD. Associate Professor in the Department of Political Science and the Institute of Political Economy at Carleton University, and the Director of the Centre on North American Politics and Society. Author of *Supporting Civil Society: The Political Impact of Non-governmental Assistance to Central America* (Macmillan/St. Martin's, 1997). Author of numerous articles in journals and editor of collections on such issues as the role of nongovernmental organizations in development, global civil society, citizenship struggles in Latin America, Canadian development assistance, and the political impact of the North American Free Trade Agreement (NAFTA) on human rights and democracy in the three member states. Currently researching the gendered impact of liberalized trade, the role of civil society in trade discussions in the Americas, and the impact of NAFTA on immigration and border control policies.

AQUILES MONTOYA. Professor of Economics at the Universidad Católica (UCA), San Salvador. Author of numerous studies on community economic development, including two volumes on Segundo Montes, a model of community development set up by expatriates of the long civil war in the 1980s.

ANTHONY O'MALLEY. Adjunct Professor of International Development Studies at St. Mary's University in Halifax, Nova Scotia, Canada. President of CELACAD (Centre for Latin American and Caribbean Development). A scholar of Latin American affairs/development issues and private consultant.

JUAN TELLEZ. President, Atlantic Centre for Community Economic Development, Halifax, Nova Scotia, Canada. Adjunct Professor, International Development Studies, St. Mary's University (Halifax) and Universidad de San Simón (Cochabamba, Bolivia).

HENRY VELTMEYER. Professor of Sociology and International Development at St. Mary's University (Halifax, Nova Scotia, Canada) and Adjunct Professor in Political Science, Maestria en Ciencia Política, Universidad Autónoma de Zacatecas (Zacatecas, Mexico). Author of diverse studies on the political economy of international development and Latin American affairs. Recent publications include *América Latina: Capital global y la perspectiva del desarrollo alternativo* (UAZ/UNESCO, 2000); *Hegemonia dos Estados Unidos no novo milênio* (VOZES, 2000); *The Dynamics of Social Change in Latin America* (Macmillan, UK, 2000); and *The Labyrinth of Latin American Development* (APH, 1999).

Index

action research, 14
Administrative Decentralization Law, 29, 58
Agacino, R., 98
Agenda 21, 20
agriculture: autonomous development and, 200–202; in El Salvador, 160–63; indigenous peoples and, 198; sustainable, 192–93. *See also* peasants; rural communities
Agro-Action, 146, 147
agroecology, 202
agromining, 114–15
Alianza Democrática Nacionalista, 74
Allende, Salvador, 10, 23, 96
Alliance for Progress, 23
Altieri, Miguel, 16, 204n.9
Another Development: beginnings of the search for, 47–48; DAWN and, 18; ECLAC and, 14–16; grassroots sustainable development and, 20–21; Guimarães on, 11–13; Korten on, 16–18; microenterprise lending and, 19–20; overview of, 6–7; Razeto on, 8–9; the sustainable livelihoods approach and, 21–22; UNRISD and, 13–14; Vanek and Guillén on, 9–11
Antigonish, 11
Arnstein, Sherry, 152n.4
Asociación Costaricense de Organismos de Desarrollo, 135, 137, 138, 143
autonomous development, 200–202. *See also* autonomy
autonomy, 192–93, 200–202, 213–14, 215–16

Banzer, Hugo, 69–75, 77, 87
Barkin, David, 16
basic-needs approach, 131, 153n.9
Bell, Daniel, 1
Benjamin, Thomas, 43

Bio-Bio Region of Chile: poverty in, 110–21; the problems with outward-oriented development in, 102–10
biodiversity, 190, 199–200
Blaikie, P., 195
Boisier, S., 104
Bolivia: conclusions regarding reforms in, 89–91; decentralization and, 57–59; history from 1971 to 1985, 69–75; history from 1985 to 1989, 75–81; history from 1989 to 1992, 81–84; history from 1993 to 1997, 84–89; social experiments in, 29
Borda, Fals, 11, 13, 14
Boserup, Ester, 18
Bretton Woods, 47
Bruntland Report, 20, 23

capitalism: in Chile, 97; community-based development and, 209; ECLAC on, 14–15; effects on rural communities of, 184–88; the Latin American social structure and, 36; the new development model in Chile and, 100–102; in the 1980s, 210. *See also* neoliberalism
Cárdenas, Victor Hugo, 84
CARE, 130
Caritas, 153n.8
Catholic Church, the, 130, 132–33, 134, 137. *See also* Catholic Relief Services
Catholic Relief Services, 130, 136–41
Center for International Private Enterprise, 33n.6
Central Obrera Boliviana, 57, 69, 71, 72, 73, 74, 76–77
Centro de Capacitación y Desarrollo, 137, 146–50
Centro de Ecología y Desarrollo, 204n.10
Chambers, Robert, 22
charity, 134
Chiapas, Mexico, 42, 43, 44
Chicago Boys, the, 76

 Kumarian Press is dedicated to publishing and distributing books and other media that will have a positive social and economic impact on the lives of peoples living in "Third World" conditions no matter where they live.

Kumarian Press publishes books about Global Issues and International Development, such as Conflict Resolution, Environment, Globalization, Human Rights, Nongovernmental Organizations, Political Economy, and Women and Gender.

To receive a complimentary catalog or to request writer's guidelines call or write:

Kumarian Press, Inc.
1294 Blue Hills Avenue
Bloomfield, CT 06002
U.S.A.

Inquiries: (860) 243-2098
Fax: (860) 243-2867
Order toll free: (800) 289-2664

e-mail: kpbooks@aol.com
Internet: www.kpbooks.com